THE JOHN HARVARD LIBRARY

AN

THE WORKS OF
ANNE BRADSTREET

Edited by Jeannine Hensley
Foreword by Adrienne Rich

THE BELKNAP PRESS OF
HARVARD UNIVERSITY PRESS
Cambridge, Massachusetts
London, England

CONTENTS

THE WORKS OF
ANNE BRADSTREET

[POEMS PRINTED IN THE FIRST TWO EDITIONS]

ANNE BRADSTREET AND
HER POETRY

BY ADRIENNE RICH

1630: the expected sea-voyage with its alternations of danger and boredom, three months of close quarters and raw nerves, sickness and hysteria and salt meats; finally the wild coast of Massachusetts Bay, the blazing heat of an American June, the half-dying, famine-ridden frontier village of Salem, clinging to the edge of an incalculable land-mass.

"I found a new world and new manners, at which my heart rose. But after I was convinced it was the way of God, I submitted to it and joined to the church at Boston." Sixty years later she was to write that. Other hearts had hesitated, at the first view of the same world and its manners. Anne Bradstreet's heart rose against much that lay before her, much too that had come along with her in the *Arbella*. She was eighteen, two years married, out of a civilized and humane background. Her father, Thomas Dudley, a man of education and worldly experience, had been steward to an earl; her mother, by Cotton Mather's account, "a gentlewoman whose extraction and estates were considerable." Her own education had been that of the clever girl in the cultivated seventeenth century house: an excellent library, worldly talk, the encouragement of a literate father who loved history. Her husband was a Cambridge man, a Nonconformist minister's son. Her father, her husband, each was to serve as Governor of Massachusetts; she came to the wilderness as a woman of rank.

Younger, Anne Bradstreet had struggled with a "carnall heart." Self-scrutiny, precisianism, were in any event expected of Puritan young people. But her doubts, her "sitting loose from God," were underscored by uncommon intelligence and curiosity. Once in Massachusetts, in a society coarsened by hardship and meagre in consolations, any religious doubt must at times have made everything seem dubious. Her father wrote back to England a year after their arrival:

If there be any endued with grace . . . let them come over . . . For others, I conceive they are not yet fitted for this business.
. . . There is not a house where is not one dead, and some houses many . . . the natural causes seem to be in the want of warm lodging and good diet, to which Englishmen are habituated at home, and the sudden increase of heat which they endure that are landed here in summer . . . for those only these two last years died of fevers who landed in June or July, as those of Plymouth, who landed in winter, died of the scurvy.[1]

To read and accept God's will, not only in the deaths of friends, but in one's own frequent illness, chronic lameness, political tension between one's father and Governor Winthrop, four changes of house in eight years, difficulty in conceiving a child, private and public anxiety and hardship, placed a peculiar burden of belief and introspection on an intellectually active, sensually quick spirit.

Seventeenth-century Puritan life was perhaps the most self-conscious ever lived in its requirements of the individual understanding: no event so trivial that it could not speak a divine message, no disappointment so heavy that it could not serve as a "correction," a disguised blessing. Faith underwent its hourly testing, the domestic mundanities were episodes in the drama; the piecemeal thoughts of a woman stirring a pot, clues to her "justification" in Christ. A modern consciousness looks almost enviously upon the intense light of significance under which those lives were lived out: "everything had a meaning then," we say, as if that had ever held alert and curious minds back from perverse journeys:

1 Augustine Jones, *Thomas Dudley, Second Governor of Massachusetts* (Boston, 1899), p. 449.

When I have got over this Block, then have I another put in my way,
That admitt this be the true God whom we worship, and that be his
word, yet why may not the Popish religion be the right? They have
the same God, the same Christ, the same word: they only interpret it
one way, we another.

Thus Anne Bradstreet described in her old age, for her
children, what the substance of doubt had been. And if Arch-
bishop Laud and the Hierarchists back in England were right,
what was one doing, after all, on that stretch of intemperate
coast, hoarding fuel, hoarding corn, dragging one's half-sick
self to the bedsides of the dying? What was the meaning of it
all? One's heart rose in rebellion.

Still, she was devotedly, even passionately married, and
through husband and father stood close to the vital life of
the community. (Her father was a magistrate at the trial of
Anne Hutchinson, the other, heretical, Anne, who threatened
the foundations of the colony and "gloried" in her excom-
munication.) And her mind was alive. Thomas Dudley's
library had passed to the New World, and the early childless
years, for all their struggles with theology and primitive sur-
roundings, left time, energy to go on reading and thinking.
The Bible was the air she and everyone else breathed; but she
also knew Raleigh's *History of the World,* Camden's *Annals
of Queen Elizabeth, Piers Plowman,* Sidney's poems; and she
was deeply impressed by Joshua Sylvester's translation of
Guillaume Du Bartas' *La Sepmaine du Creation.*[2]

The Divine Weekes and Works, as this elephantine poem
was called in English, was an acknowledged popular master-
piece. Du Bartas, the leading French Calvinist poet, was
admired as a peer of Ronsard. Sylvester was not his only
English translator: Philip Sidney among others had been
moved to undertake a version. Sylvester's own poetry had
been praised—in verse blurbs—by Samuel Daniel and Ben

2 See Jones, *Thomas Dudley,* p. 260, for a partial listing of books in Dudley's
library.

Jonson.[3] Milton had pillaged *The Divine Weekes* in compos-
ing *Paradise Lost*. Anne Bradstreet was thus showing no pro-
vinciality of taste in her response to Du Bartas. His poem was,
in fact, as one scholar has exhaustively shown, a perfect flea-
market of ideas, techniques, and allusions for the Puritan
poet.[4] Crammed with popular science, catalogues of diseases,
gems, fauna, and flora, groaning with hypotheses on the free
will of angels, or God's occupation before the First Day,
quivering with excesses, laborious and fascinating as some
enormous serpent winding endlessly along and forever earth-
bound, *The Divine Weekes* has, yet, a vitality of sheer con-
viction about it; one can understand its mesmeric attraction
for an age unglutted by trivial or pseudo-momentous informa-
tion. And this poem, sublime at least in its conception, was
directly concerned with the most gripping drama recognized
by the seventeenth-century mind.

One thing is clear, when one actually reads Anne Brad-
street's early verse by the side of her master Du Bartas:
however much she may have admired his "haughty Stile and
rapted wit sublime," she almost never lapsed into his voice.
Her admiration was in large measure that of a neophyte
bluestocking for a man of wide intellectual attainments; in
emulating him she emulated above all:

> Thy Art in natural Philosophy,
> Thy Saint-like mind in grave Divinity,
> Thy piercing skill in high Astronomy,
> And curious insight in Anatomy: . . .
> Thy Physick, musick and state policy . . .

She was influenced more by Du Bartas' range and his ency-
clopaedic conception of poetry, than by his stylistic qualities.
That early verse of hers, most often pedestrian, abstract,
mechanical, rarely becomes elaborately baroque; at its best her

---

[3] *The Complete Works of Joshua Sylvester* (Edinburgh, 1880), I, xxxvi ff.,
13 ff.

[4] See George Coffin Taylor, *Milton's Use of Du Bartas* (Cambridge, 1934).

style, even in these apprentice pieces, has a plain modesty and directness which owe nothing to Du Bartas.[5] She feels herself in his shadow, constantly disclaims the ability to write like him, even if she would; but she seems further to have had reservations about mere imitation of even so stylish a model: "My goods are true (though poor) I love no stealth."

Versifying was not an exceptional pursuit in that society; poetry, if edifying in theme, was highly recommended to the Puritan reader. (A century later Cotton Mather was finding it necessary to caution the orthodox against "a Boundless and Sickly Appetite, for the Reading of Poems, which now the Rickety Nation swarms withal.")[6] Unpublished verse manuscripts circulated in New England before the first printing press began operation. By her own admission, Anne Bradstreet began her verse-making almost accidentally:

> My subject's bare, my brain is bad,
> Or better lines you should have had:
> The first fell in so naturally,
> I knew not how to pass it by . . .

Thus ends her *Quaternion,* or four poems of four books each, written somewhere between 1630 and 1642. Her expositions of "The Humours," "The Ages of Man," "The Seasons," and "The Elements," and above all her long historical poem, "The Four Monarchies," read like a commonplace book put into iambic couplets, the historical, scientific journal of a young woman with a taste for study. Had she stopped writing after the publication of these verses, or had she simply continued in the same vein, Anne Bradstreet would survive in the catalogues of Women's Archives, a social curiosity or at best a literary fossil. The talent exhibited in them was of a

5 To judge from its "Dedication," her *Quaternion* may have owed its inception as much to a poem written by her father on "The Four Parts of the World" as to *The Divine Weekes.*

6 Kenneth Murdock quotes this in his *Literature and Theology in Colonial New England* (Cambridge, 1949) from Mather's *Manductio ad Ministerium,* 1726.

kind acceptable to her time and place, but to a later eye indistinct from masses of English verse of the period.

The seventeenth-century Puritan reader was not, however, in search of "new voices" in poetry. If its theme was the individual in his experience of God, the final value of a poem lay in its revelation of God and not the individual. Least of all in a woman poet would radical powers be encouraged. Intellectual intensity among women gave cause for uneasiness: the unnerving performance of Anne Hutchinson had disordered the colony in 1636, and John Winthrop wrote feelingly in 1645 of

a godly young woman, and of special parts, who was fallen into a sad infirmity, the loss of her understanding, and reason, which had been growing upon her divers years, by occasion of her giving herself wholly to reading and writing, and written many books.

Anne Bradstreet's early work may be read, or skimmed, against this background. Apart from its technical amateurishness, it is remarkably impersonal even by Puritan standards. She was receiving indelible impressions during those years between her arrival in New England and the publication of her verses in 1650. But she appears to have written by way of escaping from the conditions of her experience, rather than as an expression of what she felt and knew. New England never enters her book except as the rather featureless speaker in a "Dialogue Between Old and New England"; the landscape, the emotional weather of the New World are totally absent; the natural descriptions in her "Four Seasons" woodenly reproduce England, like snow-scenes on Australian Christmas cards. Theology, a subject with which her prose memoir tells us she was painfully grappling, is touched on in passing. Personal history—marriage, childbearing, death—is similarly excluded from the book which gave her her contemporary reputation. These long, rather listless pieces seem to have been composed in a last compulsive effort to stay in contact with the history, traditions, and values of her former world; nostalgia for English culture, surely, kept her scribbling at those academic pages, long after her conviction had run out. Present experience was still too raw, one sought relief from its daily impact in turning Raleigh and Camden into rhymed couplets, recalling a scenery and a culture denied by the wilderness. Yet it is arguable that the verse which gained her serious acceptance in her own time was a psychological stepping-stone to the later poems which have kept her alive for us.

When, in 1650, Anne Bradstreet's brother-in-law returned to England, he carried along without her knowledge a manuscript containing the verses she had copied out for family circulation. This he had published in London under the title, *The Tenth Muse, Lately Sprung Up In America*. There was considerable plotting among friends and family to launch the book. Nathaniel Ward, the "Simple Cobbler of Agawam" and former neighbor of the Bradstreets, wrote a blurb in verse, rather avuncular and condescending. Woodbridge, the brother-in-law, himself undertook to explain in a foreword that the book

is the Work of a Woman, honoured, and esteemed where she lives, for her gracious demeanour, her eminent parts, her pious conversation, her courteous disposition, her exact diligence in her place, and discreet managing of her Family occasions, and more than so, these Poems are but the fruit of some few houres, curtailed from her sleepe and other refreshments.

Mixed feelings entered the woman's proud and self-critical soul when the printed volume was laid, with due mystery and congratulation, in her lap. "The Author To Her Book" makes this abundantly clear. *She* had not given the "rambling brat" leave to stray beyond the family circle. Fond relatives, "less wise than true," had connived under her nose to spread abroad what they knew she had "resolved in such a manner should never see the Sun." The seductions of print, the first glamor of success, were paid for by the exposure of weakness, by irritation at the printer's errors which only compounded her own. Ward's jocular praise—"a right Du Bartas Girle . . . I muse whither at length these Girles would go"—surely stung the woman who wrote:

> If what I do prove well, it won't advance.
> They'l say it's stoln, or else it was by chance.

But she was a spirited woman with a strong grasp on reality; and temperament, experience, and the fact of having reached a wider audience converged at this period to give Anne Bradstreet a new assurance. Her poems were being read seriously by strangers, though not in the form she would have chosen to send them out. Her intellectual delight was no longer vulnerable to carping ("Theyl say my hand a needle better fits"); it was a symptom neither of vanity nor infirmity; she had carried on her woman's life conscientiously while composing her book. It is probable that some tension of self-distrust was relaxed, some inner vocation confirmed, by the publication and praise of *The Tenth Muse*. But the word "vocation" must be read in a special sense. Not once in her prose memoir does she allude to her poems, or to the publication of her book; her story, as written out for her children, is the familiar Puritan drama of temptation by Satan and correction by God. She would not have defined herself, even by aspiration, as an artist. But she had crossed the line between the amateur and the artist, where private dissatisfaction begins and public approval, though gratifying, is no longer of the essence. For the poet of her time and place, poetry might be merely a means to a greater end; but the spirit in which she wrote was not that of a dilettante.

Her revisions to *The Tenth Muse* are of little aesthetic interest. Many were made on political grounds, although a reading of North's Plutarch is supposed to have prompted insertions in "The Four Monarchies." What followed, however, were the poems which rescue Anne Bradstreet from the Women's Archives and place her conclusively in literature. A glance at the titles of her later poems reveals to what extent a real change in her active sensibility had taken place after 1650. No more Ages of Man, no more Assyrian monarchs; but poems in response to the simple events in a woman's life: a fit of sickness; her son's departure for England; the arrival of letters from her absent husband; the burning of their Andover house; a child's or grandchild's death; a walk in the woods and fields near the Merrimac River. At moments her heart still rises, the lines give back a suppressed note of outrage:

> By nature Trees do rot when they are grown,
> And Plumbs and Apples thoroughly ripe do fall,
> And Corn and grass are in their season mown,
> And time brings down what is both strong and tall.
> But plants new set to be eradicate,
> And buds new blown, to have so short a date,
> Is by his hand alone that guides nature and fate.

The delicacy and reticence of her expression at its best are seen in her poem, "Before The Birth of One of Her Children," which voices woman's age-old fear of death in childbirth, in the seventeenth century a thoroughly realistic apprehension. The poem is consequently a practical document, a little testament. Neither bathos nor self-indulgence cloud the economy of these lines; they are honest, tender and homely as a letter out of a marriage in which the lovers are also friends. The emotional interest of the poem lies in the human present and future; only in its conclusion does it gesture toward a hoped-for immortality. And the writer's pangs arise, not from dread of what lies after death, but from the thought of leaving a husband she loves and children half-reared.

That there is a God my reason would soon tell me by the wondrous works that I see, the vast frame of the heaven and the earth, the order of all things, night and day, summer and winter, spring and autumn, the daily providing for this great household upon the earth, the pre-serving and directing of all to its proper end.

This theme, from her prose memoir, might be a text for the first part of her "Contemplations," the most skilled and appealing of her long poems. In its stanzas the poet wanders through a landscape of clarity and detail, exalting God's glory in nature; she becomes mindful, however, of the passing of temporal pleasure and the adversity that lies the other side of ease and sweetness. The landscape is more American than literary; it is clearly a sensuous resource and solace for the poet; but her art remains consistent in its intentions: "not to set forth myself, but the glory of God." It is of importance to bear this in mind, in any evaluation of Anne Bradstreet; it gives a peculiar poignancy to her more personal verse, and suggests an organic impulse toward economy and modesty of tone. Her several poems on recovery from illness (each with its little prose gloss recounting God's "correction" of her soul through bodily fevers and faintings) are in fact curiously im-personal as poetry; their four-foot-three-foot hymn-book metres, their sedulous meekness, their Biblical allusions, are the pure fruit of convention. Yet other occasional poems, such as "Upon the Burning of Our House," which spring from a similar motif, are heightened and individualized by references to things intimately known, life-giving strokes of personal fact:

> When by the ruins oft I past
> My sorrowing eyes aside did cast,
> And here and there the places spy
> Where oft I sat and long did lie:
> Here stood that trunk, and there that chest,
> There lay that store I counted best.
> My pleasant things in ashes lie,
> And them behold no more shall I.
> Under thy roof no guest shall sit,
> Nor at thy table eat a bit.
> No pleasant tale shall e'er be told,

Nor things recounted done of old.
No candle e'er shall shine in thee,
Nor bridegroom's voice e'er heard shall be.

Upon the grounds of a Puritan aesthetic either kind of poem won its merit solely through doctrinal effectiveness; and it was within a Puritan aesthetic that Anne Bradstreet aspired and wrote. What is remarkable is that so many of her verses satisfy a larger aesthetic, to the extent of being genuine, delicate minor poems.

Until Edward Taylor, in the second half of the century, these were the only poems of more than historical interest to be written in the New World. Anne Bradstreet was the first non-didactic American poet, the first to give an embodiment to American nature, the first in whom personal intention appears to precede Puritan dogma as an impulse to verse. Not that she could be construed as a Romantic writing out of her time. The web of her sensibility stretches almost invisibly within the framework of Puritan literary convention; its texture is essentially both Puritan and feminine. Compared with her great successor, Taylor, her voice is direct and touching, rather than electrifying in its tensions or highly colored in its values. Her verses have at every point a transparency which precludes the metaphysical image; her eye is on the realities before her, or on images from the Bible. Her individualism lies in her choice of material rather than in her style.

The difficulty displaced, the heroic energy diffused in merely living a life, is an incalculable quantity. It is pointless, finally, to say that Poe or Hart Crane might have survived longer or written differently had either been born under a better star or lived in more encouraging circumstances. America has from the first levied peculiarly harsh taxes on its poets—physical, social, moral, through absorption as much as through rejection. John Berryman admits that in coming to write his long poem, *Homage to Mistress Brad-*

street, "I did not choose her—somehow she chose me—one
point of connection being the almost insuperable difficulty of
writing high verse at all in a land that cared and cares so little
for it."[7] Still, with all stoic recognition of the common prob-
lem in each succeeding century including the last half-hour,
it is worth observing that Anne Bradstreet happened to be
one of the first American women, inhabiting a time and place
in which heroism was a necessity of life, and men and women
were fighting for survival both as individuals and as a com-
munity. To find room in that life for any mental activity
which did not directly serve certain spiritual ends, was an
act of great self-assertion and vitality. To have written poems,
the first good poems in America, while rearing eight children,
lying frequently sick, keeping house at the edge of wilderness,
was to have managed a poet's range and extension within
confines as severe as any American poet has confronted. If
the severity of these confines left its mark on the poetry of
Anne Bradstreet, it also forced into concentration and perma-
nence a gifted energy that might, in another context, have
spent itself in other, less enduring directions.

[7] From an interview in *Shenandoah,* Autumn, 1965. Berryman's *Homage
to Mistress Bradstreet* (1956) reincarnates as only a great poem can the poetic
facts of early New England.

POSTSCRIPT

By ADRIENNE RICH

I wrote this foreword for the first printing of *The Works of Anne
Bradstreet,* published in 1967. Reading and writing about Bradstreet,
I began to feel that furtive, almost guilty spark of identification so
often kindled in me, in those days, by the life of another woman writer.
There were real parallels between her life and mine. Like her, I had
learned to read and write in my father's library; like her, I had known
the ambiguities of patronizing compliments from male critics; like
her, I suffered from chronic lameness; but above all, she was one of
the few women writers I knew anything about who had also been a

mother. The tension between creative work and motherhood had occupied a decade of my life, although it is barely visible in the essay I wrote in 1966. This essay, in fact, shows the limitations of a point of view which took masculine history and literature as its center (e.g., the condescending references to "Women's Archives" on pp. xiii and xvii) and which tried from that perspective to view a woman's life and work.

Ten years later, lecturing at Douglass College on American women poets, I could raise questions which were unavailable to me when I wrote the Bradstreet essay: What did it really mean for women to come to a "new world"; in what sense and to what extent *was* it "new" for them? Do the lives of the women of a community change simply because that community migrates to another continent? (The question would have to be asked differently for the poet Phyllis Wheatley, brought to the "new world" as a slave.) What has been the woman poet's relationship to nature, in a land where both women and nature have, from the first, been raped and exploited? Much has been written, by white American male writers, of the difficulties of creating "great literature" at the edge of wilderness, in a society without customs and traditions. Were the difficulties the same for women? Could women attempt the same solutions? To what strategies have women poets resorted in order to handle dangerous and denigrated female themes and experiences? What did the warning of the midwife heretic Anne Hutchinson's fate mean for Anne Bradstreet? To what extent is Bradstreet's marriage poetry an expression of individual feeling, and where does it echo the Puritan ideology of marriage, including married love as the "duty" of every god-fearing couple? Where are the stress-marks of anger, the strains of self-division, in her work?

If such questions were unavailable to me in 1966, it was partly because of the silence surrounding the lives of women—not only our creative work, but the very terms on which that work has been created; and partly for lack of any intellectual community which would take those questions seriously. Yet they were there; unformed. I believe any woman for whom the feminist breaking of silence has been a transforming force can also look back to a time when the faint, improbable outlines of unaskable questions, curling in her brain cells, triggered a shock of recognition at certain lines, phrases, images, in the work of this or that woman, long dead, whose life and experience she could only dimly try to imagine.

NOTE: This postscript first appeared in Adrienne Rich's *On Lies, Secrets and Silence* (Norton, 1979).

ANNE BRADSTREET'S WREATH OF THYME

By JEANNINE HENSLEY

A frontier is no friendly place for literary creation; yet within a year after landing with John Winthrop in Massachusetts, America's first English poet was writing, and the fruits of her pen from the next forty odd years remain for us today. Although she shared the frontier experiences, she ignored most of the signs of a New World to write of the lore of the Old World and of hope for the next. She praised God and ignored the Indians; she eulogized her husband and ignored colonial politics. Ridiculed by some, patronized as a curiosity by others, her little book of verse has survived to gain some warm admirers in its third century. She was not a great poet, but her poetry has endured, and deserves the wreath of "thyme" that she requested.

I

Anne Bradstreet was born in 1612 in England, the daughter of Thomas Dudley and Dorothy Yorke Dudley. Her sixty years of life were devoted to piety and often interrupted by illness. At sixteen she suffered the smallpox. Shortly after recovering, she married Simon Bradstreet, whom she had known since childhood. About two years later she and Simon and her parents sailed to Massachusetts on the ship *Arbella*. The Bradstreets lived in Cambridge (then called Newtown), then moved to Ipswich, and finally to Andover, where Anne spent the rest of her life. Although her first child was not born until several years after her marriage, he was eventually followed by seven others, all but one of whom outlived their mother. Thomas Dudley, her father, became the second governor of the colony, and seven years after her death, which occurred on September 16, 1672, her husband became governor.

The home life of the Dudley and Bradstreet families must have been not only scholarly but poetic. At least three other members of her family also wrote verse. Governor Dudley wrote three poems, one on "The State of Europe," one "On the Four Parts of the World," and one on his farewell thoughts, found in his pocket at his death. Anne's sister, Mercy Woodbridge, is known to have written a poem to Anne about her book, but no one has mentioned seeing the manuscript copy since 1829, when Samuel Kettell wrote that it was "respectable, but has no striking passage."[1] In the next generation, Anne's son Samuel wrote poems in his almanac for 1657; one topic was the wooing of Apollo and Tellus (the sun and the earth) in a longer poem. Under "February" were also four lines of verse, and there may have been more in the pages now missing.[2] Of all these, only Samuel's verses and Governor Dudley's farewell poem remain today.

Versifying was, in fact, very common in colonial New England. H. S. Jantz in *The First Century of New England Verse* has made a long and impressive list of the results. The Dudley family, with the three poets already mentioned plus John Woodbridge (Mercy's husband) and Anne herself, was a remarkably verse-conscious group, especially if one also includes the slightly more distant relatives John Rogers and John Norton; but only when one considers them as a family is their interest unique. Of course, most of these Puritan rhymes were occasional verse, elegies, anagrams, and paraphrases of scripture; with a few minor exceptions, the only seventeenth-century American poets of interest to the modern reader are Edward Taylor, Anne Bradstreet, and perhaps Michael Wigglesworth.

Most of what we know about Anne herself we know from her own writings. While much information survives in documents and published works about the Dudley family and about her father and husband and their descendants, direct personal in-

---

[1] *Specimens of American Poetry* (Boston, 1829), I, xvii-xviii; H. S. Jantz, *The First Century of New England Verse* (Worcester, Massachusetts, 1944), pp. 38-9.

[2] A copy of this work is at the American Antiquarian Society in Worcester, Massachusetts: the longer poem is quoted in Perry Miller and Thomas H. Johnson, *The Puritans* (New York, 1938), p. 632; see also Jantz, *Verse*, pp. 66 and 183.

formation is sadly lacking in historical sources. There are no portraits of her, and no certain knowledge of her burial place. As to her person we have only her brother-in-law's lines (which are in fact about her poems) that "There needs no painting to that comely face,/ That in its native beauty hath such grace." At the very least, it must be assumed that she had not been permanently marked by the smallpox, for if she had, the lines would be unnecessarily cruel. If we judge her by her own work, we must discover that her longer, more public works evidence her piety, filial duty, feminism, and interest in and wide reading of history, natural science, and literature; the personal lyrics, along with these public poems, reveal the sincerity of her passion for her husband and her concern for her children. But we also see a charming and very human woman who loves her tables and trunks and chests, allows her sometimes excessive humility to turn into feministic irony, and through her dread of dying in childbirth lets us see that her deeper fear is a jealous one that her husband might remarry.

Although Anne often wrote of the afflictions which God sent to remind her of the things higher than this world, she had a reasonably happy life. We know of her frequent illness, the deaths of some of her grandchildren, and her husband's absences "upon Public employment," but we also know that her children fared well and that her husband was one of those rare men who can inspire a woman to passionate poetry. She knew her good fortune and wrote, "Compare with me ye women if you can." Governor Bradstreet's portrait shows an attractive man with long hair and the glow of good living—not a dour ascetic, rather more like a Cavalier than the popular idea of the typical Puritan.

But if her poetry shows her to be a woman of charm, humor, passion, and wit, her purpose in writing exemplifies the Puritan ideals for literature, not unlike Milton's intent to "justify God's ways to man." Anne Bradstreet said, "I have not studied in this you read to show my skill, but to declare the truth, not to set forth myself, but the glory of God." It is significant that this specifically concerns a body of prose and poetry meant to advise her children spiritually, but it explains most of her other works as well. Whether she was drawing a picture of the world or teaching her children moral living, she dedicated poet and poem to her father, to her husband, or to God.

Around these three masculine figures most of her loving devotion centered; only twice did she escape to worship her feministic Muse. Her love for her father (Governor Thomas Dudley) led her to envision him a stern and wrathful, but awfully just judge to whom she owed all and to whose judgment she submitted herself and her poetry. Her husband, whom she called "My head, my heart, mine eyes, my life, nay more," corresponds in one poem to the sun, a being she knew had been a deity; she exclaimed in her admiration for the "bridegroom" sun in "Contemplations" that she herself would have called him a god if she had not known better. Literary convention makes God the Father and the Bridegroom, but Anne Bradstreet found comfort in the idea. She nestled in the thought that her Heavenly Father had provided especially for her soul's gain certain punishments—fever, fainting spells, the burning of her house—to remind her when she had forgotten her duty to reject the vanity of this world. Her rejection of vanity appeared partly as she set forth the truth and the glory of God while she maintained her own humility through simplicity of poetic style. In her characteristic attitude she worshiped the archetypical male.

Anne Bradstreet's earlier works, those published in *The Tenth Muse*, were actually given to her father, and the bulk of them is a compilation of facts (often compiled with grace and charm), a picture of seventeenth-century interests, and of special interest to him as politician, ex-soldier, dabbler in verse, and "magazine of history." The Quaternions follow the structure of Thomas Dudley's own "On the Four Parts of the World," now lost. The topics fulfill the practical Puritan's need for worldly information about history, heroes, natural philosophy, and the political arguments between old England and New. They must have pleased the eminently practical Dudley, the obstinate, the conservative, the driver of hard bargains—in short, that primeval Yankee. But a Puritan's duty to achieve success was a part of his duty to God—a proper use of the talents given him and a reflection of God's favor. If Governor Dudley appeared harsh to most, his daughter explains that the good loved him while the bad feared him. To her he was "pious, just, and wise." We may see in this why God was her kind, careful parent, while for many Puritans he seems to have been a God of terror.

Anne may not have suffered personally from the narrowness of Puritan doctrine. When she wrote later that upon first arriving at Boston her "heart rose" against the "new world and new manners," but that she "submitted" and "joined the church at Boston," she was probably suggesting that she overcame her wordly distaste by doing her spiritual duty. Life in frontier Boston would have been crude and nasty for a girl brought up in the grand house of an English nobleman; the Lady Arbella died shortly after Winthrop's party landed, and Anne's health had been delicate, too. The little journal (now in the North Andover library) which she later prepared for her children gives evidence that she had religious doubts, especially about atheism and Catholicism; she appears to have made a genuine attempt to consider the truth in Catholic doctrine. But the poetry for public view blazed out with the vigor one expects of a colonial New Englander against "bloody Popish, hellish miscreants" and "Rome's whore." She resolved her doubts, perhaps, through her writing,[3] and her thinking and writing on the subject seem less strange for her time and place if we relate them to the basic Protestant ideal that each Christian must find the road to truth for himself, even though in practice colonial New England had little patience with Quakers and others such as Anne Hutchinson whose progress led them to unorthodox truths.

Whether or not Anne Bradstreet found religious comfort through writing poetry or overcame her disgust at Boston through joining the church, she certainly sought help from her God through versified prayers in such personal troubles as fainting, fevers, her husband's trips to Boston and to England, her son's stay in England, and the burning of her house.

II

Despite the Puritan interest in didactic poetry, the meager printing facilities of early New England were devoted to other matters of greater religious and political importance. Books of

[3] Elizabeth Wade White, "The Tenth Muse—A Tercentenary Appraisal of Anne Bradstreet," *William and Mary Quarterly*, VIII (July, 1951), 362-63.

any sort were few and precious. The Bradstreet library of over 800 books (destroyed along with some of the poet's manuscripts on July 12, 1666, when the house burned) showed the family's affluence and scholarliness. We have no list of the burned volumes, but among them may have been works by writers the poet mentions: Sylvester's Du Bartas, Spenser, Sidney, Camden, Raleigh, Speed, Usher, and Dr. Crooke. Among the poets, her favorites seem to have been Du Bartas and Sidney, and among the historians Raleigh, whom she paraphrases through many long passages of "The Four Monarchies."[4] However great her interest in other poets' work, she had little enough opportunity to read that of her English contemporaries.

As for American poetry, except for the *Bay Psalm Book*, no volume of poetry had been printed in New England before *The Tenth Muse* was published in London in 1650. One sometimes hears of a 1640 edition, printed in Cambridge. There is no evidence that such an edition ever appeared; yet the rumor has persisted from early in the nineteenth century to the present. The error still appears occasionally.

The first edition of Anne Bradstreet's poems was published in 1650 after John Woodbridge, the poet's brother-in-law, had taken the manuscript to London. Having been his neighbor at Ipswich, Nathaniel Ward may have directed Woodbridge to his own bookseller, Stephen Bowtell, who published his *Simple Cobler of Aggawam* in 1647. The dedication to Governor Dudley suggests that the manuscript was given to him; so Woodbridge could easily have taken it to England without the poet's knowledge or permission. Woodbridge's epistle to the reader and dedicatory poem both imply that Anne did not know of the publication and might not be entirely pleased to see her work in print. Such disclaimers were standard in that era and were often untrue, but nothing indicates that Anne Bradstreet had any foreknowledge of the publication of *The Tenth Muse*.

She had been dead six years before the second edition was printed, but it seems clear that this edition contains the poet's

---

[4] Excellent examples of parallel passages are found in John Harvard Ellis' Introduction to *The Works of Anne Bradstreet* (New York, 1867), pp. xliv-v.

own corrections, made because she was dissatisfied with *The Tenth Muse*.[5] The identity of the editor of the 1678 edition has been a mystery, although it was probably no secret in 1678. But someone must have prepared for the press those poems found among the poet's papers after her death, and the most likely person to have done that appears to have been John Rogers, Anne Bradsteet's nephew-in-law, who in 1682 became president of Harvard College.[6] Reason tells us that her family provided the

[5] First, according to the title page, the second edition was "Corrected by the Author." Second, in the second edition inconsistencies in *The Tenth Muse* are corrected; for instance, the dedication to her father is modified to refer to all four Quaternions. Third, many of the revisions that appear in the second edition are of the same kind as those in the holograph manuscript now owned by the Stephens Memorial Library in North Andover, Massachusetts; most of the changes would seem to be hers. Fourth, internal evidence in "An Apology" and "The Author to her Book" shows that she had extended the "Four Monarchies" in a manuscript which burned with her house, and that she was displeased with the errors in the first edition and was revising it. The last lines of "The Author to her Book" indicate that she intended a second edition. Fifth, pages 237-251 in the second edition contain poems prefaced by this note: "Several other Poems made by the Author upon Diverse Occasions, were found among her Papers after her Death, which she never meant should come to public view; amongst which, these following (at the desire of some friends that knew her well) are here inserted." We may infer that the other poems including those appearing for the first time in this edition were meant for publication. Sixth, other than those "found among her papers," the second edition adds six new poems by Anne Bradstreet to those already printed in *The Tenth Muse*. These six are all concerned with subjects the poet would have considered public; religion, filial piety, or literary comments related to her work. My conclusion is that she revised and added to the first edition in the hope of publishing a second, and that when she died she left her work in much the same form in which it appears in the 1678 edition and in this edition.

[6] Two persons, John Rogers and John Norton, have been suggested. Being the authors of the two new poems in the 1678 edition, they are easily connected with it. Norton is more often mentioned; the reasons given are that he was a relative of Governor Bradstreet's second wife and that he might have wanted to publish his own poem. His poem is, however, only a funeral elegy, full of hyperbole and empty of knowledge of Anne Bradstreet's poems. John Rogers was a scholar of experience and a near relative to Anne, but more telling than that is his own poem. Like Norton's poem it is more gracious than critical, but it displays a knowledge of Mrs. Bradstreet's work, which Norton's does not. More than that, he writes that he has walked "twice through the Muses Grove" and "twice drunk the Nectar of your lines." These phrases could refer to a second reading, but more probably they refer to the second edition. His final couplet is less ambiguous,

printed poems, the corrections, and those poems not yet printed, but neither the title page nor tradition reveals an editor's name. A third edition, simply reprinted from the second, was published anonymously in 1758.

In 1867 John Harvard Ellis reprinted the text of the 1678 edition, using one copy of that edition and one of the 1650 edition; he documented most of the substantial changes between these editions. Also, he published the contents of a manuscript, handed down in the Bradstreet family, which was filled with poems and prose by Anne Bradstreet. None of the manuscript prose or poetry had appeared in earlier editions. In his edition Ellis altered the spelling and punctuation of the manuscript material, but he used "antique" type to reproduce the appearance of the 1678 edition as much as possible. His edition was reprinted in 1932 and in 1963.

In 1897 a publication committee headed by Frank E. Hopkins edited a "modern" type edition of the complete works. This edition, with an introduction by Charles Eliot Norton, is based on the text of the 1678 edition. It corrects punctuation, spelling, and printing errors without noting corrections. Because it does not document changes between the first two editions it is less valuable than Ellis' edition. In 1965 a facsimile of *The Tenth Muse* (the 1650 edition) was printed with an introduction by Josephine K. Piercy.

Fortunately most of Anne Bradstreet's poems can be dated either by dates affixed to them in one of the first two editions or in the Andover manuscript, so that we can see her artistic development. The dates of publication, however, are misleading, since the earliest poem appeared first in the second edition, and many of the manuscript pieces (unpublished until the Ellis edition) were written earlier than some poems published in the 1678 edition.

especially when one knows that one whole errata leaf and a fragment of another remain in copies of this edition. He wrote:

I'le please my self, though I my self disgrace,
What errors here be found, are in *Errataes* place.

He was referring to the errata leaf and assuming the responsibility for the state of the text. Only the editor could know the errors and assume the responsibility.

In "The Author to Her Book," the metaphor of the book as a child expresses how the poet felt when she saw her work in print. It was her own child, even if she was ashamed of its errors, and she would clean it up, dress it in the best "homespun cloth" she could find, and send it out among strangers. Besides revising her previously published work for the intended second edition, she added six new poems. The longest of these is "Contemplations" in thirty-five ababccc stanzas, which has achieved critical approval though it is uneven and lacking in unity; some of the stanzas are, however, charming. Another of the six, "The Author to Her Book," displays a wit quite in keeping with the seventeenth-century, or even Elizabethan, standard. The basic metaphor, though old since the Romans, seems newborn and viable from Anne Bradstreet's pen.

The friends who included the thirteen poems found among her papers were correct in their judgment that most of these were worth publishing. Among these are the poems to her children and grandchildren and those to her husband; some of the latter are now often considered her best work. Three of the thirteen refer to deaths which occurred in the autumn of 1669 and are dated in their subtitles; one of the poems in the Andover Manuscript is also dated, August 31, 1669; so Mrs. Bradstreet must have been writing less than three years before her death on September 12, 1672. After her house at Andover burned in 1666 and destroyed most of her papers, including the remainder of the unfinished "Four Monarchies," she may have stopped adding to those works she intended to publish. None of the poems on "public" topics can be dated after that time. In "An Apology," which immediately follows the "Four Monarchies" in the 1678 edition, she explained, "But 'fore I could accomplish my desire,/ My papers fell a prey to th' raging fire." And she wrote that she would attempt no more additions to that poem.

In preparation for a second edition the poet not only polished her work, she also altered it to suit historical events and changes. For instance, in "The Four Elements," lines were added to mention the great fire of London in 1666 and the rebuilding of the city. The account of recent political events in "Old Age" changed; Cromwell was called a "Usurper," a politically wise epithet since the monarchy had been restored. She also modified statements about which she had probably read more. For example, Ellis says that North's *Plutarch* influenced some of the changes in the "Four Monarchies."[7] And while she seemed even more sure of her enthusiasm for Sidney, the revised poem does not assert a family relationship as the earlier version did.

III

The general approval which *The Tenth Muse* received should have prompted the poet to a second edition, even if desire to correct its errors did not. But Mrs. Bradstreet may never have known that her little book was listed among the "most vendible books" in England. Although we have no contemporary reference to her or her poetry which is not somewhere between admiration and adulation, she must have sensed what people were likely to say about females who showed scholarly inclinations. The fate of Anne Hutchinson must have made lively gossip, and poor Mrs. Hopkins, who, according to John Winthrop, read and wrote too much and so became insane, was surely a subject for scandal. Reason enough to fear "each carping tongue who says my hand a needle better fits." But even Nathaniel Ward, a misogynist who had once commented on certain women's "squirrel brains,"[8] had only praise, if rather amusingly qualified: "It half revives my chill frost-bitten blood,/ To see a woman once, do aught that's good." The general prejudice against women who possessed "wit and learning" must have annoyed Anne Bradstreet; several defensively feministic comments appear in "The Prologue" and the poem on Queen Elizabeth. In the former she is full of humility ("Men can do best, and women know it well") both for her sex and for herself ("Give Thyme or Parsley wreath, I ask no bayes"), but she is also bitter ("If what I do prove well, it won't advance,/ They'll say it's stol'n, or else it was by chance"). There is still personal humility in the latter poem, but the pride of an English woman glows about the great monarch:

7 *Bradstreet*, pp. xlviii-ix.
8 Theodore de la Guard (pseud.), *The Simple Cobler of Aggawam in America* . . . (London, 1647), p. 24.

> Now say, have women worth? or have they none?
> Or had they some, but with our Queen is't gone?
> . . . .
> Let such as say our sex is void of reason,
> Know tis a slander now, but once was treason.

It is unfortunate that other parts of this poem do not equal these in vigor and wit.

The Tenth Muse was, however, popular. If the poems dedicatory are more gallant than trustworthy, there is other evidence. Eight years after its publication, *The Tenth Muse* was listed in the bookseller London's catalogue along with Phineas Fletcher, "Mr. Milton's Poems," Du Bartas, Walton's *Compleat Angler,* Browne's *Religio Medici,* and "Mr. Shaksper's Poems." J. Kester Svendsen asserts that this is a carefully selected, bookseller's list.[9] Some fifteen years later "a very learned English woman who had tutored the daughters of Charles I" wrote, "How excellent a Poet Mrs. Bradstreet is (now in America) her works do testify."[10] And scarcely any mention of *The Tenth Muse* since Ellis' edition has failed to observe that Milton's nephew Edward Phillips in his *Theatarum Poetarum* wrote that memory of it was "not yet wholly extinct."[11]

Back in New England, Cotton Mather in his *Magnalia Christi Americana* compared the poet to the learned ladies of the Old World and called her poems "a Monument for her Memory beyond the Statliest Marbles."[12] In the next generation another significant New England poet, Edward Taylor, had only one book of poetry, Anne Bradstreet's, in his own library.[13]

Looking back over the generations of critics who have roundly thrashed her little book, one must wonder whether Anne Brad-

[9] "Anne Bradstreet in England: A Bibliographical Note," *American Literature,* XIII (March, 1941), 63-65.

[10] Mrs. Batsua Makin, *An Essay to Revive the Ancient Education of Gentlewomen in Religion, Manners, Arts and Tongues* (London, 1673), quoted in White, "Tenth Muse," *WMQ,* p. 365.

[11] London, 1675; Ellis, *Bradstreet,* p. lvi.

[12] Ed. Thomas Robbins, 2nd American ed. (Hartford, 1853), I, 134.

[13] Probate Records, Northhampton, Massachusetts, January 13, 1729/30, mentioned in Thomas H. Johnson, "Edward Taylor: A Puritan 'Sacred Poet,'" *New England Quarterly,* X (June, 1937), 321.

street's ghost would envy Edward Taylor's two centuries of
obscurity. She might compare her critics to the "beetle-headed"
Puritans who reviled Sidney. In short, she has suffered from the
same critical ignorance and misinterpretation that most Puritan
writing has. One cause of this condescension has been a failure to
respect the purposes of the Puritan writers. The man who
achieved his own purpose and the common purpose of his milieu
is a success to himself and his age; the extent to which we admire
his purpose is something else again, a topic worthy of discussion
only if it does not ignore that success. Especially we have been
guilty of the misapplication of critical standards. Certainly Anne
Bradstreet summed up the goal of Puritan writing in the follow-
ing, written to her children: "I have not studied in this you read
to show my skill, but to declare the Truth, not to set forth my
self, but the glory of God."

In the century following her own, Anne Bradstreet was not
forgotten; in 1758 a reprinting of the second edition appeared.
With the growth of literary activity in the nineteenth century in
America came much more critical attention, but most of it was
patronizing, condescending, and not very perceptive. Even John
Harvard Ellis apologized for her poems:

If it is denied that they evince much poetic genius, it must, at least,
be acknowledged that they are remarkable, when the time, place, and
circumstances under which they were composed, are taken into consid-
eration. They are quaint and curious; they contain many beautiful
and original ideas, not badly expressed; and they constitute a singular
and valuable relic of the earliest literature of the country. It is im-
portant that the reader should bear in mind the peculiarly un-
propitious circumstances under which they were written.[14]

Among the nineteenth-century scholars, Moses Coit Tyler most
nearly approved of Anne Bradstreet. He admired her satire,
sarcasm, and irony aimed at "the traditional disparagement by
men of the intelligence of her sex." While deploring the sad effect
of her sect and literary era on her output, he is willing to admit
that "amid all this lamentable rubbish, there is often to be found
such an ingot of pure poetry, as proves her to have had, indeed,

[14] *Bradstreet*, p. xlii.

the poetic endowment." His strangest condemnation is that she and the other New England seventeenth-century poets were followers of the "fantastic" school of the "later euphuists": "The worst lines of Anne Bradstreet and of the other American verse-writers in the seventeenth century, can be readily matched for fantastic perversion, and for total absence of beauty, by passages from the poems of John Donne, George Herbert, Crashaw, Cleveland, Waller, Quarles, Thomas Coryat, John Taylor, and even Herrick, Cowley, and Dryden."[15]

To another critic her work is "not a piece of literature . . . only . . . a curiosity . . . a pitiful indication of the literary poverty of the days and land in which it was popular." The only merit he concedes to her poems is that they are not "so bad as they might have been."[16]

Even Charles Eliot Norton, who wrote the introduction to the 1897 edition of her poems, did not suppose that anyone would, at that time, read her verses for their aesthetic value, and the best opinion he offers is that "now and then a single verse shows a true, if slight, capacity for poetic expression." While he admits her "good sense and good feeling" and "something of ingenuity and skill," he sees no inspiration in the bulk of her work. Otherwise, his critical opinion is that the chief interest in her work is antiquarian rather than aesthetic.

Conrad Aiken brought an abrupt critical change with his anthology of American poetry in 1929.[17] In this and subsequent expanded editions he dedicates space to the various poets on the basis of "sheer excellence or intensity" rather than range. His printing several of her poems without comment seems to have had a salutary effect on her literary reputation. That a serious editor could fill twelve pages with her poetry on aesthetic grounds alone,

[15] *A History of American Literature During the Colonial Time* (New York, 1897), I, 282-83. Elizabeth Wade White says he "thunders at her earlier works in a way that will delight, rather than terrify, the modern student of English poetry." "Tenth Muse," *WMQ,* p. 371.

[16] Charles F. Richardson, *American Literature 1607-1885* (New York, 1888), II, 7.

[17] *American Poetry, 1671-1928: A comprehensive Anthology* (New York, 1929); also his later *An Anthology of Famous English and American Poetry* (New York, 1945).

with no apologies for filial piety or anti-chauvinistic protestations, was reconsideration enough. Aiken gives no more space than that to Bryant, Holmes, and Lowell together, and only six pages to Whittier, and eight each to Emerson and Longfellow. Probably few readers share quite that much enthusiasm with Aiken, but it is no longer necessary to treat Anne Bradstreet with condescension.

As Samuel Eliot Morison has said, her "poetry . . . has endured, and will endure."[18] Anne Bradstreet now stands with Edward Taylor as one of the two true poets of seventeenth-century New England, and modern collections of American poetry would be foolish to ignore her lyrics. While statements about her ability usually evade direct evaluation and refer rather to her sincerity, personal charm, and whimsicality—none of these attributes being irrelevant, however—we must now affirm that our first poet was a genuine, if minor, poet.

Has she influenced other poets? What influence her poems had on Edward Taylor is difficult to say. Some scholars have seen her genius for homely household metaphor "reincarnated in Emily Dickinson." Since, however, reincarnation is not an acceptable method of transmitting literary influence, we must find the greatest influence in John Berryman's *Homage to Mistress Bradstreet* (London, 1959). (John Norton wrote, in a funeral elegy to Anne Bradstreet printed in the 1678 edition of her poems, ". . . time will a poet raise/ Born under better Stars, shall sing thy praise.") Berryman's poem of fifty-nine stanzas is full of knowledge of colonial New England, Bradstreetiana, and phrases borrowed from Anne Bradstreet's prose and verse, the Winthrop papers, and Helen Campbell's biography. It is also modern poetry of merit, full of multiple implication and suggestion, and showing adept handling of metrical techniques. Berryman's sympathy for Anne Bradstreet is evident, and his interpretations (e.g., that her heart rose because of Lady Arbella's death) are novel and consistent. *Homage to Mistress Bradstreet* is certainly clear evidence that Anne has influenced a modern poet who has read her work carefully.

[18] *Builders of the Bay Colony* (Boston, 1930), p. 335.

A NOTE ON THE TEXT

The following text reproduces carefully the second edition, *Several Poems*, published in 1678 by John Foster in Boston. Although many of these poems were first printed in 1650 by Stephen Bowtell in London, the author, as has been mentioned before, had no control over that edition. She corrected it, added to it, and planned for a revised edition; and even though it was not printed until six years after she died, the 1678 edition must contain more nearly the form in which she intended her work to appear. In preparing this John Harvard Library edition, all known copies of the first and second editions have been compared and the variants documented. The copy of *Several Poems* owned by the Massachusetts Historical Society is the copy text.

Since the present edition is intended for those who wish to read the work of Anne Bradstreet in a clear and accurate form, no attempt has been made to reproduce the peculiarities of seventeenth-century type, such as the swash *s*, and the spelling and punctuation have been modernized. So many variations occurred between the 1650 and 1678 editions that the notes which appear at the end of the text of the cloth edition indicate only those of special interest or importance. All variations among copies of either first or second editions have been noted. The notes also show readings given on the errata leaf, which remains complete only in the Prince copy of the 1678 edition at the Boston Public Library. I have regarded the errata leaf readings as primary and preferred the readings of the second edition to those of the first, with certain clearly marked exceptions.

I have not attempted to show variations in font. Ornamental initials, larger type, and type ornaments are ignored. Running titles, catchwords, page numbers, and signatures are omitted, but variants in pagination and signature are in the notes. I have numbered the lines of the poems, but in other ways the text follows that of the second edition unless it is marked otherwise.

The prose and poetry listed in the Contents as "The Andover

Manuscripts" appeared first in John Harvard Ellis' 1867 edition of the *Works of Anne Bradstreet*. They come originally from a small notebook now belonging to the Stephens Memorial Library in North Andover, Massachusetts. The book is about six-by-three-and-three-fourths inches in size, leather bound, and much worn. Part is in Mrs. Bradstreet's own handwriting, and part is in her son Simon Bradstreet's. It contains also a Latin translation of the dedication and first four meditations by Mrs. Bradstreet's great-grandson, Simon Bradstreet. I have omitted the Latin translation and certain notes by Simon, but all other contents of the book have been included.

To verify the accuracy of the portions in Simon's handwriting I have compared them with a second manuscript of the same material belonging to Houghton Library and in his sister Sarah Hubbard's hand; it contains the same items in the same order except the passage dated "May 11, 1661." I have expanded all abbreviations, and the present line divisions do not follow the original manuscript. Modern spelling and punctuation have been used, but no words are changed. Any doubtful passages are mentioned in the notes.

For this edition I have changed the order of the items to approach the order in which they were written. The material in Simon's hand comes first, except for the poem on the burning of the house in 1666. Then follow the holograph meditations, dated 1664. Last come the verses on the burning of the house and "As Weary Pilgrim" dated 1669.

THE WORKS OF
ANNE BRADSTREET

[EPISTLE TO THE READER,

BY JOHN WOODBRIDGE]

Kind Reader:

Had I opportunity but to borrow some of the author's wit, 'tis possible I might so trim this curious work with such quaint expressions, as that the Preface might bespeak thy further perusal; but I fear 'twill be a shame for a man that can speak so little, to be seen in the title-page of this woman's book, lest by comparing the one with the other, the reader should pass his sentence that it is the gift of women not only to speak most but to speak best; I shall leave therefore to commend that, which with any ingenious reader will too much commend the author, unless men turn more peevish then women, to envy the excellency of the inferior sex. I doubt not but the reader will quickly find more than I can say, and the worst effect of his reading will be unbelief, which will make him question whether it be a woman's work, and ask, is it possible? If any do, take this as an answer from him that dares avow it: it is the work of a woman, honoured, and esteemed where she lives, for her gracious demeanour, her eminent parts, her pious conversation, her courteous disposition, her exact diligence in her place, and discrete managing of her family occasions, and more than so, these poems are the fruit but of some few hours, curtailed from her sleep and other refreshments. I dare add little lest I keep thee too long; if thou wilt not believe the worth of these things (in their kind) when a man says it, yet believe it from a woman when thou seest it. This only I shall annex, I fear the displeasure of no person in the publishing of these poems but the author, without whose knowledge, and contrary to her expectation, I have presumed to bring to public view, what she resolved should (in such a manner) never see the sun; but I found that divers had gotten some scattered papers, affected them well, were likely to have sent forth broken pieces, to the author's prejudice, which I thought to prevent, as well as to pleasure those that earnestly desired the view of the whole.

[INTRODUCTORY VERSES, BY NATHANIEL WARD, JOHN ROGERS, AND OTHERS]

Mercury showed Apollo Bartas' book,
Minerva this, and wished him well to look,
And tell uprightly, which did which excell,
He viewed and viewed, and vowed he could not tell.
They bid him hemisphere his mouldy nose,   5
With's cracked leering glasses, for it would pose
The best brains he had in's old pudding-pan,
Sex weighed, which best, the woman, or the man?
He peered, and poured, and glared, and said for wore,
I'm even as wise now, as I was before: 10
They both 'gan laugh, and said it was no mar'l
The Auth'ress was a right Du Bartas girl.
Good sooth quoth the old Don, tell ye me so,
I muse whither at length these girls will go;
It half revives my chill frost-bitten blood,   15
To see a woman once do ought that's good;
And shod by Chaucer's boots, and Homer's furs,
Let men look to't, lest women wear the spurs.

N. Ward.

TO MY DEAR SISTER, THE AUTHOR OF THESE POEMS

Though most that know me dare (I think) affirm
I ne'er was born to do a poet harm,
Yet when I read your pleasant witty strains,   5
It wrought so strongly on my addle brains;
That though my verse be not so finely spun,
And so (like yours) cannot so neatly run,
Yet am I willing, with upright intent,
To show my love without a compliment.   10

There needs no painting to that comely face,
That in its native beauty hath such grace;
What I (poor silly I) prefix therefore,
Can but do this, make yours admired the more;
And if but only this I do attain,   15
Content, that my disgrace may be your gain.
  If women, I with women may compare,
Your works are solid, others weak as air;
Some books of women I have heard of late,
Perused some, so witless, intricate,   20
So void of sense, and truth, as if to err
Were only wished (acting above their sphere)
And all to get, what (silly souls) they lack,
Esteem to be the wisest of the pack;
Though (for your sake) to some this be permitted,   25
To print, yet wish I many better witted;
Their vanity make this to be enquired,
If women are with wit and sense inspired:
Yet when your works shall come to public view,
'Twill be affirmed, 'twill be confirmed by you: 30
And I, when seriously I had revolved
What you had done, I presently resolved,
Theirs was the person's, not the sex's failing,
And therefore did bespeak a modest veiling.
You have acutely in Eliza's ditty,   35
Acquitted women, else I might with pity,
Have wished them all to women's works to look,
And never more to meddle with their book.
What you have done, the sun shall witness bear,
That for a woman's work 'tis very rare;   40
And if the nine, vouchsafe the tenth a place,
I think they rightly may yield you that grace.
  But lest I should exceed, and too much love,
Should too too much endeared affection move,
To super-add in praises, I shall cease,   45
Lest while I please myself I should displease
The longing reader, who may chance complain,
And so requite my love with deep disdain;

That I your silly servant, stand in the porch,
Lighting your sunlight, with my blinking torch;   50
Hindering his mind's content, his sweet repose,
Which your delightful poems do disclose,
When once the casket's op'ned; yet to you
Let this be added, then I'll bid adieu,
If you shall think it will be to your shame   55
To be in print, then I must bear the blame;
If't be a fault, 'tis mine, 'tis shame that might
Deny so fair an infant of its right
To look abroad; I know your modest mind,
How you will blush, complain, 'tis too unkind: 60
To force a woman's birth, provoke her pain,
Expose her labours to the world's disdain.
I know you'll say, you do defy that mint,
That stamped you thus, to be a fool in print.
'Tis true, it doth not now so neatly stand,   65
As if 'twere polished with your own sweet hand;
'Tis not so richly decked, so trimly tired,
Yet it is such as justly is admired.
If it be folly, 'tis of both, or neither,
Both you and I, we'll both be fools together;   70
And he that says, 'tis foolish (if my word
May sway) by my consent shall make the third,
I dare outface the world's disdain for both,
If you alone profess you are not wroth;
Yet if you are, a woman's wrath is little,   75
When thousands else admire you in each tittle.

I. W.

UPON THE AUTHOR: BY
A KNOWN FRIEND

Now I believe tradition, which doth call
The Muses, Virtues, Graces, females all;
Only they are not nine, eleven nor three;

Our auth'ress proves them but one unity.
Mankind take up some blushes on the score;
Monopolize perfection no more;
In your own arts, confess yourselves outdone,
The moon hath totally eclipsed the sun,
Not with her sable mantle muffling him;
But her bright silver makes his gold look dim:
Just as his beams force our pale lamps to wink,
And earthly fires, within their ashes shrink.

                                        B. W.

I cannot wonder at Apollo now,
That he with female laurel crowned his brow.
That made him witty; had I leave to choose,
My verse should be a page unto your Muse.

                                        C. B.

Arm, arm, soldados arm; horse,
    Horse, speed to your horses;
Gentle-women, make head, they vent
    their plots in verses;
They write of monarchies, a most se-
    ditious word,
It signifies oppression, tyranny, and
    sword:
March amain to London, they'll rise, for
    there they flock,
But stay a while, they seldom rise till
    ten o'clock.
                                R. Q.

IN PRAISE OF THE AUTHOR, MISTRESS ANNE BRADSTREET, VIRTUES TRUE AND LIVELY PATTERN, WIFE OF THE WORSHIPFUL SIMON BRADSTREET ESQ.

AT PRESENT RESIDING IN THE OCCIDENTAL PARTS OF THE WORLD IN AMERICA, ALIAS NOV-ANGLIA   10

What golden splendent star is this so bright,
One thousand miles thrice told, both day and night,
(From th' Orient first sprung) now from the West
That shines: swift-winged Phoebus, and the rest
Of all Jove's fiery flames surmounting far   15
As doth each planet, every falling star;
By whose divine and lucid light most clear
Nature's dark secret mysteries appear;
Heavens, earths, admired wonders, noble acts
Of Kings and Princes most heroic facts,   20
And what e'er else in darkness seemed to die,
Revives all things so obvious now to th' eye,
That he who these its glittering rayes views o're,
Shall see what's done in all the world before.

N. H.

UPON THE AUTHOR

'Twere extreme folly should I dare attempt,
To praise this author's worth with compliment;
None but herself must dare commend her parts,
Whose sublime brain's the synopsis of arts.

Nature and skill, here both in one agree,
To frame this masterpiece of poetry:
False fame, belie their sex no more, it can
Surpass, or parallel, the best of man.

C. B.

ANOTHER
TO MRS. ANNE BRADSTREET,
AUTHOR OF THIS POEM

I've read your poem, Lady, and admire,
Your sex to such a pitch should e'er aspire;
Go on to write, continue to relate,
New histories, of monarchy and state:
And what the Romans to their poets gave,
Be sure such honour, and esteem you'll have.

H. S.

AN ANAGRAM

Anna Bradestreate   Dear neat An Bartas.
So Bartas like thy fine spun poems been,
That Bartas' name will prove an epicene.

ANOTHER

Anne Bradstreate   Artes bred neat An.

UPON
MRS. ANNE BRADSTREET
HER POEMS, ETC.

Madam, twice through the Muses' grove I walked,
Under your blissful bowers, I shrouding there,   5
It seemed with nymphs of Helicon I talked:
For there those sweet-lipped sisters sporting were,
Apollo with his sacred lute sat by,
On high they made their heavenly sonnets fly,
Posies around they strowed, of sweetest poesy.   10

2

Twice have I drunk the nectar of your lines,
Which high sublimed my mean born phantasy,
Flushed with these streams of your Maronean wines
Above myself rapt to an ecstasy:
Methought I was upon Mount Hiblas' top,   15
There where I might those fragrant flowers lop,
Whence did sweet odors flow, and honey spangles drop.

3

To Venus' shrine no altars raised are,
Nor venomed shafts from painted quiver fly,
Nor wanton doves of Aphrodite's car   20
Are fluttering there, nor here forlornly lie,
Lorn paramours, not chatting birds tell news
How sage Apollo, Daphne hot pursues,
Or stately Jove himself is wont to haunt the stews.

4

Nor barking satyr's breath, nor dreary clouds   25
Exhaled from Styx, their dismal drops distil
Within these fairy, flow'ry fields, nor shrouds

The screeching night raven, with his shady quill:
But lyric strings here Orpheus nimbly hits,
Arion on his saddled dolphin sits,   30
Chanting as every humour, age and season fits.

5

Here silver swans, with nightingales set spells
Which sweetly charm the traveler, and raise
Earth's earthed monarchs from their hidden cells,
And to appearance summons lapsed days,   35
There heav'nly air becalms the swelling frays,
And fury fell of elements allays,
By paying every one due tribute of his praise.

6

This seemed the site of all those verdant vales,
And purled springs, whereat the nymphs do play,   40
With lofty hills, where poets rear their tales,
To heavenly vaults, which heav'nly sound repay
By echo's sweet rebound, here ladies kiss,
Circling nor songs, nor dances circle miss;
But whilst those sirens sung, I sunk in sea of bliss.   45

7

Thus welt'ring in delight, my virgin mind
Admits a rape; truth still lies undescried,
It's singular, that plural seemed, I find,
'Twas fancy's glass alone that multiplied;
Nature with art, so closely did combine,   50
I thought I saw the Muses treble trine,
Which proved your lonely Muse superior to the nine.

8

Your only hand those poesies did compose,
Your head the source, whence all those springs did flow,

Your voice, whence change's sweetest notes arose,   55
Your feet that kept the dance alone, I trow.
Then veil your bonnets, poetasters all,
Strike, lower amain, and at these humbly fall,
And deem yourselves advanced to be her pedestal.

9

Should all with lowly Congies laurels bring,   60
Waste Flora's magazine to find a wreath,
Or Pineus' banks, 'twere too mean offering;
Your Muse a fairer garland doth bequeath
To guard your fairer front; here 'tis your name
Shall stand immarbled; this your little frame   65
Shall great Colossus be, to your eternal fame.

I'll please my self, though I my self disgrace,
What errors here be found, are in Errata's place.

J. Rogers.

TO HER MOST HONOURED FATHER
THOMAS DUDLEY ESQ. THESE
HUMBLY PRESENTED

Dear Sir, of late delighted with
   the sight

Of your four Sisters clothed in black
   and white,

T.D. On
the four
parts of   5
the world.

Of fairer dames the sun ne'er saw the face;
Though made a pedestal for Adam's race;
Their worth so shines in these rich lines you show,
Their parallels to find I scarcely know;
To climb their climes, I have nor strength nor skill.   10
To mount so high requires an eagle's quill;
Yet view thereof did cause my thoughts to soar;
My lowly pen might wait upon these four.
I bring my four times four, now meanly clad
To do their homage unto yours, full glad;   15
Who for their age, their worth and quality
Might seem of yours to claim precedency;
But by my humble hand thus rudely penned,
They are your bounden handmaids to attend,
These same are they from whom we being have,   20
These are of all, the life, the nurse, the grave,
These are the hot, the cold, the moist, the dry,
That sink, that swim, that fill, that upwards fly,
Of these consists our bodies, clothes, and food,
The world, the useful, hurtful, and the good.   25
Sweet harmony they keep, yet jar oft times,
Their discord doth appear by these harsh rimes;

Yours did contest for wealth, for arts, for age,
My first do show their good, and then their rage,
My other fours do intermixed tell   30
Each other's faults, and where themselves excel;
How hot and dry contend with moist and cold,
How air and earth no correspondence hold,
And yet in equal tempers, how they 'gree
How divers natures make one unity.   35
Something of all (though mean) I did intend
But feared you'ld judge Du Bartas was my friend.
I honour him, but dare not wear his wealth;
My goods are true (though poor), I love no stealth,
But if I did, I durst not send them you   40
Who must reward a thief, but with his due.
I shall not need mine innocence to clear,
These ragged lines will do't when they appear:
On what they are, your mild aspect I crave;
Accept my best, my worst vouchsafe a grave.   45

From her that to yourself more duty owes
Than water in the boundless ocean flows.

March 20, 1642.

ANNE BRADSTREET

THE
PROLOGUE

1

To sing of wars, of captains, and of kings,
Of cities founded, commonwealths begun,
For my mean pen are too superior things: 5
Or how they all, or each their dates have run
Let poets and historians set these forth,
My obscure lines shall not so dim their worth.

2

But when my wond'ring eyes and envious heart
Great Bartas' sugared lines do but read o'er,   10
Fool I do grudge the Muses did not part
'Twixt him and me that overfluent store;
A Bartas can do what a Bartas will
But simple I according to my skill.

3

From schoolboy's tongue no rhet'ric we expect,   15
Nor yet a sweet consort from broken strings,
Nor perfect beauty where's a main defect:
My foolish, broken, blemished Muse so sings,
And this to mend, alas, no art is able,
'Cause nature made it so irreparable.   20

4

Nor can I, like that fluent sweet tongued Greek,
Who lisped at first, in future times speak plain.

By art he gladly found what he did seek,
A full requital of his striving pain.
Art can do much, but this maxim's most sure: 25
A weak or wounded brain admits no cure.

5

I am obnoxious to each carping tongue
Who says my hand a needle better fits,
A poet's pen all scorn I should thus wrong,
For such despite they cast on female wits: 30
If what I do prove well, it won't advance,
They'll say it's stol'n, or else it was by chance.

6

But sure the antique Greeks were far more mild
Else of our sex, why feigned they those nine
And poesy made Calliope's own child;   35
So 'mongst the rest they placed the arts divine:
But this weak knot they will full soon untie,
The Greeks did nought, but play the fools and lie.

7

Let Greeks be Greeks, and women what they are
Men have precedency and still excel,   40
It is but vain unjustly to wage war;
Men can do best, and women know it well.
Preeminence in all and each is yours;
Yet grant some small acknowledgement of ours.

8

And oh ye high flown quills that soar the skies,   45
And ever with your prey still catch your praise,
If e'er you deign these lowly lines your eyes,

Give thyme or parsley wreath, I ask no bays;
This mean and unrefined ore of mine
Will make your glist'ring gold but more to shine.   50

THE
FOUR ELEMENTS

The Fire, Air, Earth, and Water did contest
Which was the strongest, noblest, and the best,
Who was of greatest use and might'est force;   5
In placid terms they thought now to discourse,
That in due order each her turn should speak;
But enmity this amity did break.
All would be chief, and all scorned to be under,
Whence issued winds and rains, lightning and thunder;   10
The quaking earth did groan, the sky looked black,
The fire, the forced air, in sunder crack;
The sea did threat the heavens, the heavens the earth,
All looked like a chaos or new birth:
Fire broiled Earth, and scorched Earth it choked.   15
Both by their darings, Water so provoked
That roaring in it came, and with its source
Soon made the combatants abate their force.
The rumbling, hissing, puffing was so great
The world's confusion it did seem to threat   20
Till gentle Air contention so abated
That betwixt hot and cold she arbitrated;
The others' difference, being less, did cease;
All storms now laid, and they in perfect peace.
That Fire should first begin, the rest consent,   25
The noblest and most active element.

Fire

What is my worth, both ye and all men know,
In little time I can but little show,
But what I am, let learned Grecians say;   30
What I can do, well skilled mechanics may:

The benefit all living by me find,
All sorts of artists, here declare your mind.
What tool was ever framed, but by my might?
Ye martialists, what weapons for your fight   35
To try your valour by, but it must feel
My force? your sword, and gun, your lance of steel,
Your cannon's bootless and your powder too.
Without mine aid, alas, what can they do?
The adverse wall's not shaked, the mine's not blown,   40
And in despite the city keeps her own;
But I with one granado or petard
Set ope those gates, that 'fore so strong were barred.
Ye husband-men, your coulters made by me
Your hoes, your mattocks, and what e'er you see   45
Subdue the earth, and fit it for your grain
That so it might in time requite your pain:
Though strong limbed Vulcan forged it by his skill
I made it flexible unto his will;
Ye cooks, your kitchen implements I frame   50
Your spits, pots, jacks, what else I need not name
Your daily food I wholesome make, I warm
Your shrinking limbs, which winter's cold doth harm;
Ye Paracelsians too, in vain's your skill
In chemistry, unless I help you still.   55
And you philosophers, if e'er you made
A transmutation, it was through mine aid.
Ye silversmiths, your ore I do refine,
What mingled lay with earth, I cause to shine;
But let me leave these things, my flame aspires   60
To match on high with the celestial fires;
The sun an orb of fire was held of old,
Our sages new another tale have told:
But be he what they will, yet his aspect
A burning fiery heat we find reflect,   65
And of the self same nature is with mine.

Cold sister Earth, no witness needs but thine:
How doth his warmth, refresh thy frozen back
And trim thee brave, in green, after thy black.
Both man and beast rejoice at his approach,   70
And birds do sing, to see his glittering coach
And though nought but sal'manders live in fire
And fly Pyrausta called, all else expire.
Yet men and beasts, astronomers will tell
Fixed in heavenly constellations dwell,   75
My planets of both sexes whose degree
Poor heathen judged worthy a diety:
There's Orion armed attended by his dog;
The Theban stout Alcides with his club;
The valiant Perseus, who Medusa slew,   80
The horse that killed Belerophon, then flew.
My crab, my scorpion, fishes you may see
The maid with balance, wain with horses three,
The ram, the bull, the lion, and the beagle,
The bear, the goat, the raven, and the eagle   85
The crown, the whale, the archer, Bernice hair,
The hydra, dolphin, boys that water bear,
Nay more than these, rivers 'mongst stars are found,
Eridanus, where Phaeton was drowned.
Their magnitude, and height, should I recount   90
My story to a volume would amount;
Out of a multitude these few I touch,
Your wisdom out of little gather much.
I'll here let pass my choler, cause of wars
And influence of divers of those stars,   95
When in conjunction with the sun do more
Augment his heat, which was too hot before.
The summer ripening season I do claim
And man from thirty unto fifty frame.
Of old when sacrifices were divine,   100
I of acceptance was the holy sign.

'Mong all my wonders which I might recount,
There's none more strange than Aetna's sulphry mount.
The choking flames, that from Vesuvius flew,
The overcurious second Pliny slew,   105
And with the ashes that it sometimes shed
Apulia's 'jacent parts were covered.
And though I be a servant to each man,
Yet by my force, master my masters can.
What famous towns to cinders have I turned?   110
What lasting forts my kindled wrath hath burned?
The stately seats of mighty kings by me
In confused heaps of ashes may you see.
Where's Ninus' great walled town, and Troy of old?
Carthage, and hundred more in stories told   115
Which when they could not be o'recome by foes
The army through my help victorious rose;
And stately London (our great Britain's glory)
My raging flame did make a mournful story,
But maugre all, that I, or foes could do   120
That Phoenix from her bed is risen new.
Old sacred Zion, I demolished thee.
So great Diana's temple was by me,
And more than brutish Sodom, for her lust
With neighbouring towns, I did consume to dust;   125
What shall I say of lightening and of thunder,
Which kings and mighty ones amaze with wonder,
Which made a Caesar, (Rome's) the world's proud head,
Foolish Caligula creep under's bed.
Of meteors, *ignis fatuus* and the rest,   130
But to leave those to th' wise, I judge it best.
The rich I oft make poor, the strong I maim,
Not sparing life when I can take the same;
And in a word, the world I shall consume
And all therein, at that great day of doom;   135
Not before then, shall cease my raging ire

And then because no matter more for fire;
Now sisters pray proceed, each in your course,
As I, impart your usefulness and force.

Earth

140

The next in place Earth judged to be her due,
Sister (quoth she) I come not short of you,
In wealth and use I do surpass you all,
And Mother Earth of old men did me call:
Such is my fruitfulness, an epithet,   145
Which none ere gave, or you could claim of right,
Among my praises this I count not least,
I am th' original of man and beast.
To tell what sundry fruits my fat soil yields
In vineyards, gardens, orchards, and cornfields,   150
Their kinds, their tastes, their colors, and their smells
Would so pass time I could say nothing else:
The rich, the poor, wise, fool, and every sort
Of these so common things can make report.
To tell you of my countries and my regions,   155
Soon would they pass not hundreds but legions:
My cities famous, rich, and populous,
Whose numbers now are grown innumerous.
I have not time to think of every part,
Yet let me name my Grecia, 'tis my heart.   160
For learning, arms, and arts I love it well,
But chiefly 'cause the Muses there did dwell.
I'll here skip o're my mountains reaching skies,
Whether Pyrenean, or the Alps, both lies
On either side the country of the Gauls,   165
Strong forts, from Spanish and Italian brawls.
And huge great Taurus, longer than the rest,
Dividing great Armenia from the least;
And Hemus whose steep sides none foot upon,

But farewell all for dear mount Helicon. 170
And wondrous high Olympus, of such fame,
That heav'n itself was oft called by that name.
Parnassus sweet, I dote too much on thee,
Unless thou prove a better friend to me:
But I'll leap o're these hills, not touch a dale, 175
Nor will I stay, no not in Tempe Vale,
I'll here let go my lions of Numidia,
My panthers and my leopards of Libia,
The behemoth and rare found unicorn,
Poison's sure antidote lies in his horn, 180
And my hyaena (imitates man's voice).
Out of great numbers I might pick my choice,
Thousands in woods and plains, both wild and tame,
But here or there, I list now none to name:
No, though the fawning dog did urge me sore, 185
In his behalf to speak a word the more,
Whose trust and valour I might here commend;
But time's too short and precious so to spend.
But hark you wealthy merchants, who for prize
Send forth your well-manned ships where sun doth rise, 190
After three years when men and meat is spent,
My rich commodities pay double rent.
Ye Galenists, my drugs that come from thence,
Do cure your patients, fill your purse with pence;
Besides the use of roots, of herbs and plants, 195
That with less cost near home supply your wants.
But mariners where got you ships and sails,
And oars to row, when both my sisters fails?
Your tackling, anchor, compass too is mine,
Which guides when sun nor moon nor stars do shine. 200
Ye mighty kings, who for your lasting fames
Built cities, monuments, called by your names,
Were those compiled heaps of massy stones
That your ambition laid, ought but my bones?

Ye greedy misers, who do dig for gold,   205
For gems, for silver, treasures which I hold,
Will not my goodly face your rage suffice
But you will see what in my bowels lies?
And ye artificers, all trades and sorts,
My bounty calls you forth to make reports,   210
If ought you have, to use, to wear, to eat,
But what I freely yield, upon your sweat?
And choleric sister, thou for all thine ire
Well knowest my fuel must maintain thy fire.
As I ingenuously with thanks confess,   215
My cold thy fruitful heat doth crave no less,
But how my cold dry temper works upon
The melancholy constitution;
How the autumnal season I do sway,
And how I force the grey-head to obey,   220
I should here make a short, yet true narration,
But that thy method is mine imitation.
Now must I show mine adverse quality,
And how I oft work man's mortality:
He sometimes finds, maugre his toiling pain,   225
Thistles and thorns where he expected grain.
My sap to plants and trees I must not grant,
The vine, the olive, and the figtree want:
The corn and hay do fall before they're mown,
And buds from fruitful trees as soon as blown;   230
Then dearth prevails, that nature to suffice
The mother on her tender infant flies;
The husband knows no wife, nor father sons,
But to all outrages their hunger runs:
Dreadful examples soon I might produce,   235
But to such auditors 'twere of no use.
Again when delvers dare in hope of gold
To ope those veins of mine, audacious bold:
While they thus in mine entrails love to dive,

Before they know, they are interred alive.   240
Y'affrighted wights appalled, how do ye shake,
When once you feel me your foundation quake?
Because in the abyss of my dark womb
Your cities and your selves I oft intomb:
O dreadful sepulcher! that this is true   245
Dathan and all his company well knew,
So did that Roman, far more stout than wise,
Bur'ing himself alive for honour's prize.
And since fair Italy full sadly knows
What she hath lost by these remed'less woes.   250
Again what veins of poison in me lie,
Some kill outright, and some do stupefy:
Nay into herbs and plants it sometimes creeps,
In heats and colds and grippes and drowsy sleeps:
Thus I occasion death to man and beast   255
When food they seek, and harm mistrust the least.
Much might I say of the hot Libyan sand
Which rise like tumbling billows on the land
Wherein Cambyses' army was o'erthrown;
(But windy sister, 'twas when you have blown).   260
I'll say no more, but this thing add I must,
Remember sons, your mould is of my dust
And after death whether interred or burned
As Earth at first so into Earth returned.

Water   265

Scarce Earth had done, but th' angry water moved;
Sister (quoth she) it had full well behoved
Among your boastings to have praised me,
Cause of your fruitfulness, as you shall see:
This your neglect shows your ingratitude   270
And how your subtlety would men delude.
Not one of us (all knows) that's like to thee

Ever in craving from the other three.
But thou art bound to me above the rest,
Who am thy drink, thy blood, thy sap and best: 275
If I withold, what art thou? dead dry lump,
Thou bear'st no grass nor plant nor tree, nor stump.
Thy extreme thirst is moistened by my love
With springs below, and showers from above
Or else thy sunburnt face, and gaping chaps   280
Complain to th' heavens, if I withhold my drops.
Thy bear, thy tiger, and thy lion stout,
When I am gone, their fierceness none needs doubt;
Thy camel hath no strength, thy bull no force;
Nor mettle's found, in the courageous horse;   285
Hinds leave their calves, the elephant the fens;
The wolves and savage beasts forsake their dens.
The lofty eagle and the stork fly low,
The peacock and the ostrich share in woe,
The pine, the cedar, yea, and Daphne's tree   290
Do cease to flourish in this misery.
Man wants his bread and wine, and pleasant fruits;
He knows such sweets lies not in earth's dry roots,
Then seeks me out, in river and in well
His deadly malady I might expell: 295
If I supply, his heart and veins rejoice,
If not, soon ends his life, as did his voice;
That this is true, Earth thou canst not deny;
I call thine Egypt, this to verify,
Which by my fatting Nile, doth yield such store   300
That she can spare, when nations round are poor.
When I run low, and not o'erflow her brinks
To meet with want, each woeful man bethinks:
And such I am, in rivers, showers and springs.
But what's the wealth that my rich ocean brings?   305
Fishes so numberless I there do hold,
If thou shouldst buy, it would exhaust thy gold:

There lives the oily whale, whom all men know,
Such wealth but not such like, earth thou may'st show,
The dolphin, loving music, Arian's friend,   310
The witty barbel, whose craft doth her commend
With thousands more, which now I list not name;
Thy silence of thy beasts doth cause the same.
My pearls that dangle at thy darling's ears,
Not thou, but shellfish yield, as Pliny clears.   315
Was ever gem so rich found in thy trunk,
As Egypt's wanton Cleopatra drunk?
Or hast thou any colour can come nigh
The Roman purple, double Tyrian dye?
Which Caesar's consuls, tribunes all adorn,   320
For it to search my waves they thought no scorn.
Thy gallant rich perfuming ambergris
I lightly cast ashore as frothy fleece,
With rolling grains of purest massy gold,
Which Spain's Americans do gladly hold.   325
Earth, thou hast not moe countries, vales and mounds
Than I have fountains, rivers, lakes, and ponds.
My sundry seas, Black, White, and Adriatic,
Ionian, Baltic, and the vast Atlantic,
Aegean, Caspian, golden rivers five,   330
Asphaltis lake where nought remains alive:
But I should go beyond thee in my boasts,
If I should name more seas than thou hast coasts.
And be thy mountains n'er so high and steep,
I soon can match them with my seas as deep.   335
To speak of kinds of waters I neglect,
My diverse fountains and their strange effect;
My wholesome baths, together with their cures;
My water Sirens with their guileful lures.
Th' uncertain cause of certain ebbs and flows,   340
Which wond'ring Aristotle's wit n'er knows.
Nor will I speak of waters made by art,

Which can to life restore a fainting heart.
Nor fruitful dews, nor drops distilled from eyes,
Which pity move, and oft deceive the wise: 345
Nor yet of salt and sugar, sweet and smart,
Both when we list to water we convert.
Alas thy ships and oars could do no good
Did they but want my ocean and my flood.
The wary merchant on his weary beast   350
Transfers his goods from south to north and east,
Unless I ease his toil, and do transport
The wealthy freight unto his wished port.
These be my benefits, which may suffice:
I now must show what ill there in me lies.   355
The phlegmy constitution I uphold,
All humors, tumors which are bred of cold:
O'er childhood, and o'er winter I bear sway,
And Luna for my regent I obey.
As I with showers oft times refresh the earth,   360
So oft in my excess I cause a dearth,
And with abundant wet so cool the ground,
By adding cold to cold no fruit proves sound.
The farmer and the grazier do complain
Of rotten sheep, lean kine, and mildewed grain,   365
And with my wasting floods and roaring torrent,
Their cattle, hay, and corn I sweep down current.
Nay many times my ocean breaks his bounds,
And with astonishment the world confounds,
And swallows countries up, n'er seen again,   370
And that an island makes which once was main:
Thus Britain fair ('tis thought) was cut from France,
Sicily from Italy by the like chance,
And but one land was Africa and Spain
Until proud Gibraltar did make them twain.   375
Some say I swallowed up (sure 'tis a notion)
A mighty country in th' Atlantic Ocean.

I need not say much of my hail and snow,
My ice and extreme cold, which all men know,
Whereof the first so ominous I rained, 380
That Israel's enemies therewith were brained;
And of my chilling snows such plenty be,
That Caucasus' high mounts are seldom free.
Mine ice doth glaze Europe's great rivers o'er,
Till sun release, their ships can sail no more. 385
All know that inundations I have made,
Wherein not men, but mountains seemed to wade;
As when Achaia all under water stood,
That for two hundred years it n'er proved good.
Deucalion's great deluge with many moe, 390
But these are trifles to the flood of Noe,
Then wholly perished Earth's ignoble race,
And to this day impairs her beauteous face.
That after times shall never feel like woe,
Her confirmed sons behold my coloured bow. 395
Much might I say of wracks, but that I'll spare,
And now give place unto our sister Air.

Air

Content (quoth Air) to speak the last of you,
Yet am not ignorant first was my due: 400
I do suppose you'll yield without control
I am the breath of every living soul.
Mortals, what one of you that loves not me
Abundantly more than my sisters three?
And though you love Fire, Earth and Water well 405
Yet Air beyond all these you know t' excell.
I ask the man condemned, that's near his death,
How gladly should his gold purchase his breath,
And all the wealth that ever earth did give,
How freely should it go so he might live: 410

No Earth, thy witching trash were all but vain,
If my pure air thy sons did not sustain.
The famished, thirsty man that craves supply,
His moving reason is, give least I die,
So loth he is to go though nature's spent 415
To bid adieu to his dear element.
Nay what are words which do reveal the mind?
Speak who or what they will they are but wind.
Your drums, your trumpets, and your organs sound,
What is't but forced air which doth rebound, 420
And such are echoes and report of th' gun
That tells afar th' exploit which it hath done.
Your songs and pleasant tunes, they are the same,
And so's the notes which nightingales do frame.
Ye forging smiths, if bellows once were gone, 425
Your red hot work more coldly would go on.
Ye mariners, 'tis I that fill your sails,
And speed you to your port with wished gales.
When burning heat doth cause you faint, I cool,
And when I smile, your ocean's like a pool. 430
I help to ripe the corn, I turn the mill,
And with myself I every vacuum fill.
The ruddy sweet sanguine is like to air,
And youth and spring, sages to me compare.
My moist hot nature is so purely thin, 435
No place so subtly made, but I get in.
I grow more pure and pure as I mount higher,
And when I'm thoroughly rarified turn Fire:
So when I am condensed, I turn to Water,
Which may be done by holding down my vapour. 440
Thus I another body can assume,
And in a trice my own nature resume.
Some for this cause of late have been so bold
Me for no element longer to hold.
Let such suspend their thoughts, and silent be, 445

For all philosophers make one of me;
And what those sages either spake or writ
Is more authentic than our modern wit.
Next of my fowls such multitudes there are,
Earth's beasts and Water's fish scarce can compare.   450
Th' ostrich with her plumes, th' eagle with her eyn,
The phoenix too (if any be) are mine,
The stork, the crane, the partridge, and the pheasant
The thrush, the wren, the lark a prey to th' peasant.
With thousands more which now I may omit   455
Without impeachment to my tale or wit.
As my fresh air preserves all things in life,
So when corrupt, mortality is rife:
Then fevers, purples, pox, and pestilence,
With divers moe, work deadly consequence;   460
Whereof such multitudes have died and fled,
The living scarce had power to bury dead;
Yea so contagious countries have me known
That birds have not 'scaped death as they have flown,
Of murrain, cattle numberless did fall,   465
Men feared destruction epidemical.
Then of my tempests felt at sea and land,
Which neither ships nor houses could withstand,
What woeful wracks I've made may well appear,
If nought were known but that before Algier,   470
Where famous Charles the Fifth more loss sustained
Than in his long hot war which Milan gained.
Again what furious storms and hurricanoes
Know western isles, as Christophers, Barbadoes,
Where neither houses, trees, nor plants I spare;   475
But some fall down, and some fly up with air.
Earthquakes so hurtful, and so feared of all,
Imprisoned I am the original.
Then what prodigious sights I sometimes show,
As battles pitched in th' air, as countries know,   480

Their joining, fighting, forcing, and retreat,
That earth appears in heaven, O wonder great!
Sometimes red flaming swords and blazing stars,
Portentous signs of famines, plagues, and wars.
Which make the mighty monarchs fear their fates   485
By death or great mutation of their states.
I have said less than did my sisters three,
But what's their worth or force, the same's in me.
To add to all I've said was my intent,
But dare not go beyond my element.   490

OF THE FOUR HUMOURS IN MAN'S CONSTITUTION

The former four now ending their discourse,
Ceasing to vaunt their good, or threat their force,
Lo! other four step up, crave leave to show   5
The native qualities that from them flow:
But first they wisely showed their high descent,
Each eldest daughter to each element.
Choler was owned by Fire, and Blood by Air,
Earth knew her black swarth child, Water her fair: 10
All having made obeisance to each mother,
Had leave to speak, succeeding one the other:
But 'mongst themselves they were at variance,
Which of the four should have predominance.
Choler first hotly claimed right by her mother,   15
Who had precedency of all the other;
But Sanguine did disdain what she required,
Pleading herself was most of all desired.
Proud Melancholy, more envious than the rest,
The second, third, or last could not digest.   20
She was the silentest of all the four,
Her wisdom spake not much, but thought the more.
Mild Phlegm did not contest for chiefest place,
Only she craved to have a vacant space.
Well, thus they parle and chide; but to be brief,   25
Or will they, nill they, Choler will be chief.
They seeing her impetuosity
At present yielded to necessity.

Choler

To show my high descent and pedigree,   30
Yourselves would judge but vain prolixity;

It is acknowledged from whence I came,
It shall suffice to show you what I am;
My self and mother one, as you shall see,
But she in greater, I in less degree.   35
We both once masculines, the world doth know,
Now feminines awhile; for love we owe
Unto your sisterhood, which makes us render
Our noble selves in a less noble gender.
Though under Fire we comprehend all heat,   40
Yet man for Choler is the proper seat:
I in his heart erect my regal throne,
Where monarch like I play and sway alone.
Yet many times unto my great disgrace
One of yourselves are my compeers in place,   45
Where if your rule prove once predominant,
The man proves boyish, sottish, ignorant:
But if you yield subservience unto me
I make a man, a man in th' highest degree:
Be he a soldier, I more fence his heart   50
Than iron corslet 'gainst a sword or dart.
What makes him face his foe without appall,
To storm a breach, or scale a city wall,
In dangers to account himself more sure
Than timorous hares whom castles do immure?   55
Have you not heard of worthies, demi-gods?
Twixt them and others what is't makes the odds
But valour? whence comes that? from none of you,
Nay milksops, at such brunts you look but blue.
Here's sister ruddy, worth the other two,   60
Who much will talk, but little dares she do,
Unless to court and claw, to dice and drink,
And there she will out-bid us all, I think,
She loves a fiddle better than a drum,
A chamber well, in field she dares not come,   65
She'll ride a horse as bravely as the best,

And break a staff, provided 't be in jest;
But shuns to look on wounds, and blood that's spilt,
She loves her sword only because it's gilt.
Then here's our sad black sister, worse than you.   70
She'll neither say she will, nor will she do;
But peevish malecontent, musing she sits,
And by misprisions like to lose her Wits:
If great persuasions cause her meet her foe,
In her dull resolution she's so slow,   75
To march her pace to some is greater pain
Than by a quick encounter to be slain.
But be she beaten, she'll not run away,
She'll first advise if't be not best to stay.
Now let's give cold white sister Phlegm her right,   80
So loving unto all, she scorns to fight:
If any threaten her, she'll in a trice
Convert from water to congealed ice:
Her teeth will chatter, dead and wan's her face,
And 'fore she be assaulted, quits the place.   85
She dares not challenge, if I speak amiss,
Nor hath she wit or heat to blush at this.
Here's three of you all see now what you are,
Then yield to me preeminence in war.
Again who fits for learning, science, arts?   90
Who rarifies the intellectual parts,
From whence fine spirits flow and witty notions?
But 'tis not from our dull, slow sister's motions:
Nor sister Sanguine, from thy moderate heat,
Poor spirits the liver breeds, which is thy seat.   95
What comes from thence, my heat refines the same
And through the arteries sends it o're the frame:
The vital spirits they're called, and well they may
For when they fail, man turns unto his clay.
The animal I claim as well as these,   100
The nerves, should I not warm, soon would they freeze,

But Phlegm herself is now provoked at this,
She thinks I never shot so far amiss.
The brain she challengeth, the head's her seat;
But know'ts a foolish brain that wanteth heat.   105
My absence proves it plain, her wit then flies
Out at her nose, or melteth at her eyes.
Oh who would miss this influence of thine
To be distilled, a drop on every line?
Alas, thou hast no spirits, thy company   110
Will feed a dropsy, or a tympany,
The palsy, gout, or cramp, or some such dolour:
Thou wast not made, for soldier or for scholar;
Of greasy paunch, and bloated cheeks go vaunt,
But a good head from these are dissonant.   115
But Melancholy, wouldst have this glory thine,
Thou sayst thy wits are staid, subtle and fine;
'Tis true, when I am midwife to thy birth
Thy self's as dull, as is thy mother Earth:
Thou canst not claim the liver, head, nor heart   120
Yet hast thy seat assigned, a goodly part
The sink of all us three, the hateful spleen;
Of that black region, nature made thee queen;
Where pain and sore obstruction thou dost work,
Where envy, malice, thy companions lurk.   125
If once thou'rt great, what follows thereupon
But bodies wasting, and destruction?
So base thou art, that baser cannot be,
Th' excrement adustion of me.
But I am weary to dilate your shame,   130
Nor is't my pleasure thus to blur your name,
Only to raise my honour to the skies,
As objects best appear by contraries.
Both arms and arts I claim, and higher things,
The princely qualities befitting kings,   135
Whose profound heads I line with policies,

They're held for oracles, they are so wise,
Their wrathful looks are death, their words are laws;
Their courage friend and foe and subject awes;
But one of you, would make a worthy king   140
Like our sixth Henry (that same virtuous thing)
That when a varlet struck him o're the side,
"Forsooth you are to blame," he grave replied.
Take Choler from a prince, what is he more
Than a dead lion, by beasts triumphed o're.   145
Again you know how I act every part
By th' influence, I still send from the heart:
It's not your muscles, nerves, nor this nor that
Does ought without my lively heat, that's flat:
Nay th' stomach, magazine to all the rest,   150
Without my boiling heat cannot digest:
And yet to make my greatness, still more great
What differences, the sex, but only heat?
And one thing more, to close up my narration:
Of all that lives, I cause the propagation.   155
I have been sparing what I might have said;
I love no boasting, that's but children's trade.
To what you now shall say I will attend,
And to your weakness gently condescend.

Blood   160

Good sisters, give me leave, as is my place,
To vent my grief, and wipe off my disgrace:
Yourselves may plead your wrongs are no whit less,
Your patience more than mine, I must confess.
Did ever sober tongue such language speak,   165
Or honesty such ties unfriendly break?
Dost know thy self so well, us so amiss?
Is't arrogance or folly causeth this?
I'll only show the wrong thou'st done to me,

Then let my sisters right their injury.   170
To pay with railings is not mine intent,
But to evince the truth by argument.
I will analyse this thy proud relation,
So full of boasting and prevarication,
Thy foolish incongruities I'll show,   175
So walk thee till thou'rt cold, then let thee go.
There is no soldier but thy self (thou sayest),
No valour upon earth, but what thou hast.
Thy silly provocations I despise,
And leave't to all to judge, where valour lies.   180
No pattern, nor no patron will I bring
But David, Judah's most heroic king,
Whose glorious deeds in arms the world can tell,
A rosy cheek musician thou knowest well;
He knew well how to handle sword and harp,   185
And how to strike full sweet, as well as sharp,
Thou laugh'st at me for loving merriment,
And scorn'st all knightly sports at tournament.
Thou sayst I love my sword, because it's gilt,
But know, I love the blade more than the hilt.   190
Yet do abhor such temerarious deeds,
As thy unbridled, barbarous Choler breeds.
Thy rudeness counts good manners vanity,
And real compliments base flattery.
For drink, which of us twain like it the best,   195
I'll go no further than thy nose for test:
Thy other scoffs, not worthy of reply
Shall vanish as of no validity:
Of thy black calumnies this is but part,
But now I'll show what soldier thou art.   200
And though thou'st used me with opprobrious spite,
My ingenuity must give thee right.
Thy Choler is but rage when 'tis most pure,
But useful when a mixture can endure;

As with thy mother Fire, so 'tis with thee,   205
The best of all the four when they agree:
But let her leave the rest, then I presume
Both them and all things else she would consume.
Whilst us for thine associates thou tak'st,
A soldier most complete in all points mak'st: 210
But when thou scorn'st to take the help we lend,
Thou art a fury or infernal fiend.
Witness the execrable deeds thou'st done,
Nor sparing sex nor age, nor sire nor son;
To satisfy thy pride and cruelty,   215
Thou oft hast broke bounds of humanity,
Nay should I tell, thou would'st count me no blab,
How often for the lie, thou'st given the stab.
To take the wall's a sin of so high rate,
That nought but death the same may expiate,   220
To cross thy will, a challenge doth deserve
So shed'st that blood, thou'rt bounden to preserve.
Wilt thou this valour, courage, manhood call?
No, know 'tis pride most diabolical.
If murthers be thy glory, 'tis no less,   225
I'll not envy thy feats, nor happiness:
But if in fitting time and place 'gainst foes
For countries' good thy life thou dar'st expose,
Be dangers n'er so high, and courage great,
I'll praise that prowess, fury, choler, heat: 230
But such thou never art when all alone,
Yet such when we all four are joined in one.
And when such thou art, even such are we,
The friendly coadjutors still of thee.
Nextly the spirits thou dost wholly claim,   235
Which natural, vital, animal we name:
To play philosopher I have no list,
Nor yet physician, nor anatomist,
For acting these, I have no will nor art,

Yet shall with equity, give thee thy part.   240
For natural, thou dost not much contest;
For there is none (thou sayst) if some not best;
That there are some, and best, I dare aver,
Of greatest use, if reason do not erre;
What is there living, which don't first derive   245
His life now animal, from vegetive?
If thou giv'st life, I give the nourishment,
Thine without mine, is not, 'tis evident:
But I without thy help, can give a growth
As plants, trees, and small embryon know'th   250
And if vital spirits do flow from thee,
I am as sure, the natural, from me;
Be thine the nobler, which I grant, yet mine
Shall justly claim priority of thine.
I am the fountain which thy cistern fills   255
Through warm blue conduits of my venial rills.
What hath the heart, but what's sent from the liver?
If thou'rt the taker, I must be the giver.
Then never boast of what thou dost receive;
For of such glory I shall thee bereave.   260
But why the heart should be usurped by thee,
I must confess seems something strange to me:
The spirits through thy heat made perfect are,
But the material's none of thine, that's clear:
Their wondrous mixture is of blood and air,   265
The first myself, second my mother fair.
But I'll not force retorts, nor do thee wrong,
Thy fiery yellow froth is mixt among,
Challenge not all, 'cause part we do allow;
Thou know'st I've there to do as well as thou: 270
But thou wilt say I deal unequally,
There lives the irascible faculty,
Which without all dispute, is Choler's own;
Besides the vehement heat, only there known,

Can be imputed unto none but Fire,   275
Which is thy self, thy mother and thy sire;
That this is true, I easily can assent
If still you take along my aliment,
And let me be your partner, which is due,
So shall I give the dignity to you.   280
Again, stomach's concoction thou dost claim,
But by what right, nor dost, nor canst thou name
Unless as heat, it be thy faculty,
And so thou challengest her property.
The help she needs, the loving liver lends,   285
Who th' benefit o' th' whole ever intends.
To meddle further I shall be but shent,
Th' rest to our sisters is more pertinent;
Your slanders, thus refuted, takes no place,
Nor what you've said, doth argue my disgrace,   290
Now through your leaves, some little time I'll spend
My worth in humble manner to commend.
This, hot, moist, nutritive humour of mine
When 'tis untaint, pure, and most genuine
Shall chiefly take the place, as is my due,   295
Without the least indignity to you.
Of all your qualities I do partake,
And what you single are, the whole I make.
Your hot, moist, cold, dry natures are but four,
I moderately am all, what need I more;   300
As thus, if hot then dry, if moist, then cold,
If this you can't disprove, then all I hold.
My virtues hid, I've let you dimly see
My sweet complexion proves the verity.
This scarlet dye's a badge of what's within   305
One touch thereof so beautifies the skin:
Nay, could I be from all your tangs but pure
Man's life to boundless time might still endure.
But here one thrusts her heat where'ts not required

So suddenly, the body all is fired, 310
And of the calm sweet temper quite bereft,
Which makes the mansion by the soul soon left.
So Melancholy seizes on a man,
With her uncheerful visage, swarth and wan,
The body dries, the mind sublime doth smother, 315
And turns him to the womb of's earthy mother:
And Phlegm likewise can show her cruel art,
With cold distempers to pain every part:
The lungs she rots, the body wears away,
As if she'd leave no flesh to turn to clay, 320
Her languishing diseases, though not quick,
At length demolishes the faberic,
All to prevent, this curious care I take,
In th' last concoction segregation make
Of all the perverse humours from mine own, 325
The bitter Choler, most malignant known,
I turn into his cell close by my side,
The Melancholy to the spleen t' abide:
Likewise the whey, some use I in the veins,
The overplus I send unto the reins: 330
But yet for all my toil, my care and skill,
It's doomed by an irrevocable will
That my intents should meet with interruption,
That mortal man might turn to his corruption.
I might here show the nobleness of mind 335
Of such as to the sanguine are inclined,
They're liberal, pleasant, kind, and courteous,
And like the liver all benignious.
For arts and sciences they are the fittest;
And maugre Choler still they are the wittiest: 340
With an ingenious working phantasy,
A most voluminous large memory,
And nothing wanting but solidity.
But why alas, thus tedious should I be,

Thousand examples you may daily see. 345
If time I have transgressed, and been too long,
Yet could not be more brief without much wrong;
I've scarce wiped off the spots proud Choler cast,
Such venom lies in words, though but a blast;
No braggs I've used, to you I dare appeal, 350
If modesty my worth do not conceal.
I've used no bitterness, nor taxed your name,
As I to you, to me do ye the same.

Melancholy

He that with two assailants hath to do, 355
Had need be armed well and active too.
Especially when friendship is pretended,
That blow's most deadly where it is intended.
Though Choler rage and rail, I'll not do so,
The tongue's no weapon to assault a foe: 360
But sith we fight with words, we might be kind
To spare our selves and beat the whistling wind,
Fair rosy sister, so might'st thou scape free;
I'll flatter for a time as thou didst me:
But when the first offender I have laid, 365
Thy soothing girds shall fully be repaid.
But Choler be thou cooled or chafed, I'll venture,
And in contention's lists now justly enter.
What moved thee thus to vilify my name,
Not past all reason, but in truth all shame: 370
Thy fiery spirit shall bear away this prize,
To play such furious pranks I am too wise:
If in a soldier rashness be so precious,
Know in a general 'tis most pernicious.
Nature doth teach to shield the head from harm, 375
The blow that's aimed thereat is latched by th' arm.
When in Battalia my foes I face,

I then command proud Choler stand thy place,
To use thy sword, thy courage and thy art
There to defend myself, thy better part.   380
This wariness count not for cowardice,
He is not truly valiant that's not wise.
It's no less glory to defend a town,
Than by assault to gain one not our own;
And if Marcellus bold be called Rome's sword,   385
Wise Fabius is her buckler, all accord:
And if thy haste my slowness should not temper,
'Twere but a mad irregular distemper;
Enough of that by our sisters heretofore,
I'll come to that which wounds me somewhat more,   390
Of learning, policy thou wouldst bereave me,
But's not thine ignorance shall thus deceive me:
What greater clerk or politician lives,
Than he whose brain a touch my humour gives?
What is too hot my coldness doth abate,   395
What's diffluent I do consolidate.
If I be partial judged or thought to err,
The melancholy snake shall it aver,
Whose cold dry head more subtilty doth yield,
Than all the huge beasts of the fertile field.   400
Again thou dost confine me to the spleen,
As of that only part I were the queen,
Let me as well make thy precincts the gall,
So prison thee within that bladder small:
Reduce the man to's principles, then see   405
If I have not more part than all you three:
What is within, without, of theirs or thine,
Yet time and age shall soon declare it mine.
When death doth seize the man, your stock is lost,
When you poor bankrupts prove then have I most.   410
You'll say here none shall e're disturb my right,
You high born, from that lump then take your flight.

Then who's man's friend, when life and all forsakes?
His mother, mine, him to her womb retakes:
Thus he is ours, his portion is the grave,   415
But while he lives, I'll show what part I have:
And first the firm dry bones I justly claim,
The strong foundation of the stately frame;
Likewise the useful spleen, though not the best,
Yet is a bowel called well as the rest: 420
The liver, stomach, owe their thanks of right,
The first it drains, of th' last quicks appetite.
Laughter (though thou say malice) flows from hence,
These two in one cannot have residence.
But thou most grossly dost mistake to think   425
The spleen for all you three was made a sink,
Of all the rest thou'st nothing there to do,
But if thou hast, that malice is from you.
Again you often touch my swarthy hue,
That black is black, and I am black 'tis true;   430
But yet more comely far I dare avow,
Than is thy torrid nose or brazen brow.
But that which shows how high your spite is bent
Is charging me to be thy excrement:
Thy loathsome imputation I defy,   435
So plain a slander needeth no reply.
When by thy heat thou'st baked thyself to crust,
And so art called black Choler or adust,
Thou witless think'st that I am thy excretion,
So mean thou art in art as in discretion: 440
But by your leave I'll let your greatness see
What officer thou art to us all three,
The kitchen drudge, the cleanser of the sinks
That casts out all that man e'er eats or drinks:
If any doubt the truth whence this should come,   445
Show them thy passage to th' duodenum;
Thy biting quality still irritates,

Till filth and thee nature exonerates.
If there thou'rt stopped, to th' liver thou turn'st in,
And thence with jaundice saffrons all the skin.   450
No further time I'll spend in confutation,
I trust I've cleared your slanderous imputation.
I now speak unto all, no more to one,
Pray here, admire, and learn instruction.
My virtues yours surpass without compare,   455
The first my constancy, that jewel rare:
Choler's too rash this golden gift to hold,
And Sanguine is more fickle manifold.
Here, there her restless thoughts do ever fly,
Constant in nothing but unconstancy.   460
And what Phlegm is, we know, like to her mother,
Unstable is the one, and so the other;
With me is noble patience also found,
Impatient Choler loveth not the sound,
What Sanguine is, she doth not heed nor care,   465
Now up, now down, transported like the air:
Phlegm's patient because her nature's tame;
But I, by virtue do acquire the same.
My temperance, chastity is eminent,
But these with you are seldom resident;   470
Now could I stain my ruddy sister's face
With deeper red, to show you her disgrace,
But rather I with silence veil her shame
Than cause her blush, while I relate the same.
Nor are ye free from this enormity,   475
Although she bear the greatest obloquy,
My prudence, judgement, I might now reveal
But wisdom 'tis my wisdom to conceal.
Unto diseases not inclined as you,
Nor cold, nor hot, ague nor pleurisy,   480
Nor cough, nor quinsy, nor the burning fever,
I rarely feel to act his fierce endeavour;

My sickness in conceit chiefly doth lie,
What I imagine that's my malady.
Chimeras strange are in my phantasy,   485
And things that never were, nor shall I see.
I love not talk, reason lies not in length,
Nor multitude of words argues our strength;
I've done, pray sister Phlegm proceed in course,
We shall expect much sound, but little force.   490

Phlegm

Patient I am, patient I'd need to be,
To bear with the injurious taunts of three,
Though wit I want, and anger I have less,
Enough of both, my wrongs now to express.   495
I've not forgot, how bitter Choler spake
Nor how her gall on me she causeless brake;
Nor wonder 'twas, for hatred there's not small,
Where opposition is diametrical.
To what is truth I freely will assent,   500
Although my name do suffer detriment,
What's slanderous repel, doubtful dispute,
And when I've nothing left to say, be mute.
Valour I want, no soldier am 'tis true,
I'll leave that manly property to you;   505
I love no thund'ring guns, nor bloody wars,
My polished skin was not ordained for scars:
But though the pitched field I've ever fled,
At home the conquerours have conquered.
Nay, I could tell you what's more true than meet,   510
That kings have laid their scepters at my feet;
When sister Sanguine paints my ivory face,
The monarchs bend and sue, but for my grace;
My lily white when joined with her red,
Princes hath slaved, and captains captived,   515

Country with country, Greece with Asia fights
Sixty-nine princes, all stout hero knights,
Under Troy's walls ten years will wear away,
Rather than lose one beauteous Helena.
But 'twere as vain to prove this truth of mine   520
As at noon day to tell the sun doth shine.
Next difference that 'twixt us twain doth lie
Who doth possess the brain, or thou or I?
Shame forced thee say the matter that was mine,
But the spirits by which it acts are thine: 525
Thou speakest truth, and I can say no less,
Thy heat doth much, I candidly confess;
Yet without ostentation I may say,
I do as much for thee another way:
And though I grant, thou art my helper here,   530
No debtor I because it's paid elsewhere.
With all your flourishes, now sisters three
Who is't that dare, or can, compare with me?
My excellencies are so great, so many,
I am confounded, fore I speak of any: 535
The brain's the noblest member all allow,
Its form and situation will avow,
Its ventricles, membranes, and wond'rous net,
Galen, Hippocrates drive to a set;
That divine offspring the immortal soul   540
Though it in all and every part be whole,
Within this stately place of eminence,
Doth doubtless keep its mighty residence.
And surely, the soul sensitive here lives,
Which life and motion to each creature gives,   545
The conjugation of the parts to th' brain
Doth show, hence flow the powers which they retain;
Within this high built citadel, doth lie
The reason, fancy, and the memory;
The faculty of speech doth here abide,   550

The spirits animal from hence do slide:
The five most noble senses here do dwell;
Of three it's hard to say which doth excel.
This point now to discuss, 'longs not to me,
I'll touch the sight, great'st wonder of the three;   555
The optic nerve, coats, humours all are mine,
The wat'ry, glassy, and the crystaline;
O mixture strange! O colour colourless,
Thy perfect temperament who can express?
He was no fool who thought the soul lay there,   560
Whence her affections, passions speak so clear.
O good, O bad, O true, O traitorous eyes
What wonderments within your balls there lies!
Of all the senses sight shall be the queen;
Yet some may wish, O had mine eyes ne'er seen.   565
Mine, likewise is the marrow of the back,
Which runs through all the spondles of the rack,
It is the substitute o' the royal brain,
All nerves, except seven pair, to it retain.
And the strong ligaments from hence arise,   570
Which joint to joint, the entire body ties.
Some other parts there issue from the brain,
Whose worth and use to tell, I must refrain:
Some curious learned Crooke may these reveal,
But modesty hath charged me to conceal.   575
Here's my epitome of excellence:
For what's the brain's is mine by consequence.
A foolish brain (quoth Choler) wanting heat,
But a mad one, say I, where 'tis too great;
Frenzy's worse than folly, one would more glad   580
With a tame fool converse than with a mad;
For learning then my brain is not the fittest,
Nor will I yield that Choler is the wittiest.
Thy judgement is unsafe, thy fancy little,
For memory, the sand is not more brittle;   585

Again, none's fit for kingly state but thou,
If tyrants be the best, I'll it allow:
But if love be as requisite as fear,
Then thou and I must make a mixture here.
Well to be brief, I hope now Choler's laid,   590
And I'll pass by what sister Sanguine said.
To Melancholy I'll make no reply,
The worst she said was instability,
And too much talk, both which I here confess
A warning good, hereafter I'll say less.   595
Let's now be friends; it's time our spite were spent,
Lest we too late this rashness do repent,
Such premises will force a sad conclusion,
Unless we agree, all falls into confusion.
Let Sanguine with her hot hand Choler hold,   600
To take her moist my moisture will be bold:
My cold, cold Melancholy's hand shall clasp;
Her dry, dry Choler's other hand shall grasp.
Two hot, two moist, two cold, two dry here be,
A golden ring, the posy UNITY.   605
Nor jars nor scoffs, let none hereafter see,
But all admire our perfect amity;
Nor be discerned, here's water, earth, air, fire,
But here's a compact body, whole entire.
This loving counsel pleased them all so well   610
That Phlegm was judged for kindness to excel.

OF THE FOUR AGES
OF MAN

Lo now four other act upon the stage,
Childhood and Youth, the Manly and Old Age;
The first son unto phlegm, grand-child to water,   5
Unstable, supple, cold, and moist's his nature.
The second, frolic, claims his pedigree
From blood and air, for hot and moist is he.
The third of fire and choler is composed
Vindicative and quarrelsome disposed.   10
The last of earth, and heavy melancholy,
Solid, hating all lightness and all folly.
Childhood was clothed in white and green to show
His spring was intermixed with some snow:
Upon his head nature a garland set   15
Of primrose, daisy and the violet.
Such cold mean flowers the spring puts forth betime
Before the sun hath thoroughly heat the clime.
His hobby striding, did not ride but run,
And in his hand an hour-glass new begun,   20
In danger every moment of a fall,
And when 'tis broke then ends his life and all:
But if he hold till it have run its last,
Then may he live out threescore years or past.
Next Youth came up in gorgeous attire,   25
(As that fond age doth most of all desire).
His suit of crimson and his scarf of green,
His pride in's countenance was quickly seen;
Garland of roses, pinks and gilliflowers
Seemed on's head to grow bedewed with showers: 30
His face as fresh as is Aurora fair,
When blushing she first 'gins to light the air.

No wooden horse, but one of mettle tried,
He seems to fly or swim, and not to ride.
Then prancing on the stage, about he wheels,   35
But as he went, death waited at his heels.
The next came up in a much graver sort,
As one that cared for a good report,
His sword by's side, and choler in his eyes,
But neither used as yet, for he was wise: 40
Of autumn's fruits a basket on his arm,
His golden god in's purse, which was his charm.
And last of all to act upon this stage
Leaning upon his staff came up Old Age,
Under his arm a sheaf of wheat he bore,   45
An harvest of the best, what needs he more?
In's other hand a glass even almost run,
Thus writ about: This out then am I done.
His hoary hairs, and grave aspect made way,
And all gave ear to what he had to say.   50
These being met each in his equipage
Intend to speak according to their age;
But wise Old Age did with all gravity
To childish Childhood give precendency,
And to the rest his reason mildly told,   55
That he was young before he grew so old.
To do as he, each one full soon assents,
Their method was that of the Elements,
That each should tell what of himself he knew,
Both good and bad, but yet no more than's true.   60
With heed now stood three ages of frail man,
To hear the child, who crying thus began.

Childhood

Ah me! conceived in sin and born with sorrow,
A nothing, here today and gone tomorrow,   65

Whose mean beginning blushing can't reveal,
But night and darkness must with shame conceal.
My mother's breeding sickness I will spare,
Her nine months weary burthen not declare.
To show her bearing pains, I should do wrong,   70
To tell those pangs which can't be told by tongue:
With tears into the world I did arrive;
My mother still did waste as I did thrive,
Who yet with love and all alacrity,
Spending, was willing to be spent for me.   75
With wayward cries I did disturb her rest,
Who sought still to appease me with the breast:
With weary arms she danced and "By By" sung,
When wretched I, ingrate, had done the wrong.
When infancy was past, my childishness   80
Did act all folly that it could express,
My silliness did only take delight
In that which riper age did scorn and slight.
In rattles, baubles, and such toyish stuff,
My then ambitious thoughts were low enough: 85
My highborn soul so straitly was confin'd,
That its own worth it did not know nor mind:
This little house of flesh did spacious count,
Through ignorance all troubles did surmount;
Yet this advantage had mine ignorance,   90
Freedom from envy and from arrogance.
How to be rich or great I did not cark,
A baron or a duke ne'er made my mark,
Nor studious was kings' favours how to buy,
With costly presents or base flattery: 95
No office coveted wherein I might
Make strong myself and turn aside weak right:
No malice bear to this or that great peer,
Nor unto buzzing whisperers gave ear:
I gave no hand nor vote for death or life,   100

I'd nought to do 'twixt King and people's strife.
No statist I, nor martialist in th' field;
Where e'er I went, mine innocence was shield.
My quarrels not for diadems did rise,
But for an apple, plum, or some such prize: 105
My strokes did cause no blood, no wounds or scars,
My little wrath did end soon as my wars:
My duel was no challenge nor did seek
My foe should welt'ring in his bowels reek.
I had no suits at law neighbours to vex, 110
Nor evidence for lands did me perplex.
I feared no storms, nor all the wind that blows,
I had no ships at sea, nor freights to lose.
I feared no drought nor wet, I had no crop,
Nor yet on future things did set my hope. 115
This was mine innocence, but ah! the seeds
Lay raked up of all the cursed weeds
Which sprouted forth in mine ensuing age,
As he can tell that next comes on the stage:
But yet let me relate before I go 120
The sins and dangers I am subject to.
Stained from birth with Adam's sinful fact,
Thence I began to sin as soon as act:
A perverse will, a love to what's forbid,
A serpent's sting in pleasing face lay hid: 125
A lying tongue as soon as it could speak,
And fifth commandment do daily break.
Oft stubborn, peevish, sullen, pout and cry,
Then nought can please, and yet I know not why.
As many are my sins, so dangers too; 130
For sin brings sorrow, sickness, death, and woe:
And though I miss the tossings of the mind,
Yet griefs in my frail flesh I still do find.
What grippes of wind mine infancy did pain,
What tortures I in breeding teeth sustain? 135

What crudities my stomach cold hath bred,
Whence vomits, flux, and worms have issued?
What breaches, knocks and falls I daily have,
And some perhaps I carry to my grave;
Sometimes in fire, sometimes in water fall,   140
Strangely preserved, yet mind it not at all:
At home, abroad my danger's manifold,
That wonder 'tis, my glass till now doth hold.
I've done; unto my elders I give way,
For 'tis but little that a child can say.   145

Youth

My goodly clothing, and my beauteous skin
Declare some greater riches are within:
But what is best I'll first present to view,
And then the worst in a more ugly hue: 150
For thus to do we on this stage assemble,
Then let not him that hath most craft dissemble.
My education and my learning such,
As might myself and others profit much;
With nurture trained up in virtue's schools,   155
Of science, arts, and tongues I know the rules,
The manners of the court I also know,
And so likewise what they in th' country do.
The brave attempts of valiant knights I prize,
That dare scale walls and forts reared to the skies.   160
The snorting horse, the trumpet, drum I like,
The glitt'ring sword, the pistol, and the pike:
I cannot lie intrenched before a town,
Nor wait till good success our hopes doth crown:
I scorn the heavy corslet, musket-proof;   165
I fly to catch the bullet that's aloof.
Though thus in field, at home to all most kind,
So affable, that I can suit each mind.

I can insinuate into the breast,
And by my mirth can raise the heart depressed.   170
Sweet music raps my brave harmonious soul,
My high thoughts elevate beyond the pole:
My wit, my bounty, and my courtesy
Make all to place their future hopes on me.
This is my best; but Youth is known, alas!   175
To be as wild as is the snuffing ass:
As vain as froth, or vanity can be,
That who would see vain man, may look on me.
My gifts abused, my education lost;
My woeful parents' longing hopes are crossed;   180
My wit evaporates in merriment;
My valour in some beastly quarrel's spent;
My lust doth hurry me to all that's ill:
I know no law nor reason but my will.
Sometimes lay wait to take a wealthy purse,   185
Or stab the man in's own defence (that's worse).
Sometimes I cheat (unkind) a female heir
Of all at once, who not so wise as fair
Trusteth my loving looks and glozing tongue,
Until her friends, treasure, and honour's gone.   190
Sometimes I sit carousing others' health,
Until mine own be gone, my wit and wealth.
From pipe to pot, from pot to words and blows,
For he that loveth wine wanteth no woes.
Whole nights with ruffins, roarers, fiddlers spend,   195
To all obscenity mine ears I lend;
All counsel hate, which tends to make me wise,
And dearest friends count for mine enemies.
If any care I take 'tis to be fine,
For sure my suit more than my virtues shine   200
If time from lewd companions I can spare,
'Tis spent to curl, and pounce my new-bought hair.
Some new Adonis I do strive to be;

Sardanapalus now survives in me.
Cards, dice, and oaths concomitant I love,   205
To plays, to masques, to taverns still I move.
And in a word, if what I am you'd hear,
Seek out a British brutish cavalier:
Such wretch, such monster am I, but yet more,
I have no heart at all this to deplore,   210
Rememb'ring not the dreadful day of doom,
Nor yet that heavy reckoning soon to come.
Though dangers do attend me every hour,
And ghastly Death oft threats me with his power,
Sometimes by wounds in idle combats taken,   215
Sometimes with agues all my body shaken:
Sometimes by fevers all my moisture drinking,
My heart lies frying and mine eyes are sinking,
Sometimes the quinsy, painful pleurisy,
With sad affrights of death doth menace me: 220
Sometimes the twofold pox me sore be-mars
With outward marks and inward loathsome scars,
Sometimes the frenzy strangely mads my brain,
That oft for it in bedlam I remain.
Too many my diseases to recite,   225
That wonder 'tis, I yet behold the light,
That yet my bed in darkness is not made,
And I in black oblivion's den now laid.
Of aches full my bones, of woe my heart,
Clapt in that prison, never thence to start.   230
Thus I have said, and what I've been, you see,
Childhood and Youth are vain, yea vanity.

Middle Age

Childhood and Youth (forgot) I've sometimes seen
And now am grown more staid who have been green: 235
What they have done, the same was done by me,

As was their praise or shame, so mine must be.
Now age is more; more good you may expect,
But more mine age, the more is my defect.
When my wild oats were sown and ripe and mown,   240
I then received an harvest of mine own.
My reason then bad judge how little hope
Such empty seed should yield a better crop;
Then with both hands I grasped the world together.
Thus out of one extreme into another,   245
But yet laid hold on virtue seemingly;
Who climbs without hold climbs dangerously.
Be my condition mean, I then take pains
My family to keep, but not for gains.
A father I, for children must provide;   250
But if none, then for kindred near allied.
If rich, I'm urged then to gather more,
To bear a port i' th' world, and feed the poor.
If noble, then mine honour to maintain,
If not, riches nobility can gain.   255
For time, for place, likewise for each relation
I wanted not, my ready allegiance.
Yet all my powers for self ends are not spent,
For hundreds bless me for my bounty lent,
Whose backs I've clothed, and bellies I have fed   260
With mine own fleece, and with my household bread;
Yea, justice have I done, was I in place,
To cheer the good, and wicked to deface.
The proud I crushed, th' oppressed I set free,
The liars curbed, but nourished verity.   265
Was I a pastor, I my flock did feed,
And gently lead the lambs as they had need.
A captain I, with skill I trained my band,
And showed them how in face of foes to stand.
A soldier I, with speed I did obey,   270
As readily as could my leader say.

Was I a labourer, I wrought all day
As cheerfully as e'er I took my pay.
Thus hath mine age in all sometimes done well,
Sometimes again, mine age been worse than hell.   275
In meanness, greatness, riches, poverty,
Did toil, did broil, oppressed, did steal and lie.
Was I as poor as poverty could be,
Then baseness was companion unto me,
Such scum as hedges and highways do yield,   280
As neither sow, nor reap, nor plant, nor build.
If to agriculture I was ordained,
Great labours, sorrows, crosses I sustained.
The early cock did summon but in vain
My wakeful thoughts up to my painful gain: 285
My weary beast rest from his toil can find,
But if I rest the more distressed my mind.
If happiness my sordidness hath found,
'Twas in the crop of my manured ground,
My thriving cattle and my new-milch-cow,   290
My fleeced sheep, and fruitful farrowing sow:
To greater things I never did aspire,
My dunghill thoughts or hopes could reach no higher.
If to be rich or great it was my fate,
How was I broiled with envy and with hate?   295
Greater than was the great'st was my desire,
And thirst for honour, set my heart on fire:
And by ambition's sails I was so carried,
That over flats, and sands, and rocks I hurried,
Oppressed and sunk and staved all in my way   300
That did oppose me, to my longed bay.
My thirst was higher than nobility,
I oft longed sore to taste on royalty:
Then kings must be deposed or put to flight,
I might possess that throne which was their right;   305
There set, I rid my self straight out of hand

Of such competitors as might in time withstand.
Then thought my state firm founded sure to last,
But in a trice 'tis ruined by a blast,
Though cemented with more than noble blood,   310
The bottom nought, and so no longer stood.
Sometimes vainglory is the only bait
Whereby my empty soul is lured and caught.
Be I of wit, of learning, and of parts,
I judge I should have room in all men's hearts.   315
And envy gnaws if any do surmount,
I hate not to be held in high'st account.
If Bias like I'm stripped unto my skin,
I glory in my wealth I have within.
Thus good and bad, and what I am you see,   320
Now in a word, what my diseases be.
The vexing stone in bladder and in reins,
The strangury torments me with sore pains.
The windy colic oft my bowels rend,
To break the darksome prison where it's penned.   325
The cramp and gout doth sadly torture me,
And the restraining, lame sciatica.
The asthma, megrim, palsy, lethargy,
The quartan ague, dropsy, lunacy:
Subject to all distempers, that's the truth,   330
Though some more incident to Age or Youth.
And to conclude, I may not tedious be,
Man at his best estate is vanity.

Old Age

What you have been, ev'n such have I before: 335
And all you say, say I, and somewhat more.
Babe's innocence, youth's wildness I have seen,
And in perplexed Middle Age have been;
Sickness, dangers, and anxieties have past,

And on this stage am come to act my last.   340
I have been young, and strong and wise as you:
But now *"Bis pueri senes"* is too true.
In every age I've found much vanity,
An end of all perfection now I see.
It's not my valour, honour, nor my gold   345
My ruined house now falling can uphold.
It's not my learning, rhetoric, wit so large,
Hath now the power, death's warfare to discharge.
It's not my goodly state nor bed of down
That can refresh, or ease, if conscience frown.   350
Nor from alliance can I now have hope,
But what I have done well, that is my prop;
He that in youth is godly, wise, and sage,
Provides a staff then to support his age.
Mutations great, some joyful and some sad,   355
In this short pilgrimage I oft have had.
Sometimes the Heavens with plenty smiled on me
Sometime again rained all adversity.
Sometimes in honour, sometimes in disgrace,
Sometime an abject, then again in place.   360
Such private changes oft mine eyes have seen,
In various times of state I've also been.
I've seen a kingdom flourish like a tree,
When it was ruled by that celestial she;
And like a cedar, others so surmount   365
That but for shrubs they did themselves account.
Then saw I France and Holland saved, Callais won,
And Philip and Albertus half undone.
I saw all peace at home, terror to foes,
But ah, I saw at last those eyes to close,   370
And then methought the day at noon grew dark
When it had lost that radiant sun-like spark:
In midst of griefs I saw our hopes revive,
(For 'twas our hopes then kept our hearts alive)

We changed our queen for king under whose rays   375
We joyed in many blest and prosperous days.
I've seen a prince, the glory of our land,
In prime of youth seized by heaven's angry hand,
Which filled our hearts with fears, with tears our eyes,
Wailing his fate, and our own destinies.   380
I've seen from Rome an execrable thing,
A plot to blow up nobles and their king,
But saw their horrid fact soon disappointed,
And land and nobles saved with their anointed.
I've princes seen to live on other's lands;   385
A royal one by gifts from strangers' hands,
Admired for their magnanimity,
Who lost a princedom and a monarchy.
I've seen designs for Ree and Rochelle crossed,
And poor Palatinate forever lost.   390
I've seen unworthy men advanced high,
(And better ones suffer extremity)
But neither favour, riches, title, state,
Could length their days or once reverse their fate;
I've seen one stab'd, and some to lose their heads,   395
And others fly, struck both with guilt and dread.
I've seen, and so have you, for 'tis but late,
The desolation of a goodly state,
Plotted and acted so that none can tell
Who gave the counsel, but the prince of hell,   400
Three hundred thousand slaughtered innocents,
By bloody Popish, hellish miscreants:
Oh may you live, and so you will I trust
To see them swill in blood until they burst.
I've seen a king by force thrust from his throne,   405
And an usurper subtly mount thereon.
I've seen a state unmoulded, rent in twain,
But yet may live to see't made up again.
I've seen it plundered, taxed, and soaked in blood,

But out of evil you may see much good.   410
What are my thoughts, this is no time to say.
Men may more freely speak another day.
These are no old-wives' tales, but this is truth,
We old men love to tell what's done in youth.
But I return from whence I stepped awry,   415
My memory is bad, my brain is dry:
Mine almond tree, grey hairs, do flourish now,
And back once straight, apace begins to bow:
My grinders now are few, my sight doth fail,
My skin is wrinkled, and my cheeks are pale,   420
No more rejoice at music's pleasing noise,
But waking glad to hear the cock's shrill voice:
I cannot scent savours of pleasant meat,
Nor sapors find in what I drink or eat:
My arms and hands once strong have lost their might;   425
I cannot labour, much less can I fight.
My comely legs as nimble as the roe
Now stiff and numb, can hardly creep or go,
My heart sometimes as fierce as lion bold,
Now trembling is, all fearful sad and cold;   430
My golden bowl and silver cord e'er long
Shall both be broke, by racking death so strong:
Then shall I go whence I shall come no more,
Sons, nephews, leave my farewell to deplore.
In pleasures and in labours I have found   435
That earth can give no consolation sound;
To great, to rich, to poor, to young, to old,
To mean, to noble, fearful, or to bold:
From king to beggar, all degrees shall find
But vanity, vexation of the mind.   440
Yea, knowing much, the pleasant'st life of all,
Hath yet among those sweets some bitter gall;
Though reading others' works doth much refresh,
Yet studying much brings weariness to th' flesh:

My studies, labours, readings all are done,   445
And my last period now ev'n almost run.
Corruption my father I do call,
Mother and sisters both, the worms that crawl
In my dark house, such kindred I have store,
Where I shall rest till heavens shall be no more,   450
And when this flesh shall rot and be consumed,
This body by this soul shall be assumed:
And I shall see with these same very eyes,
My strong Redeemer coming in the skies.
Triumph I shall o'er sin, o'er death, o'er hell,   455
And in that hope I bid you all farewell.

THE FOUR SEASONS OF THE YEAR

Spring

Another four I've left yet to bring on,
Of four times four the last quaternion, 5
The Winter, Summer, Autumn, and the Spring,
In season all these seasons I shall bring:
Sweet Spring like man in his minority,
At present claimed, and had priority.
With smiling face and garments somewhat green, 10
She trimmed her locks, which late had frosted been,
Nor hot nor cold she spake, but with a breath
Fit to revive the numbed earth from death.
Three months (quoth she) are 'lotted to my share
March, April, May of all the rest most fair. 15
Tenth of the first, Sol into Aries enters,
And bids defiance to all tedious winters,
Crosseth the line, and equals night and day,
Still adds to th' last till after pleasant May;
And now makes glad the dark'ned northern wights 20
Who for some months have seen but starry lights.
Now goes the plowman to his merry toil,
He might unloose his winter locked soil:
The seedsman, too, doth lavish out his grain,
In hope the more he casts, the more to gain: 25
The gard'ner now superfluous branches lops,
And poles erects for his young clamb'ring hops;
Now digs, then sows his herbs, his flowers, and roots,
And carefully manures his trees of fruits.
The Pleiades their influence now give, 30
And all that seemed as dead afresh doth live.

The croaking frogs, whom nipping winter killed,
Like birds now chirp, and hop about the field,
The nightingale, the blackbird, and the thrush
Now tune their lays, on sprays of every bush.   35
The wanton frisking kid, and soft-fleeced lambs
Do jump and play before their feeding dams,
The tender tops of budding grass they crop,
They joy in what they have, but more in hope:
For though the frost hath lost his binding power,   40
Yet many a fleece of snow and stormy shower
Doth darken Sol's bright eye, makes us remember
The pinching north-west wind of cold December.
My second month is April, green and fair,
Of longer days and a more temperate air: 45
The sun in Taurus keeps his residence,
And with his warmer beams glanceth from thence.
This is the month whose fruitful show'rs produces
All set and sown for all delights and uses:
The pear, the plum, and appletree now flourish;   50
The grass grows long the hungry beast to nourish.
The primrose pale and azure violet
Among the verdurous grass hath nature set,
That when the Sun on's love (the earth) doth shine
These might as lace set out her garment fine.   55
The fearful bird his little house now builds
In trees and walls, in cities, and in fields.
The outside strong, the inside warm and neat,
A natural artificer complete.
The clucking hen her chirping chickens leads,   60
With wings and beak defends them from the gledes.
My next and last is fruitful pleasant May,
Wherein the earth is clad in rich array,
The sun now enters loving Gemini,
And heats us with the glances of his eye,   65
Our thicker raiment makes us lay aside

Lest by his fervor we be torrified.
All flowers the Sun now with his beams discloses,
Except the double pinks and matchless roses.
Now swarms the busy, witty, honey-bee,   70
Whose praise deserves a page from more than me.
The cleanly housewife's dairy's now in th' prime,
Her shelves and firkins filled for winter time.
The meads with cowslips, honeysuckles dight;
One hangs his head, the other stands upright;   75
But both rejoice at th' heavens' clear smiling face,
More at her showers, which water them a space.
For fruits my season yields the early cherry,
The hasty peas, and wholesome cool strawberry.
More solid fruits require a longer time;   80
Each season hath his fruit, so hath each clime:
Each man his own peculiar excellence,
But none in all that hath preëminence.
Sweet fragrant Spring, with thy short pittance fly,
Let some describe thee better than can I.   85
Yet above all this privilege is thine,
Thy days still lengthen without least decline.

Summer

When Spring had done, the Summer did begin,
With melted tawny face, and garments thin,   90
Resembling Fire, Choler, and Middle Age,
As Spring did Air, Blood, Youth in's equipage.
Wiping the sweat from off her face that ran,
With hair all wet she puffing thus began;
Bright June, July and August hot are mine,   95
In th' first Sol doth in crabbed Cancer shine.
His progress to the north now's fully done,
Then retrograde must be my burning sun,
Who to his southward tropic still is bent,

Yet doth his parching heat but more augment 100
Though he decline, because his flames so fair
Have thoroughly dried the earth and heat the air.
Like as an oven that long time hath been heat,
Whose vehemency at length doth grow so great,
That if you do withdraw her burning store, 105
'Tis for a time as fervent as before.
Now go those frolic swains, the shepherd lads,
To wash the thick clothed flocks with pipes full glad;
In the cool streams they labour with delight
Rubbing their dirty coats till they look white; 110
Whose fleece when finely spun and deeply dyed
With robes thereof kings have been dignified.
Blest rustic swains, your pleasant quiet life,
Hath envy bred in kings that were at strife,
Careless of worldly wealth you sing and pipe, 115
Whilst they're embroiled in wars and troubles rife,
Which made great Bajazet cry out in's woes:
Oh, happy shepherd, which hath not to lose
Orthobulus, nor yet Sebastia great,
But whistleth to thy flock in cold and heat. 120
Viewing the sun by day, the moon by night
Endymion's, Diana's dear delight,
Upon the grass resting your healthy limbs,
By purling brooks looking how fishes swims.
If pride within your lowly cells e'er haunt, 125
Of him that was shepherd, then king go vaunt.
This month the roses are distilled in glasses,
Whose fragrant smell all made perfumes surpasses.
The cherry, gooseberry are now in th' prime,
And for all sorts of peas, this is the time. 130
July my next, the hottest in all the year,
The sun through Leo now takes his career,
Whose flaming breath doth melt us from afar,

Increased by the star Canicular.
This month from Julius Caesar took its name,   135
By Romans celebrated to his fame.
Now go the mowers to their slashing toil,
The meadows of their riches to despoil,
With weary strokes, they take all in their way,
Bearing the burning heat of the long day.   140
The forks and rakes do follow them amain,
Which makes the aged fields look young again.
The groaning carts do bear away this prize
To stacks and barns where it for fodder lies.
My next and last is August fiery hot   145
(For much, the southward sun abateth not).
This month he keeps with Virgo for a space;
The dried earth is parched with his face.
August of great Augustus took its name,
Rome's second emperor of lasting fame.   150
With sickles now the bending reapers go
The rustling tress of terra down to mow;
And bundles up in sheaves, the weighty wheat,
Which after manchet makes for kings to eat.
The barley, rye, and peas should first had place,   155
Although their bread have not so white a face.
The carter leads all home with whistling voice,
He plowed with pain, but reaping doth rejoice;
His sweat, his toil, his careful, wakeful nights,
His fruitful crop abundantly requites.   160
Now's ripe the pear, pear-plum, and apricock,
The prince of plums, whose stone's as hard as rock.
The Summer seems but short, the Autumn hastes
To shake his fruits of most delicious tastes
Like good old Age, whose younger juicy roots   165
Hath still ascended to bear goodly fruits.
Until his head be gray, and strength be gone,

Yet then appears the worthy deeds he'th done:
To feed his boughs exhausted hath his sap,
Then drops his fruits into the eater's lap.   170

Autumn

Of Autumn months September is the prime,
Now day and night are equal in each clime;
The twelfth of this Sol riseth in the line,
And doth in poising Libra this month shine.   175
The vintage now is ripe, the grapes are pressed,
Whose lively liquor oft is cursed and blest;
For nought so good, but it may be abused,
But it's a precious juice when well it's used.
The raisins now in clusters dried be,   180
The orange, lemon dangle on the tree:
The pomegranate, the fig are ripe also,
And apples now their yellow sides do show.
Of almonds, quinces, wardens, and of peach,
The season's now at hand of all and each.   185
Sure at this time, time first of all began,
And in this month was made apostate Man:
For then in Eden was not only seen,
Boughs full of leaves, or fruits unripe or green,
Or withered stocks, which were all dry and dead,   190
But trees with goodly fruits replenished;
Which shows nor Summer, Winter, nor the Spring
Our grand-sire was of paradise made king;
Nor could that temp'rate clime such difference make,
If cited as the most judicious take.   195
October is my next, we hear in this
The northern winter-blasts begin to hiss.
In Scorpio resideth now the sun,
And his declining heat is almost done.
The fruitless trees all withered now do stand,   200

Whose sapless yellow leaves, by winds are fanned,
Which notes when youth and strength have past their prime
Decrepit age must also have its time.
The sap doth slily creep towards the earth
There rests, until the sun give it a birth.   205
So doth old Age still tend unto his grave,
Where also he his winter time must have;
But when the Sun of righteousness draws nigh,
His dead old stock shall mount again on high.
November is my last, for time doth haste,   210
We now of winter's sharpness 'gin to taste.
This month the Sun's in Sagitarius,
So far remote, his glances warm not us.
Almost at shortest is the shortened day,
The northern pole beholdeth not one ray.   215
Now Greenland, Groanland, Finland, Lapland see
No sun, to lighten their obscurity:
Poor wretches that in total darkness lie,
With minds more dark than is the darkened sky.
Beef, brawn, and pork are now in great request,   220
And solid meats our stomachs can digest.
This time warm clothes, full diet, and good fires,
Our pinched flesh and hungry maws requires:
Old, cold, dry Age and Earth Autumn resembles,
And Melancholy which most of all dissembles.   225
I must be short, and short's the short'ned day,
What Winter hath to tell, now let him say.

Winter

Cold, moist, young phlegmy Winter now doth lie
In swaddling clouts, like new born infancy   230
Bound up with frosts, and furred with hail and snows,
And like an infant, still it taller grows;
December is my first, and now the Sun

To th' southward tropic, his swift race doth run:
This month he's housed in horned Capricorn,   235
From thence he 'gins to length the shortened morn,
Through Christendom with great festivity,
Now's held (but guessed) for blest Nativity.
Cold frozen January next comes in,
Chilling the blood and shrinking up the skin;   240
In Aquarius now keeps the long wished Sun,
And northward his unwearied course doth run:
The day much longer than it was before,
The cold not lessened, but augmented more.
Now toes and ears, and fingers often freeze,   245
And travellers their noses sometimes leese.
Moist snowy February is my last,
I care not how the winter time doth haste.
In Pisces now the golden sun doth shine,
And northward still approaches to the line.   250
The rivers 'gin to ope, the snows to melt,
And some warm glances from his face are felt,
Which is increased by the lengthened day,
Until by's heat, he drive all cold away,
And thus the year in circle runneth round: 255
Where first it did begin, in th' end it's found.

My subject's bare, my brain is bad,
Or better lines you should have had:
The first fell in so naturally,
I knew not how to pass it by;   260
The last, though bad I could not mend,
Accept therefore of what is penned,
And all the faults that you shall spy
Shall at your feet for pardon cry.

THE FOUR MONARCHIES

THE ASSYRIAN BEING THE FIRST BEGINNING UNDER NIMROD, 131 YEARS AFTER THE FLOOD

When time was young, and world in infancy,   5
Man did not proudly strive for sovereignty:
But each one thought his petty rule was high,
If of his house he held the monarchy.
This was the golden age, but after came
The boisterous son of Cush, grandchild to Ham,   10
That mighty hunter, who in his strong toils
Both beasts and men subjected to his spoils;
The strong foundation of proud Babel laid,
Erech, Accad, and Culneh also made.
These were his first, all stood in Shinar land,   15
From thence he went Assyria to command,
And mighty Nineveh, he there begun,
Not finished till he his race had run.
Resen, Caleh, and Rehoboth likewise
By him to cities eminent did rise.   20
Of Saturn, he was the original,
Whom the succeeding times a god did call,
When thus with rule, he had been dignified,
One hundred fourteen years he after died.

Belus   25

Great Nimrod dead, Belus the next his son
Confirms the rule his father had begun,
Whose acts and power is not for certainty

Left to the world by any history.
But yet this blot forever on him lies,   30
He taught the people first to idolize:
Titles divine he to himself did take,
Alive and dead, a god they did him make.
This is that Bel the Chaldees worshiped,
Whose priests in stories oft are mentioned;   35
This is that Baal to whom the Israelites
So oft profanely offered sacred rites:
This is Beelzebub, god of Ekronites,
Likewise Baalpeor of the Mohabites,
His reign was short, for as I calculate,   40
At twenty-five ended his regal date.

Ninus

His father dead, Ninus begins his reign,
Transfers his seat to the Assyrian plain;
And mighty Nineveh more mighty made,   45
Whose foundation was by his grandsire laid:
Four hundred forty furlongs walled about,
On which stood fifteen hundred towers stout.
The walls one hundred sixty foot upright,
So broad three chariots run abreast there might.   50
Upon the pleasant banks of Tygris flood
This stately seat of warlike Ninus stood;
This Ninus for a god his father canonized,
To whom the sottish people sacrificed.
This tyrant did his neighbours all oppress,   55
Where e'er he warred he had too good success.
Barzanes the great Armenian King
By force and fraud did under tribute bring.
The Median country he did also gain,
Thermus their king he caused to be slain;   60
An army of three millions he led out

Against the Bactrians (but that I doubt).
Zoroaster their king he likewise slew,
And all the greater Asia did subdue.
Semiramis from Menon did he take;   65
Then drowned himself, did Menon for her sake.
Fifty-two years he reigned (as we are told)
The world then was two thousand nineteen old.

Semiramis

This great oppressing Ninus, dead and gone,   70
His wife Semiramis usurped the throne;
She like a brave virago played the rex
And was both shame and glory of her sex:
Her birth place was Philistine's Ascalon,
Her mother Dorceta a courtezan.   75
Others report she was a vestal nun,
Adjudged to be drowned for th' crime she'd done.
Transformed into a fish by Venus' will,
Her beauteous face (they feign) retaining still.
Sure from this fiction Dagon first began,   80
Changing the woman's face into a man:
But all agree that from no lawful bed,
This great renowned empress issued:
For which she was obscurely nourished,
Whence rose that fable, she by birds was fed.   85
This gallant dame unto the Bactrian war,
Accompanying her husband Menon far,
Taking a town, such valour she did show,
That Ninus amorous of her soon did grow,
And thought her fit to make a monarch's wife,   90
Which was the cause poor Menon lost his life;
She flourishing with Ninus long did reign,
Till her ambition caused him to be slain,
That having no compeer, she might rule all,

Or else she sought revenge for Menon's fall.   95
Some think the Greeks this slander on her cast,
As on her life licentious, and unchaste,
That undeserved, they blurred her name and fame
By their aspersions, cast upon the same:
But were her virtues more or less, or none,   100
She for her potency must go alone.
Her wealth she showed in building Babylon,
Admired of all, but equalized of none;
The walls so strong, and curiously were wrought,
That after ages, skill by them were taught: 105
With towers and bulwarks made of costly stone,
Quadrangle was the form it stood upon.
Each square was fifteen thousand paces long,
An hundred gates it had of metal strong:
Three hundred sixty foot the walls in height,   110
Almost incredible, they were in breadth
Some writers say six chariots might affront
With great facility march safe upon't;
About the wall a ditch so deep and wide,
That like a river long it did abide.   115
Three hundred thousand men here day by day
Bestowed their labour, and received their pay.
But that which did all cost and art excel
The wondrous temple was, she reared to Bel,
Which in the midst of this brave town was placed,   120
Continuing till Xerxes it defaced,
Whose stately top above the clouds did rise,
From whence astrologers oft viewed the skies.
This to describe in each particular,
A structure rare I should but rudely mar.   125
Her gardens, bridges, arches, mounts and spires
All eyes that saw, or ears that hear admires,
In Shinar plain on the Euphratian flood
This wonder of the world, this Babel stood.

An expedition to the East she made,   130
Staurobates, his country to invade:
Her army of four millions did consist,
Each may believe it as his fancy list.
Her camels, chariots, galleys in such number,
As puzzles best historians to remember;   135
But this is wonderful, of all those men,
They say, but twenty e'er came back again.
The river Indus swept them half away,
The rest Staurobates in fight did slay;
This was last progress of this mighty queen,   140
Who in her country never more was seen.
The poets feigned her turned into a dove,
Leaving the world to Venus soared above:
Which made the Assyrians many a day,
A dove within their ensigns to display: 145
Forty-two years she reigned, and then she died
But by what means we are not certified.

Ninias or Zamies

His mother dead, Ninias obtains his right.
A prince wedded to ease and to delight,   150
Or else was his obedience very great,
To sit thus long (obscure) robbed of his seat.
Some write his mother put his habit on,
Which made the people think they served her son:
But much it is, in more than forty years   155
This fraud in war nor peace at all appears:
More like it is his lust with pleasures fed,
He sought no rule till she was gone and dead.
What then he did of worth can no man tell,
But is supposed to be that Amraphel   160
Who warred with Sodom's and Gomorrah's king,
'Gainst whom, his trained bands Abram did bring,

But this is far unlike, he being son
Unto a father, that all countries won
So suddenly should lose so great a state,   165
With petty kings to join confederate.
Nor can those reasons which wise Raleigh finds,
Well satisfy the most considerate minds:
We may with learned Usher better say,
He many ages lived after that day.   170
And that Semiramis then flourished
When famous Troy was so beleaguered:
What e'er he was, or did, or how it fell,
We may suggest our thoughts but cannot tell.
For Ninias and all his race are left   175
In deep oblivion, of acts bereft:
And many hundred years in silence sit,
Save a few names a new Berosus writ.
And such as care not what befalls their fames,
May feign as many acts as he did names;   180
It may suffice, if all be true that's past.
T' Sardanapalus next, we will make haste.

Sardanapalus

Sardanapalus, son to Ocrazapes,
Who wallowed in all voluptuousness,   185
That palliardizing sot that out of doors,
Ne'er showed his face but revelled with his whores,
Did wear their garbs, their gestures imitate,
And in their kind, t' excel did emulate.
His baseness knowing, and the people's hate   190
Kept close, fearing his well deserved fate;
It chanced Arbaces brave, unwarily,
His master like a strumpet clad did spy.
His manly heart disdained (in the least)
Longer to serve this metamorphosed beast;   195

Unto Belosus then, he brake his mind,
Who sick of his disease, he soon did find.
These two ruled Media and Babylon
Both for their king held their dominion;
Belosus promised Arbaces aid,   200
Arbaces him fully to be repaid.
The last, the Medes and Persians do invite
Against their monstrous king, to use their might.
Belosus, the Chaldeans doth require
And the Arabians, to further his desire: 205
These all agree, and forty thousand make,
The rule from their unworthy prince to take:
These forces mustered, and in array,
Sardanapalus leaves his apish play.
And though of wars, he did abhor the sight,   210
Fear of his diadem did force him fight:
And either by his valour, or his fate,
Arbaces' courage he did so abate,
That in despair, he left the field and fled,
But with fresh hopes Belosus succoured,   215
From Bactria, an army was at hand
Prest for this service, by the king's command:
These with celerity Arbaces meet,
And with all terms of amity them greet.
With promises their necks now to unyoke,   220
And their taxations sore all to revoke;
T' infranchise them, to grant what they could crave,
No privilege to want, subjects should have,
Only entreats them to join their force with his,
And win the crown, which was the way to bliss.   225
Won by his loving looks, more by his speech,
T' accept of what they could, they all beseech:
Both sides their hearts, their hands, and bands unite,
And set upon their prince's camp that night;
Who revelling in cups, sung care away,   230

For victory obtained the other day:
And now surprised, by this unlooked for fright,
Bereft of wits, were slaughtered down right.
The king his brother leaves, all to sustain,
And speeds himself to Nineveh amain.   235
But Salmeneus slain, the army falls:
The king's pursued unto the city walls,
But he once in, pursuers came too late,
The walls and gates their haste did terminate;
There with all store he was so well provided,   240
That what Arbaces did was but derided;
Who there encamped two years for little end,
But in the third the river proved his friend,
For by the rain was Tygris so o'erflown,
Part of that stately wall was overthrown.   245
Arbaces marches in, the town he takes,
For few or none (it seems) resistance makes:
And now they saw fulfilled a prophesy,
That when the river proved their enemy,
Their strong walled town should suddenly be taken;   250
By this accomplishment, their hearts were shaken.
Sardanapalus did not seek to fly,
This his inevitable destiny;
But all his wealth and friends together gets,
Then on himself, and them, a fire he sets.   255
This was last monarch of great Ninus' race
That for twelve hundred years had held the place;
Twenty he reigned same time, as stories tell,
That Amaziah was king of Israel.
His father was then king (as we suppose)   260
When Jonah for their sins denounced those woes.
He did repent, the threat'ning was not done,
But now accomplished in his wicked son.
Arbaces thus of all becoming lord,
Ingeniously with all did keep his word.   265

Of Babylon Belosus he made king,
With overplus of all the wealth therein.
To Bactrians he gave their liberty,
Of Ninevites he caused none to die.
But suffered with their goods, to go elsewhere,   270
Not granting them now to inhabit there:
For he demolished that city great,
And unto Media transferred his seat.
Such was his promise which he firmly made,
To Medes and Persians when he craved their aid: 275
A while he and his race aside must stand,
Not pertinent to what we have in hand;
And Belochus in's progency pursue,
Who did this monarchy begin anew.

Belosus or Belochus   280

Belosus settled in his new old seat,
Not so content but aiming to be great,
Encroaching still upon the bordering lands,
Till Mesopotamia he got in's hands.
And either by compound or else by strength,   285
Assyria he gained also at length;
Then did rebuild destroyed Nineveh,
A costly work which none could do but he,
Who owned the treasures of proud Babylon,
And those that seemed with Sardanapalus gone;   290
For though his palace did in ashes lie,
The fire those metals could not damnify;
From these with diligence he rakes,
Arbaces suffers all, and all he takes,
He thus enriched by this new tried gold.   295
Raises a Phoenix new, from grave o' th' old;
And from this heap did after ages see
As fair a town, as the first Nineveh.

When this was built, and matters all in peace
Molests poor Israel, his wealth t' increase.   300
A thousand talents of Menahem had,
Who to be rid of such a guest was glad;
In sacred writ he's known by name of Pul,
Which makes the world of difference so full.
That he and Belochus could not one be,   305
But circumstance doth prove the verity;
And times of both computed so fall out,
That these two made but one, we need not doubt:
What else he did, his empire to advance,
To rest content we must, in ignorance.   310
Forty-eight years he reigned, his race then run,
He left his new got kingdom to his son.

Tiglath Pulassar

Belosus dead, Tiglath his warlike son,
Next treads those steps, by which his father won;   315
Damascus, ancient seat of famous kings
Under subjection by his sword he brings.
Resin their valiant king he also slew,
And Syria t' obedience did subdue.
Judah's bad king occasioned this war,   320
When Resin's force his borders sore did mar,
And divers cities by strong hand did seize:
To Tiglath then, doth Ahaz send for ease,
The temple robs, so to fulfill his ends,
And to Assyria's king a present sends.   325
I am thy servant and thy son (quoth he)
From Resin, and from Pekah set me free;
Gladly doth Tiglath this advantage take,
And succours Ahaz, yet for Tiglath's sake.
Then Resin slain, his army overthrown,   330
He Syria makes a province of his own.

Unto Damascus then comes Judah's king,
His humble thankfulness (in haste) to bring,
Acknowledging th' Assyrian's high desert,
To whom he ought all loyalty of heart.   335
But Tiglath having gained his wished end,
Proves unto Ahaz but a feigned friend;
All Israel's lands beyond Jordan he takes,
In Galilee he woeful havoc makes.
Through Syria now he marched, none stopped his way,   340
And Ahaz open at his mercy lay;
Who still implored his love, but was distressed;
This was that Ahaz, who so high transgressed.
Thus Tiglath reigned, and warred twenty-seven years;
Then by his death released was Israel's fears.   345

Salmanassar or Nabanassar

Tiglath deceased, Salmanassar was next,
He Israelites, more than his father vext;
Hoshea, their last king, he did invade,
And him six years his tributary made;   350
But weary of his servitude, he sought
To Egypt's King, which did avail him nought;
For Salmanassar with a mighty host
Besieged his regal town, and spoiled his coast,
And did the people, nobles, and their king,   355
Into perpetual thraldom that time bring;
Those that from Joshua's time had been a state,
Did justice now by him eradicate: [10 years.
This was that strange, degenerated brood,
On whom, nor threats, nor mercies could do good;   360
Laden with honour, prisoners, and with spoil,
Returns triumphant victor to his soil;
He placed Israel there, where he thought best,
Then sent his colonies, theirs to invest;

Thus Jacob's sons in exile must remain,   365
And pleasant Canaan never saw again:
Where now those ten tribes are, can no man tell,
Or how they fare, rich, poor, or ill, or well;
Whether the Indians of the East, or West,
Or wild Tartarians, as yet ne'er blest,   370
Or else those Chinoes rare, whose wealth and arts
Hath bred more wonder than belief in hearts:
But what, or where they are; yet know we this,
They shall return, and Zion see with bliss.

Sennacherib   375

Sennacherib Salmanasser succeeds,
Whose haughty heart is shown in words and deeds;
His wars, none better than himself can boast,
On Henah, Arpad, and on Juah's coast;
On Hevah's and on Sheparvaim's gods,   380
'Twixt them and Israel's he knew no odds,   [7 years.
Until the thund'ring hand of heaven he felt,
Which made his army into nothing melt;
With shame then turned to Nineveh again,
And by his sons in's idol's house was slain.   385

Essarhaddon

His son, weak Essarhaddon, reigned in's place,
The fifth, and last of great Belosus' race.
Brave Merodach, the son of Baladan,
In Babylon lieutenant to this man,   390
Of opportunity advantage takes,
And on his master's ruins his house makes,
As Belosus his sovereign did unthrone,
So he's now styled the King of Babylon.
After twelve years did Essarhaddon die,   395
And Merodach assume the monarchy.

Merodach Baladan

All yield to him, but Nineveh kept free,
Until his grandchild made her bow the knee.
Ambassadors to Hezekiah sent,   [21 years. 400
His health congratulates with compliment.

Ben Merodach

Ben Merodach, successor to this king,
Of whom is little said in any thing,   [22 years.
But by conjecture this, and none but he   405
Led King Manasseh to captivity.

Nebulassar

Brave Nebulassar to this king was son,
The famous Nineveh by him was won,
For fifty years, or more, it had been free,   410
Now yields her neck unto captivity: [12 years.
A vice-roy from her foe she's glad to accept,
By whom in firm obedience she is kept.
This king's less famed for all the acts he's done,
Than being father to so great a son.   415

Nebuchadnezzar, or Nebopolassar

The famous acts of this heroic king
Did neither Homer, Hesiod, Virgil sing;
Nor of his wars have we the certainty
From some Thucydides' grave history;   420
Nor's metamorphosis from Ovid's book,
Nor his restoring from old legends took;
But by the prophets, penmen most divine,
This prince in's magnitude doth ever shine.
This was of monarchies that head of gold,   425

The richest and the dreadfulest to behold:
This was that tree whose branches filled the earth,
Under whose shadow birds and beasts had birth;
This was that king of kings, did what he pleased,
Killed, saved, pulled down, set up, or pained or eased;   430
And this was he, who when he feared the least,
Was changed from a king into a beast.
This prince the last year of his father's reign
Against Jehojakim marched with his train;
Judah's poor king, besieged and succourless,   435
Yields to his mercy, and the present 'stress;
His vassal is, gives pledges for his truth,
Children of royal blood, unblemished youth:
Wise Daniel and his fellows, 'mongst the rest,
By the victorious king to Babel's prest;   440
The temple of rich ornaments defaced,
And in his idol's house the vessels placed.
The next year he with unresisted hand
Quite vanquished Pharaoh Necho with his band;
By great Euphrates did his army fall,   445
Which was the loss of Syria withal.
Then into Egypt Necho did retire,
Which in few years proves the Assyrians' hire.
A mighty army next he doth prepare,
And unto wealthy Tyre in haste repair.   450
Such was the situation of this place,
As might not him, but all the world outface,
That in her pride she knew not which to boast
Whether her wealth, or yet her strength was most,
How in all merchandise she did excel,   455
None but the true Ezekiel need to tell.
And for her strength, how hard she was to gain,
Can Babel's tired soldiers tell with pain.
Within an island had this city seat,
Divided from the main by channel great;   460

Of costly ships and galleys she had store,
And mariners to handle sail and oar;
But the Chaldeans had nor ships nor skill,
Their shoulders must their master's mind fulfill,
Fetched rubbish from the opposite old town,   465
And in the channel threw each burden down;
Where after many essays, they made at last
The sea firm land, whereon the army passed,
And took the wealthy town; but all the gain,
Requited not the loss, the toil and pain.   470
Full thirteen years in this strange work he spent
Before he could accomplish his intent:
And though a victor home his army leads,
With peeled shoulders, and with balded heads.
When in the Tyrian war this king was hot,   475
Jehojakim his oath had clean forgot,
Thinks this the fittest time to break his bands
Whilst Babel's king thus deep engaged stands:
But he whose fortunes all were in the ebb,
Had all his hopes like to a spider's web;   480
For this great king withdraws part of his force,
To Judah marches with a speedy course,
And unexpected finds the feeble prince
Whom he chastised thus for his proud offence,
Fast bound, intends to Babel him to send,   485
But changed his mind, and caused his life there end,
Then cast him out like to a naked ass,
For this is he for whom none said alas.
His son he suffered three months to reign,
Then from his throne he plucked him down again,   490
Whom with his mother he to Babel led,
And seven and thirty years in prison fed:
His uncle he established in his place
(Who was last king of holy David's race),
But he as perjured as Jehojakim,   495

They lost more now than e'er they lost by him.
Seven years he kept his faith, and safe he dwells;
But in the eighth against his prince rebels;
The ninth came Nebuchadnezzar with power,
Besieged his city, temple, Zion's tower,   500
And after eighteen months he took them all;
The walls so strong, that stood so long, now fall.
The cursed king by flight could no wise fly
His well deserved and foretold misery;
But being caught, to Babel's wrathful king   505
With children, wives and nobles all they bring,
Where to the sword all but himself were put,
And with that woeful sight his eyes close shut.
Ah! hapless man, whose darksome contemplation
Was nothing but such ghastly meditation.   510
In midst of Babel now till death he lies;
Yet as was told ne'er saw it with his eyes.
The temple's burnt, the vessels had away,
The towers and palaces brought to decay;
Where late of harp and lute were heard the noise   515
Now Zim and Jim lift up their screeching voice.
All now of worth are captive led with tears,
And sit bewailing Zion seventy years.
With all these conquests, Babel's king rests not,
No, not when Moab, Edom he had got,   520
Kedar and Hazar, the Arabians, too,
All vassals at his hands for grace must sue.
A total conquest of rich Egypt makes,
All rule he from the ancient Pharaohs takes,
Who had for sixteen hundred years born sway,   525
To Babylon's proud king now yields the day.
Then Put and Lud do at his mercy stand.
Where e'er he goes, he conquers every land.
His sumptuous buildings passes all conceit,
Which wealth and strong ambition made so great.   530

His image Judah's captives worship not,
Although the furnace be seven times more hot.
His dreams wise Daniel doth expound full well,
And his unhappy change with grief foretell.
Strange melancholy humours on him lay,   535
Which for seven years his reason took away,
Which from no natural causes did proceed,
But for his pride, so had the heavens decreed.
The time expired, brutish remains no more,
But government resumes as heretofore;   540
In splendor, and in majesty he sits,
Contemplating those times he lost his wits.
And if by words we may guess at the heart,
This king among the righteous had a part;
Forty-four years he reigned, which being run,   545
He left his wealth and conquests to his son.

Evilmerodach

Babel's great monarch now laid in the dust,
His son possesses wealth and rule as just:
And in the first year of his royalty   550
Easeth Jehojakim's captivity:
Poor forlorn prince, who had all state forgot,
In seven and thirty years had seen no jot.
Among the conquered kings that there did lie
Is Judah's king now lifted up on high;   555
But yet in Babel he must still remain,
And native Canaan never see again;
Unlike his father, Evilmerodach
Prudence and magnanimity did lack;
Fair Egypt is by his remissness lost,   560
Arabia, and all the bordering coast.
Wars with the Medes unhappily he waged
(Within which broils rich Croesus was engaged)

His army routed, and himself there slain:
His kingdom to Belshazzar did remain.   565

Belshazzar

Unworthy Belshazzar next wears the crown,
Whose acts profane a sacred pen sets down,
His lust and cruelties in stories find,
A royal state ruled by a brutish mind.   570
His life so base and dissolute invites
The noble Persian to invade his rights,
Who with his own, and uncle's power anon,
Lays siege to's regal seat, proud Babylon.
The coward king, whose strength lay in his walls,   575
To banqueting and revelling now falls,
To show his little dread, but greater store,
To cheer his friends and scorn his foes the more.
The holy vessels thither brought long since,
They caroused in, and sacrilegious prince   580
Did praise his gods of metal, wood, and stone,
Protectors of his crown and Babylon,
But He above, his doings did deride,
And with a hand soon dashed all this pride.
The king, upon the wall, casting his eye,   585
The fingers of a hand writing did spy,
Which horrid sight, he fears, must needs portend
Destruction to his crown, to's person end.
With quaking knees and heart appalled he cries,
For the soothsayers and magicians wise,   590
This language strange to read and to unfold;
With gifts of scarlet robe, and chain of gold,
And highest dignity, next to the king,
To him that could interpret clear this thing:
But dumb the gazing astrologers stand,   595
Amazed at the writing and the hand.

None answers the affrighted king's intent,
Who still expects some fearful sad event;
As dead, alive he sits, as one undone:
In comes the queen, to cheer her heartless son.   600
Of Daniel tells, who in his grandsire's days
Was held in more account then now he was.
Daniel in haste is brought before the king,
Who doth not flatter, nor once cloak the thing;
Reminds him of his grandsire's height and fall,   605
And of his own notorious sins withal:
His drunkenness and his profaneness high,
His pride and sottish gross idolatry.
The guilty King with colour pale and dead
Then hears his *Mene* and his *Tekel* read.   610
And one thing did worthy a King (though late)
Performed his word to him that told his fate.
That night victorious Cyrus took the town,
Who soon did terminate his life and crown;
With him did end the race of Baladan,   615
And now the Persian monarchy began.

THE END OF THE ASSYRIAN MONARCHY

THE SECOND MONARCHY,
BEING THE PERSIAN, BEGAN UNDER
CYRUS, DARIUS BEING HIS UNCLE
AND FATHER-IN-LAW REIGNED
WITH HIM ABOUT TWO YEARS

Cyrus Cambyses, son of Persia's king,
Whom Lady Mandana did to him bring,
She daughter unto great Astiages, 625
He in descent the seventh from Arbaces.
Cambyses was of Achemenes race,
Who had in Persia the lieutenant's place
When Sardanapalus was overthrown,
And from that time had held it as his own. 630
Cyrus, Darius' daughter took to wife,
And so unites two kingdoms without strife.
Darius unto Mandana was brother,
Adopts her son for his, having no other.
This is of Cyrus the true pedigree, 635
Whose ancestors were royal in degree:
His mother's dream, and grandsire's cruelty,
His preservation in his misery,
His nourishment afforded by a bitch,
Are fit for such whose ears for fables itch. 640
He in his younger days an army led,
Against great Croesus then of Lydia head;
Who over-curious of war's event,
For information to Apollo went,
And the ambiguous oracle did trust, 645
So overthrown by Cyrus, as was just;
Who him pursues to Sardis, takes the town,
Where all that dare resist are slaughtered down;
Disguised Croesus hoped to 'scape i' th' throng,
Who had no might to save himself from wrong; 650

But as he passed, his son, who was born dumb,
With pressing grief and sorrow overcome,
Among the tumult, bloodshed, and the strife,
Brake his long silence, cried, "Spare Croesus' life":
Croesus thus known, it was great Cyrus' doom,   655
(A hard decree) to ashes he consume;
Then on a woodpile set, where all might eye,
He, "Solon, Solon, Solon," thrice did cry.
The reason of those words Cyrus demands,
Who Solon was, to whom he lifts his hands;   660
Then to the king he makes this true report,
That Solon sometimes at his stately court,
His treasures, pleasures, pomp and power did see,
And viewing all, at all nought moved was he:
That Croesus angry, urged him to express,   665
If ever king equalled his happiness.
Quoth he, "That man for happy we commend,
Whose happy life attains an happy end."
Cyrus with pity moved, knowing kings stand,
Now up, now down, as fortune turns her hand,   670
Weighing the age and greatness of the prince,
(His mother's uncle, stories do evince):
Gave him his life and took him for a friend,
Did to him still his chief designs commend.
Next war the restless Cyrus thought upon,   675
Was conquest of the stately Babylon,
Now treble walled, and moated so about,
That all the world they need not fear nor doubt;
To drain this ditch, he many sluices cut,
But till convenient time their heads kept shut;   680
That night Belshazzar feasted all his rout,
He cut those banks, and let the river out,
And to the walls securely marches on,
Not finding a defendant thereupon;
Enters the town, the sottish king he slays,   685

Upon earth's richest spoils his soldiers preys;
Here twenty years provision good he found,
Forty-five miles this city scarce could round;
This head of kingdoms, Chaldees' excellence,
For owls and satyrs made a residence;   690
Yet wondrous monuments this stately queen,
A thousand years had after to be seen.
Cyrus doth now the Jewish captives free,
An edict made, the temple builded be,
He with his uncle, Daniel sets on high,   695
And caused his foes in lions' den to die.
Long after this he 'gainst the Scythians goes,
And Tomris' son and army overthrows;
Which to revenge she hires a mighty power,
And sets on Cyrus, in a fatal hour;   700
There routs his host, himself she prisoner takes,
And at one blow, world's head, she headless makes,
The which she bathed, within a butt of blood,
Using such taunting words, as she thought good.
But Xenophon reports he died in's bed,   705
In honour, peace, and wealth, with a grey head;
And in his town of Passagardes lies,
Where some long after sought in vain for prize,
But in his tomb was only to be found
Two Scythian bows, a sword, and target round;   710
And Alexander coming to the same,
With honours great, did celebrate his fame.
Three daughters and two sons he left behind,
Ennobled more by birth, than by their mind;
Thirty-two years in all this prince did reign,   715
But eight whilst Babylon he did retain;
And though his conquests made the earth to groan,
Now quiet lies under one marble stone.
And with an epitaph, himself did make,
To show how little land he then should take.   720

Cambyses

Cambyses no ways like his noble sire,
Yet to enlarge his state had some desire,
His reign with blood and incest first begins,
Then sends to find a law, for these his sins;   725
That kings with sisters match, no law they find,
But that the Persian king may act his mind:
He wages war the fifth year of his reign,
'Gainst Egypt's king, who there by him was slain.
And all of royal blood, that came to hand,   730
He seized first of life, and then of land,
(But little Narus 'scaped that cruel fate,
Who grown a man, resumed again his state.)
He next to Cyprus sends his bloody host,
Who landing soon upon that fruitful coast,   735
Made Evelthon their king with bended knee,
To hold his own, of his free courtesy.
Their temple he destroys, not for his zeal,
For he would be professed god of their weal;
Yea, in his pride, he ventured so far,   740
To spoil the temple of great Jupiter:
But as they marched o'er those desert sands,
The stormed dust o'erwhelmed his daring bands;
But scorning thus, by Jove to be outbraved,
A second army he had almost graved,   745
But vain he found to fight with elements,
So left his sacrilegious bold intents.
The Egyptian Apis then he likewise slew,
Laughing to scorn that sottish calvish crew:
If all this heat had been for pious end,   750
Cambyses to the clouds we might commend.
But he that 'fore the gods himself prefers,
Is more profane than gross idolaters;
He after this, upon suspicion vain,

Unjustly caused his brother to be slain.   755
Praxaspes into Persia then is sent,
To act in secret, this his lewd intent:
His sister, whom incestuously he wed,
Hearing her harmless brother thus was dead,
His woeful death with tears did so bemoan,   760
That by her husband's charge, she caught her own;
She with her fruit at once were both undone,
Who would have born a nephew and a son.
Oh, hellish husband, brother, uncle, sire,
Thy cruelty all ages will admire.   765
This strange severity he sometimes used
Upon a judge, for taking bribes accused,
Flayed him alive, hung up his stuffed skin
Over his seat, then placed his son therein,
To whom he gave this in remembrance,   770
Like fault must look for the like recompense.
His cruelty was come unto that height,
He spared nor foe, nor friend, nor favorite.
'Twould be no pleasure, but a tedious thing
To tell the facts of this most bloody king,   775
Feared of all, but loved of few or none,
All wished his short reign past before 'twas done.
At last two of his officers he hears
Had set one Smerdis up, of the same years,
And like in feature to his brother dead,   780
Ruling, as they thought best, under this head.
The people ignorant of what was done,
Obedience yielded as to Cyrus' son.
Touched with this news to Persia he makes;
But in the way his sword just vengeance takes,   785
Unsheathes, as he his horse mounted on high,
And with a mortal trust wounds him i'th' thigh,
Which ends before begun his home-bred war:
So yields to death, that dreadful conqueror.

Grief for his brother's death he did express,   790
And more, because he died issueless.
The male line of great Cyrus now had end,
The female to many ages did extend.
A Babylon in Egypt did he make,
And Meroe built for his fair sister's sake.   795
Eight years he reigned, a short, yet too long time
Cut off in's wickedness, in's strength and prime.

The Inter-regnum between Cambyses And Darius Hystaspis

Childless Cambyses on the sudden dead,   800
The princes meet, to choose one in his stead,
Of which the chief was seven, called satraps,
Who like to kings, ruled kingdoms as they please,
Descended all of Achemenes blood,
And kinsmen in account to th' king they stood.   805
And first these noble Magi 'gree upon,
To thrust th' imposter Smerdis out of throne:
Then forces instantly they raise, and rout
This king with his conspirators so stout,
But yet 'fore this was done much blood was shed,   810
And two of these great peers in field lay dead.
Some write that sorely hurt they 'scaped away,
But so, or no, sure 'tis they won the day.
All things in peace, and rebels thoroughly quelled,
A consultation by those states was held,   815
What form of government now to erect
The old, or new, which best, in what respect.
The greater part declined a monarchy
So late crushed by their prince's tyranny,
And thought the people would more happy be,   820
If governed by an aristocracy;
But others thought (none of the dullest brain)

That better one than many tyrants reign.
What arguments they used, I know not well,
Too politic, it's like, for me to tell,   825
But in conclusion they all agree,
Out of the seven a monarch chosen be.
All envy to avoid, this was thought on,
Upon a green to meet by rising sun,
And he whose horse before the rest should neigh,   830
Of all the peers should have precedency.
They all attend on the appointed hour,
Praying to fortune for a kingly power.
Then mounting on their snorting coursers proud,
Darius' lusty stallion neighed full loud.   835
The nobles all alight, bow to their king,
And joyful acclamations shrill they ring.
A thousand times, "Long live the king," they cry,
"Let tyranny with dead Cambyses die";
Then all attend him to his royal room: 840
Thanks for all this to's crafty stable-groom.

Darius Hystaspis

Darius by election made a king,
His title to make strong, omits no thing:
He two of Cyrus' daughters then doth wed,   845
Two of his nieces takes to nuptial bed,
By which he cuts their hopes for future time,
That by such steps to kingdoms often climb.
And now a king by marriage, choice and blood:
Three strings to's bow, the least of which is good;   850
Yet firmly more, the people's hearts to bind,
Made wholesome, gentle laws which pleased each mind.
His courtesy and affability
Much gained the hearts of his nobility.
Yet notwithstanding all he did so well,   855

The Babylonians 'gainst their prince rebel.
An host he raised the city to reduce;
But men against those walls were of no use.
Then brave Zopirus for his master's good,
His manly face disfigures, spares no blood: 860
With his own hands cuts off his ears and nose,
And with a faithful fraud to th' town he goes,
Tells them how harshly the proud king had dealt,
That for their sakes his cruelty he felt;
Desiring of the prince to raise the siege,   865
This violence was done him by his liege.
This told, for entrance he stood not long;
For they believed his nose more than his tongue.
With all the city's strength they him betrust,
If he command, obey the greatest must.   870
When opportunity he saw was fit,
Delivers up the town, all in it.
To lose a nose, to win a town's no shame,
But who dares venture such a stake for th' game.
Then thy disgrace, thine honour's manifold,   875
Who doth deserve a statue made of gold.
Nor can Darius in his monarchy,
Scarce find enough to thank thy loyalty;
Yet o'er thy glory we must cast this veil,
Thy craft more than thy valor did prevail.   880
Darius in the second of his reign
An edict for the Jews published again:
The temple to rebuild, for that did rest
Since Cyrus time, Cambyses did molest.
He like a king now grants a charter large,   885
Out of his own revenues bears the charge,
Gives sacrifices, wheat, wine, oil, and salt,
Threats punishment to him that through default
Shall let the work, or keep back any thing
Of what is freely granted by the king;   890

And on all kings he pours out execrations
That shall once dare to raze those firm foundations.
They thus backed by the king, in spite of foes
Built on and prospered till their house they close,
And in the sixth year of his friendly reign,   895
Set up a temple (though a less) again.
Darius on the Scythians made a war,
Entering that large and barren country far;
A bridge he made, which served for boat and barge,
O'er Ister fair, with labour and with charge.   900
But in that desert, 'mongst his barbarous foes
Sharp wants, not swords, his valour did oppose;
His army fought with hunger and with cold,
Which to assail his royal camp was bold.
By these alone his host was pinched so sore,   905
He warred defensive, not offensive more.
The savages did laugh at his distress,
Their minds by hieroglyphics they express,
A frog, a mouse, a bird, an arrow sent,
The king will needs interpret their intent,   910
Possession of water, earth and air,
But wise Gobrias reads not half so fair:
Quoth he, "Like frogs in water we must dive,
Or like to mice under the earth must live,
Or fly like birds in unknown ways full quick,   915
Or Scythian arrows in our sides must stick."
The king, seeing his men and victual spent,
This fruitless war began late to repent,
Returned with little honour, and less gain.
His enemies scarce seen, than much less slain.   920
He after this intends Greece to invade,
But troubles in less Asia him stayed,
Which hushed, he straight so orders his affairs,
For Attica an army he prepares;
But as before, so now with ill success   925

Returned with wondrous loss, and honourless.
Athens, perceiving now their desperate state,
Armed all they could, which eleven thousand made,
By brave Miltiades, their chief, being led;
Darius' multitudes before them fled.   930
At Marathon this bloody field was fought,
Where Grecians proved themselves right soldiers stout;
The Persians to their galleys post with speed
Where an Athenian showed a valiant deed,
Pursues his flying foes, then on the sand,   935
He stays a launching galley with his hand,.
Which soon cut off, enraged, he with his left,
Renews his hold, and when of that bereft,
His whetted teeth he claps in the firm wood,
Off flies his head, down showers his frolic blood.   940
Go Persians, carry home that angry piece,
As the best trophy which ye won in Greece.
Darius light, yet heavy home returns,
And for revenge, his heart still restless burns,
His Queen Atossa, author of this stir,   945
For Grecian maids ('tis said) to wait on her.
She lost her aim, her husband he lost more,
His men, his coin, his honour, and his store;
And the ensuing year ended his life,
('Tis thought) through grief of this successless strife.   950
Thirty-six years this noble prince did reign,
Then to his second son did all remain.

Xerxes

Xerxes, Darius and Atossa's son,
Grandchild to Cyrus, now sits on the throne: 955
(His eldest brother put beside the place,
Because this was first born of Cyrus' race.)
His father not so full of lenity,

As was his son of pride and cruelty;
He with his crown receives a double war,   960
The Egyptians to reduce, and Greece to mar;
The first begun, and finished in such haste,
None write by whom, nor how, 'twas over past.
But for the last, he made such preparation,
As if to dust, he meant to grind that nation;   965
Yet all his men and instruments of slaughter
Produced but derision and laughter;
Sage Artabanus' counsel had he taken,
And's cousin young Mardonius forsaken,
His soldiers, credit, wealth at home had stayed,   970
And Greece such wondrous triumphs ne'er had made.
The first dehorts and lays before his eyes
His father's ill success, in's enterprize,
Against the Scythians and Grecians too,
What infamy to's honour did accrue.   975
Flatt'ring Mardonius on the other side,
With conquest of all Europe feeds his pride;
Vain Xerxes thinks his counsel hath most wit,
That his ambitious humour best can fit;
And by this choice unwarily posts on,   980
To present loss, future subversion.
Although he hasted, yet four years was spent
In great provisions, for this great intent:
His army of all nations was compounded,
That the vast Persian government surrounded.   985
His foot was seventeen hundred thousand strong,
Eight hundred thousand horse, to these belong
His camels, beasts for carriage numberless,
For truth's ashamed, how many to express;
The charge of all he severally commended   990
To princes, of the Persian blood descended;
But the command of these commanders all,
Unto Mardonius made their general;

He was the son of the fore-named Gobrius,
Who married the sister of Darius. 995
Such his land forces were, then next a fleet,
Of two and twenty thousand galleys meet,
Manned with Phoenicians and Pamphylians,
Cypriots, Dorians, and Cilicians,
Lycians, Carians, and Ionians, 1000
Eolians, and the Helespontines.
Besides the vessels for his transportation,
Which to three thousand came (by best relation)
Brave Artemisia, Halicarnassus' Queen
In person present for his aid was seen, 1005
Whose galleys all the rest in neatness pass,
Save the Sidonians, where Xerxes was:
But hers she kept still separate from the rest,
For to command alone, she judged was best.
O noble Queen, thy valour I commend; 1010
But pity 'twas thine aid thou here didst lend.
At Sardis in Lydia, all these do meet,
Whither rich Pythias comes Xerxes to greet,
Feasts all this multitude of his own charge,
Then gives the King a king-like gift full large, 1015
Three thousand talents of the purest gold,
Which mighty sum all wond'red to behold;
Then humbly to the king he makes request,
One of his five sons there might be released,
To be to's age a comfort and a stay, 1020
The other four he freely gave away.
The king calls for the youth, who being brought,
Cuts him in twain for whom his sire besought,
Then laid his parts on both sides of the way,
'Twixt which his soldiers marched in good array. 1025
For his great love is this thy recompense?
Is this to do like Xerxes or a prince?
Thou shame of kings, of men the detestation,

I rhetoric want to pour out execration.
First thing he did that's worthy of recount,   1030
A sea passage cut behind Athos mount.
Next o'er the Hellespont a bridge he made
Of boats together coupled, and there laid;
But winds and waves those iron bands did break;
To cross the sea such strength he found too weak;   1035
Then whips the sea, and with a mind most vain
He fetters cast therein the same to chain.
The workmen put to death the bridge that made,
Because they wanted skill the same to 've stayed.
Seven thousand galleys chained by Tyrians' skill,   1040
Firmly at last accomplished his will.
Seven days and nights his host without least stay
Was marching o'er this new devised way.
Then in Abidus plains must'ring his forces,
He glories in his squadrons and his horses.   1045
Long viewing them, thought it great happiness,
One king so many subjects should possess;
But yet this sight from him produced tears,
That none of those could live an hundred years.
What after did ensue had he foreseen,   1050
Of so long time his thoughts had never been.
Of Artabanus he again demands
How of this enterprise his thoughts now stands;
His answer was, both sea and land he feared,
Which was not vain as after soon appeared.   1055
But Xerxes resolute to Thrace goes first,
His host all Lissus drinks, to quench their thirst;
And for his cattle, all Pissyrus Lake
Was scarce enough, for each a draught to take;
Then marching on to th' strait Thermopyle,   1060
The Spartan meets him, brave Leonide;
This 'twixt the mountains lies (half acre wide)
That pleasant Thessaly from Greece divide;

Two days and nights, a fight they there maintain,
Till twenty thousand Persians fell down slain;   1065
And all that army then dismayed, had fled,
But that a fugitive discovered
How some might o'er the mountains go about,
And wound the backs of those brave warriors stout.
They thus behemmed with multitude of foes,   1070
Laid on more fiercely their deep mortal blows.
None cries for quarter, nor yet seeks to run,
But on their ground they die, each mother's son.
O noble Greeks, how now degenerate,
Where is the valour of your ancient state?   1075
When as one thousand could a million daunt;
Alas! it is Leonidas you want.
This shameful victory cost Xerxes dear,
Among the rest, two brothers he lost there;
And as at land, so he at sea was crossed,   1080
Four hundred stately ships by storms was lost;
Of vessels small almost innumerable,
The harbours to contain them was not able,
Yet thinking to out-match his foes at sea,
Enclosed their fleet i' th' strait of Eubea;   1085
But they as fortunate at sea as land,
In this strait, as the other firmly stand.
And Xerxes' mighty galleys battered so,
That their split sides witnessed his overthrow;
Then in the strait of Salamis he tried,   1090
If that small number his great force could 'bide;
But he in daring of his forward foe,
Received there a shameful overthrow.
Twice beaten thus at sea he warred no more,
But then the Phocians' country wasted sore;   1095
They no way able to withstand his force,
That brave Themistocles takes this wise course,
In secret manner word to Xerxes sends,

That Greeks to break his bridge shortly intends;
And as a friend warns him what e'er he do   1100
For his retreat, to have an eye thereto,
He hearing this, his thoughts and course home bended,
Much fearing that which never was intended.
Yet 'fore he went, to help out his expense,
Part of his host to Delphos sent from thence,   1105
To rob the wealthy temple of Apollo,
But mischief sacrilege doth ever follow.
Two mighty rocks brake from Parnassus hill,
And many thousands of those men did kill;
Which accident the rest affrighted so,   1110
With empty hands they to their master go;
He finding all to tend to his decay,
Fearing his bridge, no longer there would stay.
Three hundred thousand yet he left behind
With his Mardonius, index of his mind;   1115
Who for his sake he knew would venture far,
Chief instigator of this hapless war.
He instantly to Athens sends for peace,
That all hostility from thenceforth cease;
And that with Xerxes they would be at one,   1120
So should all favour to their state be shown.
The Spartans fearing Athens would agree,
As had Macedon, Thebes, and Thessaly,
And leave them out, this shock now to sustain,
By their ambassador they thus complain,   1125
That Xerxes' quarrel was 'gainst Athens' state,
And they had helped them as confederate;
If in their need they should forsake their friends,
Their infamy would last till all things ends;
But the Athenians this peace detest,   1130
And thus replied unto Mardon's request:
That whilst the sun did run his endless course,
Against the Persians they would bend their force;

Nor could the brave ambassador he sent,
With rhetoric gain better complement, 1135
A Macedonian born, and great commander,
No less than grandsire to great Alexander.
Mardonius proud, hearing this answer stout,
To add more to his numbers lays about;
And of those Greeks which by his skill he'd won, 1140
He fifty thousand joins unto his own;
The other Greeks which were confederate
In all one hundred and ten thousand made.
The Athenians could but forty thousand arm,
The rest had weapons would do little harm; 1145
But that which helped defects and made them bold,
Was victory by oracle foretold.
Then for one battle shortly all provide,
Where both their controversies they'll decide;
Ten days these armies did each other face, 1150
Mardonius finding victuals waste apace,
No longed dared, but bravely on-set gave,
The other not a hand nor sword would wave,
Till in the entrails of their sacrifice
The signal of their victory did rise; 1155
Which found, like Greeks they fight, the Persians fly,
And troublesome Mardonius now must die.
All's lost, and of three hundred thousand men,
Three thousand only can run home again.
For pity let those few to Xerxes go, 1160
To certify his final overthrow.
Same day the small remainder of his fleet,
The Grecians at Mycale in Asia meet.
And there so utterly they wracked the same,
Scarce one was left to carry home the fame; 1165
Thus did the Greeks consume, destroy, disperse
That army, which did fright the universe.
Scorned Xerxes, hated for his cruelty,

Yet ceases not to act his villainy.
His brother's wife solicits to his will,   1170
The chaste and beauteous dame refused still;
Some years by him in this vain suit was spent,
Nor prayers, nor gifts could win him least content;
Nor matching of her daughter to his son,
But she was still as when he first begun;   1175
When jealous Queen Amestris of this knew,
She harpy-like upon the lady flew,
Cut off her breasts, her lips, her nose, and ears,
And leaves her thus besmeared in blood and tears.
Straight comes her lord, and finds his wife thus lie,   1180
The sorrow of his heart did close his eye;
He dying to behold that wounding sight,
Where he had sometime gazed with great delight,
To see that face where rose, and lilies stood,
O'erflown with torrent of her guiltless blood,   1185
To see those breasts where chastity did dwell,
Thus cut and mangled by a hag of Hell;
With loaden heart unto the king he goes,
Tells as he could his unexpressed woes;
But for his deep complaints and showers of tears,   1190
His brother's recompense was nought but jeers;
The grieved prince finding nor right, nor love,
To Bactria his household did remove.
His brother sent soon after him a crew,
Which him and his most barbarously there slew;   1195
Unto such height did grow his cruelty,
Of life no man had least security.
At last his uncle did his death conspire,
And for that end his eunuch he did hire,
Who privately him smothered in his bed;   1200
But yet by search he was found murthered;
Then Artabanus, hirer of this deed,
That from suspicion he might be freed,

Accused Darius, Xerxes' eldest son,
To be the author of the crime was done.   1205
And by his craft ordered the matter so,
That the prince innocent to death did go:
But in short time this wickedness was known,
For which he died, and not he alone,
But all his family was likewise slain,   1210
Such justice in the Persian court did reign.
The eldest son thus immaturely dead,
The second was enthroned in's father's stead.

Artaxerxes Longimanus

Amongst the monarchs, next this prince had place,   1215
The best that ever sprung of Cyrus' race.
He first war with revolted Egypt made,
To whom the perjured Grecians lent their aid,
Although to Xerxes they not long before
A league of amity had firmly swore,   1220
Which had they kept, Greece had more nobly done
Than when the world they after overrun.
Greeks and Egyptians both he overthrows,
And pays them both according as he owes
Which done, a sumptuous feast makes like a king   1225
Where ninescore days are spent in banqueting.
His princes, nobles, and his captains calls,
To be partakers of these festivals;
His hangings white, and green, and purple dye,
With gold and silver beds, most gorgeously.   1230
The royal wine in golden cups did pass,
To drink more than he list, none bidden was:
Queen Vashti also feasts, but 'fore 'tis ended,
She's from her royalty (alas) suspended,
And one more worthy placed in her room,   1235
By Memucan's advice so was the doom.

What Esther was and did, the story read,
And how her countrymen from spoil she freed,
Of Haman's fall, and Mordecai's great rise,
The might of th' prince, the tribute of the isles. 1240
Good Ezra in the seventh year of his reign,
Did for the Jews commission large obtain,
With gold and silver, and what e'er they need;
His bounty did Darius' far exceed.
And Nehemiah in his twentieth year 1245
Went to Jerusalem his city dear,
Rebuilt those walls which long in rubbish lay,
And o'er his opposites still got the day.
Unto this king Themistocles did fly,
When under ostracism he did lie; 1250
For such ingratitude did Athens show,
This valiant knight whom they so much did owe;
Such royal bounty from his prince he found,
That in his loyalty his heart was bound.
The king not little joyful of this chance, 1255
Thinking his Grecian wars now to advance,
And for that end great preparation made
Fair Attica a third time to invade.
His grandsire's old disgrace did vex him sore,
His father Xerxes' loss and shame much more. 1260
For punishment their breach of oath did call,
This noble Greek, now fit for general.
Provisions then and season being fit,
To Themistocles this war he doth commit,
Who for his wrong he could not choose but deem 1265
His country nor his friends would much esteem;
But he all injury had soon forgot,
And to his native land could bear no hate,
Nor yet disloyal to his prince would prove,
By whom obliged by bounty and by love; 1270
Either to wrong, did wound his heart so sore,

To wrong himself by death he chose before;
In this sad conflict marching on his ways,
Strong poison took, so put an end to's days.
The king this noble captain having lost, 1275
Dispersed again his newly levied host;
Rest of his time in peace he did remain,
And died the two and forti'th of his reign.

Darius Nothus

Three sons great Artaxerxes left behind; 1280
The eldest to succeed, that was his mind;
His second brother with him fell at strife,
Still making war, till first had lost his life;
Then the survivor is by Nothus slain,
Who now sole monarch doth of all remain. 1285
The two first sons are by historians thought
By fair Queen Esther to her husband brought;
If so they were, the greater was her moan,
That for such graceless wretches she did groan.
Revolting Egypt 'gainst this king rebels, 1290
His garrisons drives out that 'mongst them dwells;
Joins with the Greeks, and so maintain their right
For sixty years, maugre the Persian's might.
A second trouble after this succeeds,
Which from remissness in Less Asia breeds. 1295
Amorges, whom for viceroy he ordained,
Revolts, treasure and people having gained,
Plunders the country, and much mischief wrought
Before things could to quietness be brought.
The king was glad with Sparta to make peace, 1300
That so he might those troubles soon appease;
But they in Asia must first restore
All towns held by his ancestors before.
The king much profit reaped by this league,

Regains his own, then doth the rebel break,   1305
Whose strength by Grecians' help was overthrown,
And so each man again possessed his own.
This king, Cambyses-like, his sister wed,
To which his pride, more than his lust him led;
For Persian kings then deemed themselves so good   1310
No match was high enough but their own blood.
Two sons she bore, the youngest Cyrus named,
A prince whose worth by Xenophon is famed;
His father would no notice of that take
Prefers his brother for his birthright's sake.   1315
But Cyrus scorns his brother's feeble wit,
And takes more on him than was judged fit.
The king provoked sends for him to th' court,
Meaning to chastise him in sharpest sort,
But in his slow approach, e'er he came there,   1320
His father died, so put an end to's fear.
'Bout nineteen years this Nothus reigned, which run,
His large dominions left to's eldest son.

Artaxerxes Mnemon

Mnemon now set upon his father's throne,   1325
Yet fears all he enjoys is not his own;
Still on his brother casts a jealous eye,
Judging his actions tends to's injury.
Cyrus on th' other side weighs in his mind,
What help in's enterprize he's like to find;   1330
His interest in th' kingdom, now next heir,
More dear to's mother than his brother far:
His brother's little love like to be gone,
Held by his mother's intercession.
These and like motives hurry him amain,   1335
To win by force what right could not obtain;
And thought it best now in his mother's time,

By lower steps towards the top to climb:
If in his enterprize he should fall short,
She to the king would make a fair report; 1340
He hoped if fraud nor force the crown would gain,
Her prevalence, a pardon might obtain.
From the lieutenant first he takes away
Some towns, commodious in Less Asia,
Pretending still the profit of the king, 1345
Whose rents and customs duly he sent in;
The king, finding revenues now amended,
For what was done seemed no whit offended.
Then next he takes the Spartans into pay,
One Greek could make ten Persians run away. 1350
Great care was his pretence those soldiers stout,
The rovers in Pisidia should drive out;
But lest some blacker news should fly to court,
Prepares himself to carry the report;
And for that end five hundred horse he chose; 1355
With posting speed on t'wards the king he goes;
But fame, more quick, arrives ere he comes there,
And fills the court with tumult, and with fear.
The old queen and the young at bitter jars,
The last accused the first for these sad wars; 1360
The wife against the mother still doth cry
To be the author of conspiracy.
The king dismayed, a mighty host doth raise,
Which Cyrus hears, and so foreslows his pace;
But as he goes his forces still augments, 1365
Seven hundred Greeks repair for his intents,
And others to be warmed by this new sun
In numbers from his brother daily run.
The fearful king at last musters his forces,
And counts nine hundred thousand foot and horses. 1370
Three hundred thousand he to Syria sent
To keep those straits, his brother to prevent.

Their captain, hearing but of Cyrus' name,
Forsook his charge to his eternal shame.
This place so made by nature and by art,   1375
Few might have kept it, had they had a heart.
Cyrus despaired a passage there to gain,
So hired a fleet to waft him o'er the main;
The 'mazed king was then about to fly
To Bactria and for a time there lie,   1380
Had not his captains sore against his will
By reason and by force detained him still.
Up then with speed a mighty trench he throws
For his security against his foes.
Six yards the depth and forty miles in length,   1385
Some fifty or else sixty foot in breadth;
Yet for his brother's coming durst not stay,
He safest was when farthest out of th' way.
Cyrus, finding his camp, and no man there,
Was not a little jocund at his fear.   1390
On this he and his soldiers careless grow,
And here and there in carts their arms they throw,
When suddenly their scouts come in and cry,
"Arm, Arm, the king with all his host is nigh."
In this confusion each man as he might   1395
Gets on his arms, arrays himself for fight,
And ranged stood by great Euphrates' side,
The brunt of that huge multitude to 'bide,
Of whose great numbers their intelligence
Was gathered by the dust that rose from thence,   1400
Which like a mighty cloud dark'ned the sky,
And black and blacker grew, as they drew nigh;
But when their order and their silence saw,
That, more than multitudes, their hearts did awe;
For tumult and confusion they expected,   1405
And all good discipline to be neglected.
But long under their fears they did not stay,

For at first charge the Persians ran away,
Which did such courage to the Grecians bring,
They all adored Cyrus for their king; 1410
So had he been, and got the victory,
Had not his too much valour put him by.
He with six hundred on a squadron set,
Of thousands six, wherein the king was yet,
And brought his soldiers on so gallantly, 1415
They ready were to leave their king and fly;
Whom Cyrus spies, cries loud, "I see the man,"
And with a full career at him he ran;
But in his speed a dart him hit i' th' eye,
Down Cyrus falls, and yields to destiny; 1420
His host in chase knows not of this disaster,
But treads down all, so to advance their master;
But when his head they spy upon a lance,
Who knows the sudden change made by this chance;
Senseless and mute they stand, yet breathe out groans, 1425
Nor Gorgon's head like this transformed to stones.
After this trance, revenge, new spirits blew,
And now more eagerly their foes pursue;
And heaps on heaps such multitudes they laid,
Their arms grew weary by their slaughters made. 1430
The king unto a country village flies,
And for a while unkingly there he lies.
At last displays his ensign on a hill,
Hoping by that to make the Greeks stand still,
But was deceived; to him they run amain, 1435
The king upon the spur runs back again;
But they too faint still to pursue their game,
Being victors oft, now to their camp they came.
Nor lacked they any of their number small,
Nor wound received, but one among them all; 1440
The king with his dispersed, also encamped,
With infamy upon each forehead stamped.

His hurried thoughts he after recollects,
Of this day's cowardice he fears th' effects.
If Greeks in their own country should declare   1445
What dastards in the field the Persians are,
They in short time might place one in his throne,
And rob him both of scepter and of crown;
To hinder their return by craft or force,
He judged his wisest and his safest course.   1450
Then sends, that to his tent they straight address,
And there all wait his mercy weaponless;
The Greeks with scorn reject his proud commands,
Asking no favor, where they feared no bands:
The troubled king his herald sends again,   1455
And sues for peace, that they his friends remain;
The smiling Greeks reply, they first must bait,
They were too hungry to capitulate;
The king great store of all provision sends,
And courtesy to th' utmost he pretends.   1460
Such terror on the Persians then did fall,
They quaked to hear them, to each other call.
The king perplexed, there dares not let them stay,
And fears as much to let them march away,
But kings ne'er want such as can serve their will,   1465
Fit instruments t' accomplish what is ill.
As Tyssaphernes, knowing his master's mind,
Their chief commanders feasts and yet more kind,
With all the oaths and deepest flattery,
Gets them to treat with him in privacy,   1470
But violates his honour and his word,
And villain-like there puts them all to th' sword.
The Greeks, seeing their valiant captains slain,
Chose Xenophon to lead them home again;
But Tissaphernes, what he could devise,   1475
Did stop the way in this their enterprize.
But when through difficulties all they brake,

The country burnt, they no relief might take.
But on they march through hunger and through cold
O'er mountains, rocks, and hills as lions bold,   1480
Nor river's course, nor Persians' force could stay,
But on to Trebizond they kept their way:
There was of Greeks settled a colony,
Who after all received them joyfully.
Thus finishing their travail, danger, pain,   1485
In peace they saw their native soil again.
The Greeks now (as the Persian king suspects)
The Asiatics' cowardice detects,
The many victories themselves did gain,
The many thousand Persians they had slain,   1490
And how their nation with facility,
Might gain the universal monarchy.
They then Dercilladus send with an host,
Who with the Spartans on the Asian Coast,
Town after town with small resistance take,   1495
Which rumour makes great Artaxerxes quake.
The Greeks by this success encouraged so,
Their King Agesilaus doth over go,
By Tissaphernes is encountered,
Lieutenant to the king, but soon he fled.   1500
Which overthrow incensed the king so sore,
That Tissaphern must be viceroy no more.
Tythraustes then is placed in his stead,
Commission hath to take the other's head,
Of that perjurious wretch this was the fate,   1505
Whom the old queen did bear a mortal hate.
Tythraustes trusts more to his wit than arms,
And hopes by craft to quit his master's harms;
He knows that many towns in Greece envies
The Spartan state, which now so fast did rise;   1510
To them he thirty thousand talents sent
With suit, their arms against their foes be bent;

They to their discontent receiving hire,
With broils and quarrels sets all Greece on fire:
Agesilaus is called home with speed,   1515
To defend, more than offend, there was need.
Their winnings lost, and peace they're glad to take
On such conditions as the king will make.
Dissention in Greece continued so long,
Till many a captain fell, both wise and strong,   1520
Whose courage nought but death could ever tame;
'Mongst these Epaminondas wants no fame,
Who had (as noble Raleigh doth evince)
All the peculiar virtues of a prince;
But let us leave these Greeks to discord bent,   1525
And turn to Persia, as is pertinent.
The king from foreign parts now well at ease,
His home-bred troubles sought how to appease;
The two queens by his means seem to abate
Their former envy and inveterate hate: 1530
But the old queen, implacable in strife,
By poison caused the young one lose her life.
The king highly enraged doth hereupon
From court exile her unto Babylon;
But shortly calls her home, her counsels prize,   1535
(A lady very wicked, but yet wise).
Then in voluptuousness he leads his life,
And weds his daughter for a second wife.
But long in ease and pleasure did not lie,
His sons sore vext him by disloyalty.   1540
Such as would know at large his wars and reign,
What troubles in his house he did sustain,
His match incestuous, cruelties of th' queen,
His life may read in Plutarch to be seen.
Forty-three years he ruled, then turned to dust,   1545
A king nor good, nor valiant, wise nor just.

Darius Ochus

Ochus, a wicked and rebellious son,
Succeeds in th' throne, his father being gone.
Two of his brothers in his father's days 1550
(To his great grief) most subtly he slays;
And being king, commands those that remain
Of brethern and of kindred to be slain.
Then raises forces, conquers Egypt land,
Which in rebellion sixty years did stand; 1555
And in the twenty-third of's cruel reign
Was by his eunuch, the proud Bagoas, slain.

Arsames or Arses

Arsames placed now in his father's stead,
By him that late his father murthered. 1560
Some write that Arsames was Ochus brother,
Enthroned by Bagoas in the room of th' other:
But why his brother 'fore his son succeed,
I can no reason give, 'cause non I read.
His brother, as 'tis said, long since was slain, 1565
And scarce a nephew left that now might reign;
What acts he did time hath not now left penned,
But most suppose in him did Cyrus end,
Whose race long time had worn the diadem,
But now's devolved to another stem. 1570
Three years he reigned, then drank of's father's cup
By the same eunuch who first set him up.

Darius Codomanus

Darius by this Bagoas set in throne
(Complotter with him in the murder done) 1575

And was no sooner settled in his reign,
But Bagoas falls to's practices again,
And the same sauce had served him no doubt,
But that his treason timely was found out,
And so this wretch (a punishment too small)   1580
Lost but his life for horrid treasons all.
This Codomanus now upon the stage
Was to his predecessors chamber page.
Some write great Cyrus' line was not yet run,
But from some daughter this new king was sprung,   1585
If so, or not, we cannot tell, but find
That several men will have their several mind;
Yet in such differences we may be bold,
With learned and judicious still to hold;
And this 'mongst all's no controverted thing,   1590
That this Darius was last Persian king,
Whose wars and losses we may better tell,
In Alexander's reign who did him quell,
How from the top of world's felicity,
He fell to depth of greatest misery.   1595
Whose honours, treasures, pleasures had short stay;
One deluge came and swept them all away.
And in the sixth year of his hapless reign,
Of all did scarce his winding sheet retain:
And last, a sad catastrophe to end,   1600
Him to the grave did traitor Bessus send.

THE END OF THE PERSIAN MONARCHY

THE THIRD MONARCHY,
BEING THE GRECIAN, BEGINNING
UNDER ALEXANDER THE GREAT 1605
IN THE *112* OLYMPIAD

Great Alexander was wise Philip's son,
He to Amyntas, kings of Macedon;
The cruel, proud Olympias was his mother,
She to Epirus' warlike king was daughter.   1610
This prince (his father by Pausanias slain)
The twenty-first of's age began to reign.
Great were the gifts of nature which he had,
His education much to those did add;
By art and nature both he was made fit,   1615
To 'complish that which long before was writ.
The very day of his nativity
To ground was burnt Diana's temple high:
An omen to their near approaching woe,
Whose glory to the earth this king did throw.   1620
His rule to Greece he scorned should be confined,
The universe scarce bounds his proud vast mind.
This is the he-goat which from Grecia came,
That ran in choler on the Persian ram,
That brake his horns, that threw him on the ground;   1625
To save him from his might no man was found;
Philip on this great conquest had an eye,
But death did terminate those thoughts so high.
The Greeks had chose him captain general,
Which honour to his son did now befall.   1630
(For as world's monarch now we speak not on,
But as the King of little Macedon.)
Restless both day and night his heart then was,
His high resolves which way to bring to pass;
Yet for a while in Greece is forced to stay,   1635

Which makes each moment seem more than a day.
Thebes and stiff Athens both 'gainst him rebel;
Their mutinies by valour doth he quell.
This done against both right and nature's laws,
His kinsmen put to death, who gave no cause; 1640
That no rebellion in his absence be,
Nor making title unto sovereignty.
And all whom he suspects or fears will climb
Now taste of death, lest they deserv't in time;
Nor wonder is't if he in blood begin, 1645
For cruelty was his parental sin.
Thus eased now of troubles and of fears,
Next spring his course to Asia he steers;
Leaves sage Antipater, at home to sway,
And through the Hellespont his ships make way. 1650
Coming to land, his dart on shore he throws,
Then with alacrity he after goes;
And with a bount'ous heart and courage brave,
His little wealth among his soldiers gave.
And being asked what for himself was left, 1655
Replied, enough, sith only hope he kept.
Thirty-two thousand made up his foot force,
To which were joined five thousand goodly horse.
Then on he marched, in's way he viewed old Troy,
And on Achilles' tomb with wondrous joy 1660
He offered, and for good success did pray
To him, his mother's ancestor, men say.
When news of Alexander came to court,
To scorn at him Darius had good sport;
Sends him a frothy and contemptuous letter, 1665
Styles him disloyal servant, and no better;
Reproves him for his proud audacity
To lift his hand 'gainst such a monarchy.
Then to's lieutenant he in Asia sends
That he be ta'n alive, for he intends 1670
To whip him well with rods, and so to bring

That boy so malipert before the king.
Ah! fond vain man, whose pen ere while
In lower terms was taught a higher style.
To River Granic Alexander hies   1675
Which in Phrygia near Propontike lies.
The Persians ready for encounter stand,
And strive to keep his men from off the land;
Those banks so steep the Greeks yet scramble up,
And beat the coward Persians from the top,   1680
And twenty thousand of their lives bereave,
Who in their backs did all their wounds receive.
This victory did Alexander gain,
With loss of thirty-four of his there slain:
Then Sardis he, and Ephesus did gain,   1685
Where stood of late, Diana's wondrous fane,
And by Parmenio (of renowned fame)
Miletus and Pamphilia overcame.
Hallicarnassus and Pisidia
He for his master takes with Lycia.   1690
Next Alexander marched towards the Black Sea
And easily takes old Gordium in his way,
Of ass-eared Midas, once the regal seat,
Whose touch turned all to gold, yea even his meat,
Where the prophetic knot he cuts in twain,   1695
Which who so doth, must lord of all remain.
Now news of Memnon's death (the king's viceroy)
To Alexander's heart's no little joy,
For in that peer, more valour did abide,
Than in Darius' multitude beside;   1700
In's stead, was Arses placed, but durst not stay,
Yet set one in his room, and ran away;
His substitute as fearful as his master,
Runs after too, and leaves all to disaster.
Then Alexander all Cilicia takes,   1705
No stroke for it he struck, their hearts so quakes.
To Greece he thirty thousand talents sends,

To raise more force to further his intends;
Then o'er he goes, Darius now to meet,
Who came with thousand thousands at his feet.   1710
Though some there be, perhaps more likely, write
He but four hundred thousand had to fight,
The rest attendants, which made up no less,
Both sexes there was almost numberless.
For this wise king had brought to see the sport,   1715
With him the greatest ladies of the court,
His mother, his beauteous queen, and daughters,
It seems to see the Macedonian slaughters.
It's much beyond my time and little art,
To show how great Darius played his part,   1720
The splendor and the pomp he marched in,
For since the world was no such pageant seen.
Sure 'twas a goodly sight there to behold,
The Persians clad in silk, and glistering gold,
The stately horses trapped, the lances gilt,   1725
As if addressed now all to run at tilt.
The holy fire was borne before the host,
For sun and fire the Persians worship most;
The priests in their strange habit follow after,
An object, not so much of fear as laughter.   1730
The king sat in a chariot made of gold,
With crown and robes most glorious to behold,
And o'er his head his golden gods on high,
Support a parti-coloured canopy.
A number of spare horses next were led,   1735
Lest he should need them in his chariot's stead;
But those that saw him in this state to lie,
Supposed he neither meant to fight nor fly.
He fifteen hundred had like women dressed;
For thus to fright the Greeks he judged was best.   1740
Their golden ornaments how to set forth,
Would ask more time than was their bodies worth,
Great Sysigambis she brought up the rear,

Then such a world of wagons did appear,
Like several houses moving upon wheels,   1745
As if she'd drawn whole Shushan at her heels:
This brave virago to the king was mother,
And as much good she did as any other.
Now lest this gold, and all this goodly stuff
Had not been spoil and booty rich enough,   1750
A thousand mules and camels ready wait,
Loaden with gold, with jewels, and with plate;
For sure Darius thought at the first sight,
The Greeks would all adore, but none would fight,
But when both armies met, he might behold   1755
That valour was more worth than pearls or gold,
And that his wealth served but for baits to 'lure
To make his overthrow more fierce and sure.
The Greeks came on and with a gallant grace
Let fly their arrows in the Persians' face.   1760
The cowards, feeling this sharp stinging charge,
Most basely ran, and left their king at large,
Who from his golden coach is glad to 'light,
And cast away his crown for swifter flight;
Of late like some immoveable he lay,   1765
Now finds both legs and horse to run away.
Two hundred thousand men that day were slain,
And forty thousand prisoners also ta'n,
Besides the queens and ladies of the court,
If Curtius be true in his report.   1770
The regal ornaments were lost, the treasure
Divided at the Macedonian's pleasure;
Yet all this grief, this loss, this overthrow,
Was but beginning of his future woe.
The royal captives brought to Alexander,   1775
T'ward them demeaned himself like a commander,
For though their beauties were unparalleled,
Conquered himself now he had conquered,
Preserved their honour, used them bounteously,

Commands no man should do them injury;   1780
And this to Alexander is more fame
Than that the Persian king he overcame.
Two hundred eighty Greeks he lost in fight,
By too much heat, not wounds (as authors write);
No sooner had this victor won the field,   1785
But all Phoenicia to his pleasure yield,
Of which the government he doth commit
Unto Parmenio of all most fit.
Darius now less lofty than before,
To Alexander writes he would restore   1790
Those mournful ladies from captivity,
For whom he offers him a ransom high;
But down his haughty stomach could not bring,
To give this conqueror the style of king.
This letter Alexander doth disdain,   1795
And in short terms sends this reply again,
A king he was, and that not only so,
But of Darius king, as he should know.
Next Alexander unto Tyre doth go,
His valour and his victories they know;   1800
To gain his love the Tyrians intend,
Therefore a crown and great provision send;
Their present he receives with thankfulness,
Desires to offer unto Hercules,
Protector of their town, by whom defended,   1805
And from whom he lineally descended.
But they accept not this in any wise,
Lest he intend more fraud than sacrifice,
Sent word that Hercules his temple stood
In the old town (which then lay like a wood).   1810
With this reply he was so deep enraged,
To win the town, his honour he engaged;
And now as Babel's king did once before,
He leaves not till he made the sea firm shore,
But far less time and cost he did expend,   1815

The former ruins forwarded his end;
Moreover had a navy at command,
The other by his men fetcht all by land.
In seven months' time he took that wealthy town,
Whose glory now a second time's brought down.   1820
Two thousand of the chief he crucified,
Eight thousand by the sword then also died,
And thirteen thousand galley slaves he made,
And thus the Tyrians for mistrust were paid.
The rule of this he to Philotas gave,   1825
Who was the son of that Parmenio brave.
Cilicia to Socrates doth give,
For now's the time captains like kings may live.
Sidon he on Ephestion bestows;
For that which freely comes, as freely goes.   1830
He scorns to have one worse than had the other,
So gives his little lordship to another.
Ephestion, having chief command of th' fleet,
At Gaza now must Alexander meet.
Darius finding troubles still increase,   1835
By his ambassadors now sues for peace,
And lays before great Alexander's eyes
The dangers, difficulties like to rise,
First at Euphrates what he's like to 'bide,
And then at Tygris and Araxis side;   1840
These he may scape, and if he so desire,
A league of friendship make firm and entire.
His eldest daughter he in marriage proffers,
And a most princely dowry with her offers.
All those rich kingdoms large that do abide   1845
Betwixt the Hellespont and Halys' side.
But he with scorn his courtesy rejects,
And the distressed king no whit respects,
Tells him, these proffers great in truth were none
For all he offers now was but his own.   1850
But quoth Parmenio, that brave commander,

Was I as great, as is great Alexander,
Darius' offers I would not reject,
But th' kingdoms and the lady soon accept.
To which proud Alexander made reply,   1855
And so, if I Parmenio was, would I.
He now to Gaza goes, and there doth meet
His favorite Ephestion with his fleet,
Where valiant Betis stoutly keeps the town,
A loyal subject to Darius' crown;   1860
For more repulse the Grecians here abide
Than in the Persian monarchy beside;
And by these walls so many men were slain,
That Greece was forced to yield supply again.
But yet this well-defended town was taken,   1865
For 'twas decreed that empire should be shaken;
Thus Betis ta'en had holes bored through his feet,
And by command was drawn through every street
To imitate Achilles in his shame,
Who did the like to Hector (of more fame).   1870
What hast thou lost thy magnanimity,
Can Alexander deal thus cruelly?
Sith valour with heroics is renowned,
Though in an enemy it should be found;
If of thy future fame thou hadst regard,   1875
Why didst not heap up honours and reward?
From Gaza to Jerusalem he goes,
But in no hostile way (as I suppose);
Him in his priestly robes high Jaddus meets,
Whom with great reverence Alexander greets;   1880
The priest shows him good Daniel's prophesy,
How he should overthrow this monarchy,
By which he was so much encouraged,
No future dangers he did ever dread.
From thence to fruitful Egypt marched with speed,   1885
Where happily in's wars he did succeed;
To see how fast he gained was no small wonder,

For in few days he brought that kingdom under.
Then to the fane of Jupiter he went,
To be installed a god was his intent.   1890
The pagan priest through hire, or else mistake,
The son of Jupiter did straight him make;
He diabolical must needs remain,
That his humanity will not retain.
Thence back to Egypt goes, and in few days;   1895
Fair Alexandria from the ground doth raise;
Then settling all things in Less Asia,
In Syria, Egypt, and Phoenicia,
Unto Euphrates marched and overgoes,
For no man's there his army to oppose;   1900
Had Betis now been there but with his band,
Great Alexander had been kept from land.
But as the king, so is the multitude,
And now of valour both are destitute.
Yet he (poor prince) another host doth muster,   1905
Of Persians, Scythians, Indians in a cluster;
Men but in shape and name, of valour none
Most fit, to blunt the swords of Macedon.
Two hundred fifty thousand by account,
Of horse and foot his army did amount;   1910
For in his multitudes his trust still lay,
But on their fortitude he had small stay;
Yet had some hope that on the spacious plain,
His numbers might the victory obtain.
About this time Darius' beautious queen,   1915
Who had sore travail and much sorrow seen,
Now bids the world adieu, with pain being spent,
Whose death her lord full sadly did lament.
Great Alexander mourns as well as he,
The more because not set at liberty;   1920
When this sad news at first Darius hears,
Some injury was offered he fears;
But when informed how royally the king

Had used her, and hers, in everything,
He prays the immortal gods they would reward   1925
Great Alexander for this good regard;
And if they down his monarchy will throw,
Let them on him this dignity bestow.
And now for peace he sues as once before,
And offers all he did and kingdoms more;   1930
His eldest daughter for his princely bride
(Nor was such match in all the world beside),
And all those countries which betwixt did lie
Phoenician Sea, and great Euphrates high,
With fertile Egypt and rich Syria,   1935
And all those kingdoms in Less Asia.
With thirty thousand talents to be paid,
For the queen mother and the royal maid;
And till all this be well performed, and sure,
Ochus his son for hostage should endure.   1940
To this stout Alexander gives no ear,
No, though Parmenio plead, yet will not hear;
Which had he done, perhaps, his fame he'd kept,
Nor infamy had waked, when he had slept,
For his unlimited prosperity   1945
Him boundless made in vice and cruelty.
Thus to Darius he writes back again,
The firmament, two suns cannot contain.
Two monarchies on earth cannot abide,
Nor yet two monarchs in one world reside;   1950
The afflicted king, finding him set to jar,
Prepares against tomorrow, for the war,
Parmenio, Alexander wished, that night
To force his camp, so vanquish them by flight.
For tumult in the night doth cause most dread,   1955
And weakness of a foe is covered,
But he disdained to steal a victory;
The sun should witness of his valour be,

And careless in his bed, next morn he lies,
By captains twice is called before he'll rise;   1960
The armies joined awhile, the Persians fight,
And spilt the Greeks some blood before their flight;
But long they stood not ere they're forced to run,
So made an end, as soon as well begun.
Forty-five thousand Alexander had,   1965
But is not known what slaughter here was made.
Some write th' other had a million, some more,
But Quintus Curtius, as was said before.
At Arbela this victory was gained,
Together with the town also obtained;   1970
Darius, stripped of all, to Media came,
Accompanied with sorrow, fear, and shame,
At Arbela left his ornaments and treasure,
Which Alexander deals as suits his pleasure.
This conqueror to Babylon then goes,   1975
Is entertained with joy and pompous shows,
With showers of flowers the streets along are strown,
And incense burnt the silver altars on.
The glory of the castle he admires,
The strong foundation and the lofty spires   1980
In this, a world of gold and treasure lay,
Which in few hours was carried all away.
With greedy eyes he views this city round,
Whose fame throughout the world was so renowned;
And to possess he counts no little bliss   1985
The towers and bowers of proud Semiramis,
Though worn by time, and razed by foes full sore,
Yet old foundations showed and somewhat more.
With all the pleasures that on earth are found,
This city did abundantly abound,   1990
Where four and thirty days he now did stay,
And gave himself to banqueting and play;
He and his soldiers wax effeminate,

And former discipline begin to hate.
Whilst revelling at Babylon he lies,   1995
Antipater from Greece sends fresh supplies.
He then to Shushan goes with his new bands,
But needs no force, 'tis rend'red to his hands.
He likewise here a world of treasure found;
For 'twas the seat of Persian kings renowned.   2000
Here stood the royal houses of delight,
Where kings have shown their glory, wealth, and might;
The sumptuous palace of Queen Esther here,
And of good Mordecai, her kinsman dear,
Those purple hangings, mixed with green and white,   2005
Those beds of gold, and couches of delight,
And furniture the richest in all lands,
Now fall into the Macedonians' hands.
From Shushan to Persepolis he goes,
Which news doth still augment Darius' woes.   2010
In his approach the governor sends word,
For his receipt with joy they all accord;
With open gates the wealthy town did stand,
And all in it was at his high command.
Of all the cities that on earth was found,   2015
None like to this in riches did abound;
Though Babylon was rich and Shushan, too,
Yet to compare with this they might not do;
Here lay the bulk of all those precious things
That did pertain unto the Persian kings;   2020
For when the soldiers rifled had their pleasure,
And taken money, plate, and golden treasure,
Statues, some gold, and silver numberless,
Yet after all, as stories do express,
The share of Alexander did amount   2025
To an hundred thousand talents by account.
Here of his own he sets a garrison
(As first at Shushan and at Babylon);

On their old governors titles he laid,
But on their faithfulness he never staid;   2030
Their place gave to his captains (as was just),
For such revolters false, what king can trust?
The riches and the pleasures of this town
Now makes this king his virtues all to drown,
That wallowing in all licentiousness,   2035
In pride and cruelty to high excess,
Being inflamed with wine upon a season,
Filled with madness, and quite void of reason,
He, at a bold proud strumpet's lewd desire,
Commands to set this goodly town on fire.   2040
Parmenio wise entreats him to desist
And lays before his eyes if he persist
His fame's dishonour, loss unto his state,
And just procuring of the Persians' hate;
But deaf to reason, bent to have his will,   2045
Those stately streets with raging flame did fill.
Then to Darius he directs his way,
Who was retired as far as Media,
And there with sorrows, fears, and cares surrounded,
Had now his army fourth and last compounded,   2050
Which forty thousand made, but his intent
Was these in Bactria soon to augment;
But hearing Alexander was so near,
Thought now this once to try his fortunes here,
And rather chose an honourable death,   2055
Than still with infamy to draw his breath;
But Bessus false, who was his chief commander,
Persuades him not to fight with Alexander.
With sage advice he sets before his eyes
The little hope of profit like to rise: 2060
If when he'd multitudes the day he lost,
Then with so few, how likely to be crossed.
This counsel for his safety he pretended,

But to deliver him to's foe intended.
Next day this treason to Darius known,   2065
Transported sore with grief and passion,
Grinding his teeth, and plucking off his hair,
Sat overwhelmed with sorrow and despair;
Then bids his servant, Artabasus true,
Look to himself, and leave him to that crew,   2070
Who was of hopes and comforts quite bereft,
And by his guard and servitors all left.
Straight Bessus comes, and with his trait'rous hands
Lays hold on's lord, and binding him with bands
Throws him into a cart, covered with hides,   2075
Who wanting means t' resist these wrongs abides,
Then draws the cart along with chains of gold,
In more despite the thralled prince to hold,
And thus t'ward Alexander on he goes.
Great recompense for this, he did propose;   2080
But some, detesting this his wicked fact,
To Alexander flies and tells this act,
Who doubling of his march, posts on amain,
Darius from that traitor's hands to gain.
Bessus gets knowledge his disloyalty   2085
Had Alexander's wrath incensed high,
Whose army now was almost within sight,
His hopes being dashed, prepares himself for flight;
Unto Darius first he brings a horse,
And bids him save himself by speedy course;   2090
The woeful king his courtesy refuses,
Whom thus the execrable wretch abuses,
By throwing darts gave him his mortal wound,
Then slew his servants that were faithful found,
Yea wounds the beasts that drew him unto death,   2095
And leaves him thus to gasp out his last breath.
Bessus, his partner in this tragedy,
Was the false governor of Media.

This done, they with their host soon speed away,
To hide themselves remote in Bactria.   2100
Darius, bathed in blood, sends out his groans,
Invokes the heav'ns and earth to hear his moans;
His lost felicity did grieve him sore,
But this unheard of treachery much more;
But above all, that neither ear nor eye   2105
Should hear nor see his dying misery;
As thus he lay, Polistrates, a Greek,
Wearied with his long march, did water seek,
So chanced these bloody horses to espy,
Whose wounds had made their skins of purple dye,   2110
To them repairs, then looking in the cart,
Finds poor Darius pierced to the heart,
Who not a little cheered to have some eye
The witness of this horrid tragedy;
Prays him to Alexander to commend   2115
The just revenge of this his woeful end,
And not to pardon such disloyalty,
Of treason, murther, and base cruelty.
If not, because Darius thus did pray,
Yet that succeeding kings in safety may   2120
Their lives enjoy, their crowns and dignity,
And not by traitors' hands untimely die.
He also sends his humble thankfulness
For all the kingly grace he did express
To's mother, children dear, and wife now gone,   2125
Which made their long restraint seem to be none;
Praying the immortal gods that sea and land
Might be subjected to his royal hand,
And that his rule as far extended be,
As men the rising, setting sun shall see;   2130
This said, the Greek for water doth entreat,
To quench his thirst, and to allay his heat;
Of all good things (quoth he) once in my power,

I've nothing left at this my dying hour,
Thy service and compassion to reward, 2135
But Alexander will, for this regard.
This said, his fainting breath did fleet away,
And though a monarch late, now lies like clay;
And thus must every son of Adam lie;
Though gods on earth like sons of men they die. 2140
Now to the East, great Alexander goes,
To see if any dare his might oppose,
For scarce the world or any bounds thereon
Could bound his boundless, fond ambition;
Such as submits again he doth restore 2145
Their riches, and their honours he makes more,
On Artabaces more than all bestowed,
For his fidelity to's master showed.
Thalestris, queen of th' Amazons, now brought
Her train to Alexander, as 'tis thought. 2150
Though most of reading best and soundest mind,
Such country there, nor yet such people find.
Than tell her errand, we had better spare;
To th' ignorant, her title will declare.
As Alexander in his greatness grows, 2155
So daily of his virtues doth he lose.
He baseness counts his former clemency,
And not beseeming such a dignity;
His past sobriety doth also hate,
As most incompatible to his state; 2160
His temperance is but a sordid thing
No ways becoming such a mighty king;
His greatness now he takes to represent
His fancied gods above the firmament.
And such as showed but reverence before, 2165
Now are commanded strictly to adore;
With Persian robes himself doth dignify,
Charging the same on his nobility;

His manners, habit, gestures, all did fashion
After that conquered and luxurious nation.   2170
His captains that were virtuously inclined
Grieved at this change of manners and of mind.
The ruder sort did openly deride
His feigned diety and foolish pride;
The certainty of both comes to his ears,   2175
But yet no notice takes of what he hears;
With those of worth he still desires esteem,
So heaps up gifts his credit to redeem;
And for the rest new wars and travails finds,
That other matters might take up their minds,   2180
And hearing Bessus makes himself a king,
Intends that traitor to his end to bring.
Now that his host from luggage might be free,
And with his burden no man burdened be,
Commands forthwith each man his fardle bring   2185
Into the market place before the king;
Which done, sets fire upon those goodly spoils,
The recompense of travails, wars, and toils.
And thus unwisely in a madding fume,
The wealth of many kingdoms did consume;   2190
But marvel 'tis that without mutiny
The soldiers should let pass this injury;
Nor wonder less to readers may it bring,
Here to observe the rashness of the king.
Now with his army doth he post away   2195
False Bessus to find out in Bactria;
But much distressed for water in their march,
The drought and heat their bodies sore did parch.
At length they came to th' river Oxus' brink,
Where so immoderately these thirsty drink,   2200
Which more mortality to them did bring
Than all their wars against the Persian king.
Here Alexander's almost at a stand,

To pass the river to the other land.
For boats here's none, nor near it any wood,   2205
To make them rafts to waft them o'er the flood;
But he that was resolved in his mind
Would without means some transportation find.
Then from the carriages the hides he takes,
And stuffiing them with straw, he bundles makes.   2210
On these together tied, in six days' space,
They all pass over to the other place.
Had Bessus had but valour to his will,
With little pain there might have kept them still;
But coward, durst not fight, nor could he fly,   2215
Hated of all for's former treachery,
Is by his own now bound in iron chains;
A collar of the same his neck contains.
And in this sort they rather drag than bring
This malefactor vile before the king,   2220
Who to Darius' brother gives the wretch,
With racks and tortures every limb to stretch.
Here was of Greeks a town in Bactria,
Whom Xerxes from their country led away,
These not a little joyed this day to see   2225
Wherein their own had got the sov'reignty,
And now revived, with hopes held up their head
From bondage long to be enfranchised.
But Alexander puts them to the sword
Without least cause from them in deed or word;   2230
Nor sex, nor age, nor one, nor other spared,
But in his cruelty alike they shared;
Nor reason could he give for this great wrong,
But that they had forgot their mother tongue.
While thus some time he spent in Bactria,   2235
And in his camp strong and securely lay,
Down from the mountains twenty thousand came
And there most fiercely set upon the same;

Repelling these, two marks of honour got
Imprinted in his leg, by arrows shot.   2240
The Bactrians against him now rebel;
But he their stubbornness in time doth quell.
From hence he to Jaxartis River goes,
Where Scythians rude his army doth oppose,
And with their outcries in an hideous sort   2245
Beset his camp, or military court;
Of darts and arrows, made so little spare,
They flew so thick, they seemed to dark the air;
But soon his soldiers forced them to a flight;
Their nakedness could not endure their might.   2250
Upon this river's bank in seventeen days
A goodly city doth completely raise,
Which Alexandria he doth likewise name,
And sixty furlongs could but round the same.
A third supply Antipater now sent,   2255
Which did his former forces much augment;
And being one hundred twenty thousand strong,
He enters then the Indian kings among.
Those that submit, he gives them rule again;
Such as do not, both them and theirs are slain.   2260
His wars with sundry nations I'll omit,
And also of the Mallians what is writ,
His fights, his dangers, and the hurts he had,
How to submit their necks at last they're glad.
To Nisa goes by Bacchus built long since,   2265
Whose feasts are celebrated by this prince;
Nor had that drunken god one who would take
His liquors more devoutly for his sake.
When thus ten days his brain with wine he'd soaked,
And with delicious meats his palate choked,   2270
To th' River Indus next his course he bends;
Boats to prepare, Ephestion first he sends,
Who coming thither long before his lord,

Had to his mind made all things to accord;
The vessels ready were at his command,   2275
And Omphis, king of that part of the land,
Through his persuasion Alexander meets,
And as his sov'reign lord him humbly greets.
Fifty-six elephants he brings to's hand,
And tenders him the strength of all his land,   2280
Presents himself first with a golden crown,
Then eighty talents to his captains down;
But Alexander made him to behold
He glory sought, no silver nor no gold;
His presents all with thanks he did restore,   2285
And of his own a thousand talents more.
Thus all the Indian kings to him submit,
But Porus stout, who will not yield as yet;
To him doth Alexander thus declare,
His pleasure is that forthwith he repair   2290
Unto his kingdom's borders, and as due,
His homage to himself as sovereign do.
But kingly Porus this brave answer sent,
That to attend him there was his intent,
And come as well provided as he could,   2295
But for the rest, his sword advise him should.
Great Alexander, vext at this reply,
Did more his valour than his crown envy,
Is now resolved to pass Hydaspes' flood,
And there by force his sovereignty make good.   2300
Stout Porus on the banks doth ready stand
To give him welcome when he comes to land.
A potent army with him like a king
And ninety elephants for war did bring.
Had Alexander such resistance seen   2305
On Tygris' side, here now he had not been.
Within this spacious river deep and wide
Did here and there isles full of trees abide.

His army Alexander doth divide,
With Ptolemy sends part to th' other side;   2310
Porus encounters them and thinks all's there,
When covertly the rest get o'er elsewhere;
And whilst the first he valiantly assailed,
The last set on his back, and so prevailed.
Yet work enough here Alexander found,   2315
For to the last stout Porus kept his ground;
Nor was't dishonour at the length to yield,
When Alexander strives to win the field.
The kingly captive 'fore the victor's brought,
In looks or gesture not abased ought,   2320
But him a prince of an undaunted mind
Did Alexander by his answers find.
His fortitude his royal foe commends,
Restores him and his bounds farther extends.
Now eastward Alexander would go still,   2325
But so to do his soldiers had no will,
Long with excessive travails wearied,
Could by no means be farther drawn or led;
Yet that his fame might to posterity
Be had in everlasting memory,   2330
Doth for his camp a greater circuit take,
And for his soldiers larger cabins make.
His mangers he erected up so high
As never horse his provender could eye.
Huge bridles made, which here and there he left,   2335
Which might be found, and for great wonders kept.
Twelve altars then for monuments he rears,
Whereon his acts and travels long appears.
But doubting wearing time might these decay,
And so his memory would fade away,   2340
He, on the fair Hydaspes' pleasant side,
Two cities built, his name might there abide,
First Nicea, the next Bucephalon,

Where he entombed his stately stallion.
His fourth and last supply was hither sent,   2345
Then down Hydaspes with his fleet he went;
Some time he after spent upon that shore,
Whither ambassadors, ninety or more,
Came with submission from the Indian kings,
Bringing their presents rare and precious things.   2350
These all he feasts in state on beds of gold,
His furniture most sumptuous to behold;
His meat and drink, attendants, everything,
To th' utmost showed the glory of a king.
With rich rewards he sent them home again,   2355
Acknowledged their masters' sovereign;
Then sailing south and coming to that shore,
Those obscure nations yielded as before.
A city here he built, called by his name,
Which could not sound too oft with too much fame.   2360
Then sailing by the mouth of Indus flood,
His galleys struck upon the flats and mud;
Which the stout Macedonians amazed sore,
Deprived at once the use of sail and oar.
Observing well the nature of the tide,   2365
In those their fears they did not long abide.
Passing fair Indus' mouth, his course he steered
To th' coast which by Euphrates' mouth appeared,
Whose inlets near unto, he winter spent,
Unto his starved soldiers small content;   2370
By hunger and by cold so many slain,
That of them all the fourth did scarce remain.
Thus winter, soldiers, and provisions spent,
From hence he then unto Gedrosia went.
And thence he marched into Carmania,   2375
And so at length drew near to Persia;
Now through these goodly countries as he passed
Much time in feasts and rioting did waste;

Then visits Cyrus' sepulcher in's way,
Who now obscure at Passagardis lay;   2380
Upon his monument his robe he spread,
And set his crown on his supposed head.
From hence to Babylon, some time there spent,
He at the last to royal Shushan went;
A wedding feast to's nobles then he makes,   2385
And Statyra, Darius' daughter, takes,
Her sister gives to his Ephestion dear,
That by this match he might be yet more near;
He fourscore Persian ladies also gave
At this same time unto his captains brave.   2390
Six thousand guests unto this feast invites,
Whose senses all were glutted with delights.
It far exceeds my mean abilities
To shadow forth these short felicities;
Spectators here could scarce relate the story,   2395
They were so rapt with this external glory.
If an ideal paradise a man would frame,
He might this feast imagine by the same;
To every guest a cup of gold he sends,
So after many days the banquet ends.   2400
Now Alexander's conquests all are done,
And his long travails past and overgone;
His virtues dead, buried, and quite forgot,
But vice remains to his eternal blot.
'Mongst those that of his cruelty did taste,   2405
Philotas was not least, nor yet the last,
Accused because he did not certify
The king of treason and conspiracy;
Upon suspicion being apprehended,
Nothing was proved wherein he had offended   2410
But silence, which was of such consequence,
He was judged guilty of the same offence,
But for his father's great deserts the king

His royal pardon gave for this foul thing.
Yet is Philotas unto judgment brought, 2415
Must suffer, not for what is proved, but thought.
His master is accuser, judge, and king,
Who to the height doth aggravate each thing,
Inveighs against his father now absent,
And's brethren who for him their lives had spent. 2420
But Philotas his unpardonable crime
No merit could obliterate or time:
He did the oracle of Jove deride,
By which his majesty was deified.
Philotas thus o'ercharged with wrong and grief 2425
Sunk in despair without hope of relief,
Fain would have spoke and made his own defence,
The king would give no ear, but went from thence.
To his malicious foes delivers him,
To wreak their spite and hate on every limb. 2430
Philotas after him sends out this cry:
O, Alexander, thy free clemency
My foes exceeds in malice, and their hate
Thy kingly word can easily terminate.
Such torments great as wit could worst invent, 2435
Or flesh and life could bear till both were spent
Were now inflicted on Parmenio's son.
He might accuse himself, as they had done,
At last he did, so they were justified,
And told the world, that for his guilt he died. 2440
But how these captains should, or yet their master
Look on Parmenio, after this disaster
They knew not, wherefore best now to be done,
Was to dispatch the father as the son.
This sound advice at heart pleased Alexander, 2445
Who was so much engaged to this commander,
As he would ne'er confess, nor yet reward,
Nor could his captains bear so great regard;

Wherefore at once, all these to satisfy,
It was decreed Parmenio should die: 2450
Polidamus, who seemed Parmenio's friend,
To do this deed they into Media send;
He walking in his garden to and fro,
Fearing no harm, because he none did do,
Most wickedly was slain without least crime 2455
(The most renowned captain of his time).
This is Parmenio who so much had done
For Philip dead and his surviving son,
Who from a petty king of Macedon
By him was set upon the Persian throne, 2460
This that Parmenio who still overcame,
Yet gave his master the immortal fame,
Who for his prudence, valour, care, and trust
Had this reward, most cruel and unjust.
The next, who in untimely death had part, 2465
Was one of more esteem, but less desert;
Clitus beloved next to Ephestion,
And in his cups his chief companion;
When both were drunk, Clitus was wont to jeer,
Alexander to rage, to kill, and swear; 2470
Nothing more pleasing to mad Clitus' tongue,
Than's master's godhead to defy and wrong;
Nothing touched Alexander to the quick,
Like this, against his diety to kick.
Both at a feast when they had tippled well, 2475
Upon this dangerous theme fond Clitus fell;
From jest to earnest, and at last so bold,
That of Parmenio's death him plainly told.
Which Alexander's wrath incensed so high,
Nought but his life for this could satisfy; 2480
From one stood by he snatched a partisan,
And in a rage him through the body ran.
Next day he tore his face for what he'd done,

And would have slain himself for Clitus gone;
This pot companion he did more bemoan,   2485
Than all the wrongs to brave Parmenio done.
The next of worth that suffered after these
Was learned, virtuous, wise Calisthenes,
Who loved his master more than did the rest,
As did appear, in flattering him the least;   2490
In his esteem a god he could not be,
Nor would adore him for a deity;
For this alone and for no other cause
Against his sovereign or against his laws,
He on the rack his limbs in pieces rent;   2495
Thus was he tortured till his life was spent.
Of this unkingly act doth Seneca
This censure pass, and not unwisely say,
Of Alexander this th' eternal crime,
Which shall not be obliterate by time.   2500
Which virtue's fame can ne'er redeem by far,
Nor all felicity of his in war.
When e'er 'tis said he thousand thousands slew,
Yea, and Calisthenes to death he drew.
The mighty Persian king he overcame,   2505
Yea, and he killed Calisthenes of fame.
All countries, kingdoms, provinces, he won
From Hellespont to th' farthest ocean.
All this he did, who knows not to be true?
But yet withal, Calisthenes he slew.   2510
From Macedon, his empire did extend
Unto the utmost bounds o' th' orient;
All this he did, yea, and much more, 'tis true,
But yet withal, Calisthenes he slew.
Now Alexander goes to Media,   2515
Finds there the want of wise Parmenio;
Here his chief favorite Ephestion dies,
He celebrates his mournful obsequies,

Hangs his physician, the reason why
He suffered his friend Ephestion die.   2520
This act (methinks) his godhead should ashame,
To punish where himself deserved blame;
Or of necessity he must imply
The other was the greatest deity.
The mules and horses are for sorrow shorn   2525
The battlements from off the walls are torn
Of stately Ecbatane who now must show,
A rueful face in this so general woe;
Twelve thousand talents also did intend,
Upon a sumptuous monument to spend.   2530
What e'er he did, or thought not so content,
His messenger to Jupiter he sent,
That by his leave his friend Ephestion
Among the demigods they might enthrone.
From Media to Babylon he went,   2535
To meet him there t' Antipater he'd sent,
That he might act also upon the stage,
And in a tragedy there end his age.
The Queen Olympias bears him deadly hate,
Not suffering her to meddle with the state,   2540
And by her letters did her son incite,
This great indignity he should requite;
His doing so, no whit displeased the king,
Though to his mother he disproved the thing.
But now Antipater had lived so long,   2545
He might well die though he had done no wrong;
His service great is suddenly forgot,
Or if remembered, yet regarded not.
The king doth intimate 'twas his intent,
His honours and his riches to augment,   2550
Of larger provinces the rule to give,
And for his counsel near the king to live.
So to be caught, Antipater's too wise,

Parmenio's death's too fresh before his eyes;
He was too subtle for his crafty foe.   2555
Nor by his baits could be ensnared so,
But his excuse with humble thanks he sends;
His age and journey long he then pretends,
And pardon craves for his unwilling stay;
He shows his grief, he's forced to disobey.   2560
Before his answer came to Babylon,
The thread of Alexander's life was spun;
Poison had put an end to's days ('twas thought)
By Philip and Cassander to him brought,
Sons to Antipater, and bearers of his cup,   2565
Lest of such like their father chance to sup;
By others thought, and that more generally,
That through excessive drinking he did die.
The thirty-third of's age do all agree,
This conqueror did yield to destiny.   2570
When this sad news came to Darius' mother,
She laid it more to heart than any other,
Nor meat, nor drink, nor comfort would she take,
But pined in grief till life did her forsake;
All friends she shuns, yea, banished the light,   2575
Till death enwrapt her in perpetual night.
This monarch's fame must last whilst world doth stand,
And conquests be talked of whilest there is land;
His princely qualities had he retained,
Unparalleled for ever had remained.   2580
But with the world his virtues overcame,
And so with black beclouded all his fame;
Wise Aristotle, tutor to his youth,
Had so instructed him in moral truth;
The principles of what he then had learned   2585
Might to the last (when sober) be discerned.
Learning and learned men he much regarded,
And curious artist evermore rewarded;

The *Iliads* of Homer he still kept,
And under's pillow laid them when he slept.   2590
Achilles' happiness he did envy,
'Cause Homer kept his acts to memory.
Profusely bountiful without desert,
For such as pleased him had both wealth and heart,
Cruel by nature and by custom, too,   2595
As oft his acts throughout his reign doth show,
Ambitious so that nought could satisfy,
Vain, thirsting after immortality,
Still fearing that his name might hap to die
And fame not last unto eternity.   2600
This conqueror did oft lament ('tis said)
There were no more worlds to be conquered.
This folly great Augustus did deride,
For had he had but wisdom to his pride,
He would have found enough there to be done,   2605
To govern that he had already won.
His thoughts are perished, he aspires no more,
Nor can he kill or save as heretofore.
A god alive, him all must idolize,
Now like a mortal helpless man he lies.   2610
Of all those kingdoms large which he had got,
To his posterity remained no jot;
For by that hand which still revengeth blood
None of his kindred nor his race long stood;
But as he took delight much blood to spill,   2615
So the same cup to his, did others fill.
Four of his captains now do all divide,
As Daniel before had prophesied.
The leopard down, the four wings 'gan to rise;
The great horn broke, the less did tyrannize.   2620
What troubles and contentions did ensue
We may hereafter show in season due.

Aridaeus

Great Alexander dead, his army's left,
Like to that giant of his eye bereft;   2625
When of his monstrous bulk it was the guide,
His matchless force no creature could abide.
But by Ulysses having lost his sight,
All men began straight to contemn his might;
For aiming still amiss, his dreadful blows   2630
Did harm himself, but never reached his foes.
Now court and camp all in confusion be,
A king they'll have, but who, none can agree;
Each captain wished this prize to bear away,
But none so hardy found as so durst say.   2635
Great Alexander did leave issue none,
Except by Artabasus' daughter one;
And Roxane fair, whom late he married,
Was near her time to be delivered.
By nature's right these had enough to claim,   2640
But meanness of their mothers barred the same,
Alleged by those who by their subtle plea
Had hope themselves to bear the crown away.
A sister Alexander had, but she
Claimed not; perhaps, her sex might hindrance be.   2645
After much tumult they at last proclaimed
His baseborn brother, Aridaeus named,
That so under his feeble wit and reign,
Their ends they might the better still attain.
This choice Perdiccas vehemently disclaimed,   2650
And babe unborn of Roxane he proclaimed;
Some wished him to take the style of king,
Because his master gave to him his ring,
And had to him still since Ephestion died
More than to th' rest his favour testified.   2655
But he refused, with feigned modesty,

Hoping to be elect more generally.
He hold on this occasion should have laid,
For second offer there was never made.
'Mongst these contentions, tumults, jealousies,   2660
Seven days the corpse of their great master lies
Untouched, uncovered, slighted, and neglected,
So much these princes their own ends respected;
A contemplation to astonish kings,
That he who late possessed all earthly things,   2665
And yet not so content unless that he
Might be esteemed for deity,
Now lay a spectacle to testify
The wretchedness of man's mortality.
After some time, when stirs began to calm,   2670
His body did the Egyptians embalm;
His countenance so lively did appear,
That for a while they durst not come so near.
No sign of poison in his entrails found,
But all his bowels, coloured well, and sound.   2675
Perdiccas, seeing Aridaeus must be king,
Under his name began to rule each thing.
His chief opponent who controlled his sway,
Was Meleager whom he would take away,
And by a wile he got him in his power,   2680
So took his life unworthily that hour,
Using the name and the command of th' king
To authorize his acts in every thing.
The princes, seeing Perdiccas' power and pride,
For their security did now provide.   2685
Antigonus for his share Asia takes,
And Ptolemy next sure of Egypt makes,
Seleucus afterward held Babylon,
Antipater had long ruled Macedon.
These now to govern for the king pretends,   2690
But nothing less each one himself intends.

Perdiccas took no province like the rest,
But held command of th' army (which was best)
And had a higher project in his head,
His master's sister secretly to wed.   2695
So to the lady covertly he sent
(That none might know, to frustrate his intent),
But Cleopatra this suitor did deny,
For Leonatus more lovely in her eye,
To whom she sent a message of her mind,   2700
That if he came good welcome he should find.
In these tumultuous days the thralled Greeks,
Their ancient liberty afresh now seeks.
And gladly would the yoke shake off, laid on
Sometimes by Philip and his conquering son.   2705
The Athenians force Antipater to fly
To Lamia where he shut up doth lie.
To brave Craterus then he sends with speed
For succours to relieve him in his need.
The like of Leonatus he requires   2710
(Which at this time well suited his desires)
For to Antipater he now might go,
His lady take in th' way, and no man know.
Antiphilus, the Athenian general,
With speed his army doth together call;   2715
And Leonatus seeks to stop, that so
He join not with Antipater their foe.
The Athenian army was the greater far
(Which did his match with Cleopatra mar)
For fighting still, while there did hope remain,   2720
This valiant chief amidst his foes was slain.
'Mongst all the princes of great Alexander
For personage, none like to this commander.
Now to Antipater Craterus goes,
Blocked up in Lamia still by his foes;   2725
Long marches through Cilicia he makes,

And the remains of Leonatus takes.
With them and his he into Grecia went,
Antipater released from prisonment.
After which time the Greeks did never more   2730
Act any thing of worth, as heretofore,
But under servitude their necks remained,
Nor former liberty or glory gained.
Now died about the end of th' Lamian War
Demosthenes, that sweet-tongued orator,   2735
Who feared Antipater would take his life
For animating the Athenian strife;
To end his days by poison, rather chose
Than fall into the hands of mortal foes.
Craterus and Antipater now join,   2740
In love and in affinity combine;
Craterus doth his daughter Phila wed
Their friendship might the more be strengthened.
Whilst they in Macedon do thus agree,
In Asia they all asunder be.   2745
Perdiccas, grieved to see the princes bold
So many kingdoms in their power to hold,
Yet to regain them how he did not know
His soldiers 'gainst those captains would not go,
To suffer them go on as they begun   2750
Was to give way himself might be undone.
With Antipater to join he sometimes thought,
That by his help, the rest might low be brought,
But this again dislikes; he would remain,
If not in style, in deed a sovereign;   2755
(For all the princes of great Alexander
Acknowledge for chief that old commander).
Desires the king to go to Macedon,
Which once was of his ancestors the throne,
And by his presence there to nullify   2760
The acts of his viceroy now grown so high.

Antigonus of treason first attaints,
And summons him to answer his complaints.
This he avoids, and ships himself and son,
Goes to Antipater and tells what's done.   2765
He and Craterus, both with him do join,
And 'gainst Perdiccas all their strength combine.
Brave Ptolemy, to make a fourth then sent
To save himself from danger imminent.
In midst of these garboils, with wondrous state   2770
His master's funeral doth celebrate;
In Alexandria his tomb he placed,
Which eating time hath scarcely yet defaced.
Two years and more, since nature's debt he paid,
And yet till now at quiet was not laid.   2775
Great love did Ptolemy by this act gain,
And made the soldiers on his side remain.
Perdiccas hears his foes are all combined,
'Gainst which to go, is not resolved in mind.
But first 'gainst Ptolemy he judged was best,   2780
Near'st unto him, and farthest from the rest.
Leaves Eumenes the Asian coast to free
From the invasions of the other three,
And with his army unto Egypt goes
Brave Ptolemy to th' utmost to oppose.   2785
Perdiccas' surly carriage and his pride
Did alienate the soldiers from his side.
But Ptolemy by affability
His sweet demeanour and his courtesy,
Did make his own, firm to his cause remain,   2790
And from the other side did daily gain.
Perdiccas in his pride did ill entreat
Python of haughty mind and courage great,
Who could not brook so great indignity,
But of his wrongs his friends doth certify;   2795
The soldiers 'gainst Perdiccas they incense,

Who vow to make this captain recompense,
And in a rage they rush into his tent,
Knock out his brains, to Ptolemy then went,
And offer him his honours and his place, 2800
With style of the Protector, him to grace.
Next day into the camp came Ptolemy,
And is received of all most joyfully.
Their proffers he refused with modesty,
Yields them to Python for his courtesy. 2805
With what he held he was now more content,
Than by more trouble to grow eminent.
Now comes there news of a great victory
That Eumenes got of the other three.
Had it but in Perdiccas' life arrived, 2810
With greater joy it would have been received.
Thus Ptolemy rich Egypt did retain,
And Python turned to Asia again.
Whilst Perdiccas encamped in Africa,
Antigonus did enter Asia, 2815
And fain would Eumenes draw to their side,
But he alone most faithful did abide.
The other all had kingdoms in their eye,
But he was true to's master's family,
Nor could Craterus, whom he much did love, 2820
From his fidelity once make him move.
Two battles fought and had of both the best,
And brave Craterus slew among the rest.
For this sad strife he pours out his complaints,
And his beloved foe full sore laments. 2825
I should but snip a story into bits
And his great acts and glory much eclipse,
To show the dangers Eumenes befell,
His stratagems wherein he did excel,
His policies, how he did extricate 2830
Himself from out of lab'rinths intricate.

He that at large would satisfy his mind,
In Plutarch's *Lives* his history may find.
For all that should be said, let this suffice,
He was both valiant, faithful, patient, wise.   2835
Python now chose protector of the state,
His rule Queen Euridice begins to hate,
Sees Aridaeus must not king it long,
If once young Alexander grow more strong,
But that her husband serve for supplement   2840
To warm his seat was never her intent.
She knew her birthright gave her Macedon,
Grandchild to him who once sat on that throne
Who was Perdiccas, Philip's eldest brother,
She daughter to his son, who had no other.   2845
Python's commands, as oft she countermands;
What he appoints, she purposely withstands.
He, wearied out at last, would needs be gone,
Resigned his place, and so let all alone.
In's room the soldiers chose Antipater,   2850
Who vext the queen more than the other far.
From Macedon to Asia he came,
That he might settle matters in the same.
He placed, displaced, controlled, ruled as he list,
And this no man durst question or resist;   2855
For all the nobles of King Alexander
Their bonnets veiled to him as chief commander.
When to his pleasure all things they had done,
The king and queen he takes to Macedon,
Two sons of Alexander, and the rest,   2860
All to be ordered there as he thought best.
The army to Antigonus doth leave,
And government of Asia to him gave.
And thus Antipater the groundwork lays,
On which Antigonus his height doth raise,   2865
Who in few years, the rest so overtops,

For universal monarchy he hopes.
With Eumenes he divers battles fought,
And by his slights to circumvent him sought;
But vain it was to use his policy,   2870
'Gainst him that all deceits could scan and try.
In this epitome too long to tell
How finely Eumenes did here excel,
And by the selfsame traps the other laid,
He to his cost was righteously repaid.   2875
But while these chieftains do in Asia fight,
To Greece and Macedon let's turn our sight.
When great Antipater the world must leave,
His place to Polisperchon did bequeath,
Fearing his son Cassander was unstaid,   2880
Too rash to bear that charge, if on him laid.
Antigonus, hearing of his decease,
On most part of Assyria doth seize.
And Ptolemy next to encroach begins,
All Syria and Phoenicia he wins;   2885
Then Polisperchon 'gins to act in's place,
Recalls Olympias the court to grace.
Antipater had banished her from thence
Into Epire for her great turbulence;
This new protector's of another mind,   2890
Thinks by her majesty much help to find.
Cassander like his father could not see
This Polisperchon's great ability,
Slights his commands, his actions he disclaims,
And to be chief himself now bends his aims;   2895
Such as his father had advanced to place,
Or by his favours any way had graced,
Are now at the devotion of the son,
Pressed to accomplish what he would have done;
Besides he was the young queen's favorite,   2900
On whom (t'was thought) she set her chief delight.

Unto these helps at home he seeks out more,
Goes to Antigonus and doth implore,
By all the bonds 'twixt him and's father past,
And for that great gift which he gave him last,   2905
By these and all to grant him some supply,
To take down Polisperchon, grown so high;
For this Antigonus did need no spurs,
Hoping to gain yet more by these new stirs,
Straight furnished him with a sufficient aid,   2910
And so he quick returns thus well appaid;
With ships at sea, an army for the land,
His proud opponent hopes soon to withstand.
But in his absence Polisperchon takes
Such friends away as for his interest makes   2915
By death, by prison, or by banishment,
That no supply by these here might be lent.
Cassander with his host to Grecia goes,
Whom Polisperchon labours to oppose;
But beaten was at sea, and foiled at land,   2920
Cassander's forces had the upper hand.
Athens, with many towns in Greece beside,
Firm (for his father's sake) to him abide.
Whilst hot in wars these two in Greece remain,
Antigonus doth all in Asia gain;   2925
Still labours Eumenes, would with him side,
But all in vain, he faithful did abide;
Nor mother could, nor sons of Alexander,
Put trust in any but in this commander.
The great ones now began to show their mind,   2930
And act as opportunity they find.
Aridaeus the scorned and simple king,
More than he bidden was could act no thing.
Polisperchon for office hoping long,
Thinks to enthrone the prince when riper grown;   2935
Euridice this injury disdains,

And to Cassander of this wrong complains.
Hateful the name and house of Alexander
Was to this proud vindicative Cassander;
He still kept locked within his memory   2940
His father's danger, with his family;
Nor thought he that indignity was small,
When Alexander knocked his head to th' wall.
These, with his love unto the amorous queen,
Did make him vow her servant to be seen.   2945
Olympias, Aridaeus deadly hates,
As all her husband's children by his mates,
She gave him poison formerly ('tis thought)
Which damage both to mind and body brought;
She now with Polisperchon doth combine,   2950
To make the king by force his seat resign,
And her young grandchild in his state enthrone,
That under him she might rule all alone.
For aid she goes t' Epire among her friends,
The better to accomplish these her ends;   2955
Euridice, hearing what she intends,
In haste unto her friend Cassander sends,
To leave his siege at Tegea and with speed
To save the king and her in this their need.
Then by entreaties, promises, and coin   2960
Some forces did procure with her to join.
Olympias soon enters Macedon,
The queen to meet her bravely marches on,
But when her soldiers saw their ancient queen,
Calling to mind what sometime she had been,   2965
The wife and mother of their famous kings,
Nor darts, nor arrows, now none shoots or flings.
The king and queen, seeing their destiny,
To save their lives t' Amphipolis do fly;
But the old queen pursues them with her hate,   2970
And needs will have their lives as well as state.

The king by extreme torments had his end,
And to the queen these presents she did send:
A halter, cup of poison, and a sword;
Bids choose her death, such kindness she'll afford.   2975
The queen with many a curse, and bitter check,
At length yields to the halter her fair neck;
Praying that fatal day might quickly haste,
On which Olympias of the like might taste.
This done, the cruel queen rests not content,   2980
'Gainst all that loved Cassander she was bent;
His brethren, kinsfolk, and his chiefest friends
That fell within her reach came to their ends.
Digged up his brother dead, 'gainst nature's right,
And threw his bones about to show her spite.   2985
The courtiers wond'ring at her furious mind,
Wished in Epire she had been still confined.
In Peloponesus then Cassander lay,
Where hearing of this news he speeds away,
With rage and with revenge he's hurried on   2990
To find this cruel queen in Macedon;
But being stopped at strait Thermopylae,
Sea passage gets, and lands in Thessaly.
His army he divides, sends post away,
Polisperchon to hold a while in play;   2995
And with the rest Olympias pursues,
For all her cruelty, to give her dues.
She with the chief o' th' court to Pydna flies,
Well fortified, and on the sea it lies.
There by Cassander she's blocked up so long,   3000
Until the famine grows exceeding strong.
Her cousin of Epire did what he might
To raise the siege and put her foes to flight.
Cassander is resolved there to remain,
So succours and endeavours proves but vain;   3005
Fain would this wretched queen capitulate,

Her foe would give no ear, such is his hate.
The soldiers, pinched with this scarcity,
By stealth unto Cassander daily fly;
Olympias means to hold out to the last,　　　　　　3010
Expecting nothing but of death to taste,
But his occasions calling him away,
Gives promise for her life, so wins the day.
No sooner had he got her in his hand,
But made in judgment her accusers stand,　　　　　3015
And plead the blood of friends and kindreds spilt,
Desiring justice might be done for guilt;
And so was he acquitted of his word,
For justice sake she being put to th' sword.
This was the end of this most cruel queen,　　　　　3020
Whose fury scarcely paralleled hath been.
The daughter, sister, mother, wife to kings,
But royalty no good conditions brings;
To husband's death ('tis thought) she gave consent,
The murtherer she did so much lament:　　　　　　3025
With garlands crowned his head, bemoaned his fates,
His sword unto Apollo consecrates.
Her outrages too tedious to relate,
How for no cause but her inveterate hate
Her husband's wives and children after's death,　　　3030
Some slew, some fried, of others stopped the breath.
Now in her age she's forced to taste that cup,
Which she had others often made to sup.
Now many towns in Macedon suppressed,
And Pellas fain to yield among the rest,　　　　　3035
The funerals Cassander celebrates,
Of Aridaeus and his queen with state;
Among their ancestors by him they're laid,
And shows of lamentation for them made.
Old Thebes he then rebuilt so much of fame,　　　　3040
And Cassandria raised after his name.

But leave him building, others in their urn,
Let's for a while, now into Asia turn.
True Eumenes endeavours by all skill
To keep Antigonus from Shushan still;   3045
Having command o' th' treasure, he can hire
Such as no threats nor favour could acquire.
In divers battles he had good success,
Antigonus came off still honourless;
When victor oft he'd been, and so might still,   3050
Peucestes did betray him by a wile
T' Antigonus, who took his life unjust,
Because he never would forgo his trust;
Thus lost he all for his fidelity,
Striving t' uphold his master's family.   3055
But to a period as that did haste,
So Eumenes (the prop) of death must taste;
All Persia now Antigonus doth gain,
And master of the treasure sole remain.
Then with Seleucus straight at odds doth fall,   3060
And he for aid to Ptolemy doth call.
The princes all begin now to envy
Antigonus his growing up so high,
Fearing his force, and what might hap ere long,
Enter into a combination strong.   3065
Seleucus, Ptolemy, Cassander joins,
Lysimachus to make a fourth combines.
Antigonus, desirous of the Greeks,
To make Cassander odious to them seeks,
Sends forth his declarations near and far,   3070
And clears what cause he had to make this war,
Cassander's outrages at large doth tell,
Shows his ambitious practices as well.
The mother of their king to death he'd put,
His wife and son in prison close had shut;   3075
And aiming now to make himself a king,

And that some title he might seem to bring,
Thessalonica he had newly wed,
Daughter to Philip their renowned head;
Had built and called a city by his name,   3080
Which none e'er did, but those of royal fame;
And in despite of their two famous kings
Hateful Olynthians to Greece rebrings.
Rebellious Thebes he had re-edified,
Which their late king in dust had damnified,   3085
Requires them therefore to take up their arms
And to requite this traitor for these harms.
Then Ptolemy would gain the Greeks likewise,
And he declares the other's injuries:
First how he held the empire in his hands,   3090
Seleucus driven from government and lands,
The valiant Eumenes unjustly slain,
And lord of royal Shushan did remain;
Therefore request their help to take him down
Before he wear the universal crown.   3095
These princes at the sea soon had a fight,
Where great Antigonus was put to flight;
His son at Gaza likewise lost the field,
So Syria to Ptolemy did yield.
And Seleucus recovers Babylon,   3100
Still gaining countries, eastward he goes on.
Demetrius with Ptolemy did fight,
And coming unawares, put him to flight;
But bravely sends the prisoners back again,
With all the spoil and booty he had ta'n.   3105
Courteous as noble Ptolemy, or more,
Who at Gaza did the like to him before.
Antigonus did much rejoice, his son
With victory, his lost repute had won.
At last these princes, tired out with wars,   3110
Sought for a peace, and laid aside their jars.

The terms of their agreement thus express
That each should hold what now he did possess,
Till Alexander unto age was grown,
Who then should be installed in the throne.   3115
This touched Cassander sore, for what he'd done,
Imprisoning both the mother and the son.
He sees the Greeks now favour their young prince,
Whom he in durance held, now, and long since,
That in few years he must be forced or glad,   3120
To render up such kingdoms as he had;
Resolves to quit his fears by one deed done,
So puts to death the mother and her son.
This Roxane for her beauty all commend,
But for one act she did, just was her end.   3125
No sooner was great Alexander dead
But she Darius' daughters murthered,
Both thrown into a well to hide her blot;
Perdiccas was her partner in this plot.
The heavens seemed slow in paying her the same,   3130
But at the last the hand of vengeance came.
And for that double fact which she had done,
The life of her must go and of her son.
Perdiccas had before for his amiss,
But by their hands who thought not once of this.   3135
Cassander's deed the princes do detest,
But 'twas in show; in heart it pleased them best.
That he is odious to the world, they're glad;
And now they were free lords of what they had.
When this foul tragedy was past and done,   3140
Polisperchon brings the other son
Called Hercules, and elder than his brother,
(But Olympias would prefer the other).
The Greeks, touched with the murther done of late,
This orphan prince 'gan to compassionate,   3145
Begin to mutter much 'gainst proud Cassander,

And place their hopes on th' heir of Alexander.
Cassander feared what might of this ensue,
So Polisperchon to his counsel drew,
And gives Peleponnesus for his hire,   3150
Who slew the prince according to desire.
Thus was the race and house of Alexander
Extinct by this inhuman wretch Cassander.
Antigonus, for all this doth not mourn,
He knows to's profit this at last will turn,   3155
But that some title now he might pretend,
To Cleopatra doth for marriage send;
Lysimachus and Ptolemy the same,
And lewd Cassander too, sticks not for shame:
She then in Lydia at Sardis lay,   3160
Where by embassage all these princes pray.
Choice above all, of Ptolemy she makes,
With his ambassador her journey takes;
Antigonus' lieutenant stays her still,
Until he further know his master's will.   3165
Antigonus now had a wolf by th' ears,
To hold her still, or let her go he fears.
Resolves at last the princess should be slain,
So hinders him of her, he could not gain;
Her women are appointed for this deed,   3170
They for their great reward no better speed,
For by command, they straight were put to death,
As vile conspirators that stopped her breath,
And now he hopes, he's ordered all so well,
The world must needs believe what he doth tell;   3175
Thus Philip's house was quite extinguished,
Except Cassander's wife who yet not dead.
And by their means who thought of nothing less,
Than vengeance just, against them to express;
Now blood was paid with blood for what was done   3180
By cruel father, mother, cruel son.

Thus may we hear, and fear, and ever say,
That hand is righteous still which doth repay.
These captains now the style of kings do take,
For to their crowns there's none can title make;   3185
Demetrius first the royal style assumed,
By his example all the rest presumed.
Antigonus himself to ingratiate,
Doth promise liberty to Athens' state;
With arms and with provision stores them well,   3190
The better 'gainst Cassander to rebel.
Demetrius thither goes, is entertained
Not like a king, but like some god they feigned;
Most grossly base was their great adulation,
Who incense burnt and offered oblation.   3195
These kings afresh fall to their wars again,
Demetrius of Ptolemy doth gain.
'Twould be an endless story to relate
Their several battles and their several fate,
Their fights by sea, their victories by land,   3200
How some when down, straight got the upper hand.
Antigonus and Seleucus then fight
Near Ephesus, each bringing all his might,
And he that conqueror shall now remain,
The lordship of all Asia shall retain;   3205
This day 'twixt these two kings ends all the strife,
For here Antigonus lost rule and life;
Nor to his son, did e'er one foot remain
Of those vast kingdoms he did sometimes gain.
Demetrius with his troops to Athens flies,   3210
Hopes to find succours in his miseries;
But they, adoring in prosperity,
Now shut their gates in his adversity.
He sorely grieved at this his desperate state
Tries foes, sith friends will not compassionate.   3215
His peace he then with old Seleucus makes,

Who his fair daughter Stratonica takes;
Antiochus, Seleucus' dear loved son,
Is for this fresh young lady quite undone,
Falls so extremely sick, all feared his life,   3220
Yet durst not say he loved his father's wife;
When his disease the skilled physician found,
His father's mind he wittily did sound,
Who did no sooner understand the same,
But willingly resigned the beautious dame.   3225
Cassander now must die, his race is run,
And leaves the ill-got kingdoms he had won.
Two sons he left, born of King Philip's daughter,
Who had an end put to their days by slaughter;
Which should succeed at variance they fell,   3230
The mother would the youngest might excel.
The eld'st enraged did play the vipers part,
And with his sword did run her through the heart.
Rather than Philip's race should longer live,
He whom she gave his life, her death shall give.   3235
This by Lysimachus was after slain,
Whose daughter he not long before had ta'en;
Demetrius is called in by th' youngest son,
Against Lysimachus who from him won.
But he a kingdom more than's friend did eye,   3240
Seized upon that and slew him trait'rously.
Thus Philip's and Cassander's race both gone,
And so falls out to be extinct in one;
And though Cassander died in his bed,
His seed to be extirpt was destined;   3245
For blood, which was decreed that he should spill,
Yet must his children pay for father's ill;
Jehu in killing Ahab's house did well,
Yet be avenged must blood of Jezreel.
Demetrius thus Cassander's kingdoms gains,   3250
And now in Macedon as king he reigns;

Though men and money both he hath at will,
In neither finds content if he sits still;
That Seleucus holds Asia grieves him sore,
Those countries large his father got before.   3255
These to recover, musters all his might,
And with his son-in-law will needs go fight;
A might navy rigged, an army stout,
With these he hopes to turn the world about,
Leaving Antigonus, his eldest son,   3260
In his long absence to rule Macedon.
Demetrius with so many troubles met,
As heaven and earth against him had been set;
Disaster on disaster him pursue,
His story seems a fable more than true.   3265
At last he's taken and imprisoned
Within an isle that was with pleasures fed,
Enjoyed what e'er beseemed his royalty,
Only restrained of his liberty;
After three years he died, left what he'd won,   3270
In Greece unto Antigonus his son.
For his posterity unto this day,
Did ne'er regain one foot in Asia;
His body Seleucus sends to his son,
Whose obsequies with wondrous pomp was done.   3275
Next died the brave and noble Ptolemy,
Renowned for bounty, valour, clemency,
Rich Egypt left, and what else he had won,
To Philadelphus his more worthy son.
Of the old heroes, now but two remain,   3280
Seleucus and Lysimachus these twain
Must needs go try their fortune and their might,
And so Lysimachus was slain in fight;
'Twas no small joy unto Seleucus' breast,
That now he had outlived all the rest;   3285
Possession of Europe thinks to take,

And so himself the only monarch make;
Whilst with these hopes in Greece he did remain,
He was by Ptolemy Ceraunus slain,
The second son of the first Ptolemy,   3290
Who for rebellion unto him did fly;
Seleucus was a father and a friend,
Yet by him had this most unworthy end.
Thus with these kingly captains have we done,
A little now how the succession run,   3295
Antigonus, Seleucus and Cassander,
With Ptolemy, reigned after Alexander;
Cassander's sons soon after's death were slain,
So three successors only did remain;
Antigonus his kingdoms lost and life,   3300
Unto Seleucus, author of that strife.
His son Demetrius, all Cassander's gains,
And his posterity, the same retains;
Demetrius' son was call'd Antigonus,
And his again was named Demetrius.   3305
I must let pass those many battles fought,
Betwixt those kings and noble Pyrrhus stout,
And his son Alexander of Epire,
Whereby immortal honour they acquire;
Demetrius had Philip to his son   3310
(Part of whose kingdoms Titus Quintius won);
Philip had Perseus, who was made a thrall
T' Emilius the Roman general;
Him with his sons in triumph lead did he,
Such riches too as Rome did never see;   3315
This of Antigonus, his seed's the fate,
Whose empire was subdued to th' Roman state.
Longer Seleucus held the royalty,
In Syria by his posterity;
Antiochus Soter his son was named,   3320
To whom the old Berosus (so much famed)

His book of Assur's monarchs dedicates,
Tells of their names, their wars, their riches, fates;
But this is perished with many more,
Which oft we wish was extant as before.   3325
Antiochus Theos was Soter's son,
Who a long war with Egypt's king begun;
The affinities and wars Daniel sets forth,
And calls them there the kings of south and north,
This Theos murthered was by his lewd wife;   3330
Seleucus reigned, when he had lost his life.
A third Seleucus next sits on the seat,
And then Antiochus, surnamed The Great,
Whose large dominions after was made small,
By Scipio the Roman general;   3335
Fourth Seleucus Antiochus succeeds,
And next Epiphanes whose wicked deeds,
Horrid massacres, murthers, cruelties,
Amongst the Jews we read in Maccabees.
Antiochus Eupater was the next,   3340
By rebels and impostors daily vext;
So many princes still were murthered,
The royal blood was nigh extinguished;
Then Tygranes the great Armenian king,
To take the government was called in;   3345
Lucullus, him, (the Roman general)
Vanquished in fight and took those kingdoms all;
Of Greece and Syria thus the rule did end,
In Egypt next, a little time we'll spend.
First Ptolemy being dead, his famous son,   3350
Called Philadelphus, did possess the throne.
At Alexandria a library did build,
And with seven hundred thousand volumes filled;
The seventy-two interpreters did seek,
They might translate the Bible into Greek.   3355
His son was Evergetes the last prince,

That valour showed, virtue, or excellence;
Philopater was Evergetes' son,
After Epiphanes sat on the throne;
Philometor, Evergetes again, 3360
And after him did false Lathurus reign.
Then Alexander in Lathurus' stead,
Next Auletes, who cut off Pompey's head.
To all these names, we Ptolemy must add,
For since the first, they still that title had. 3365
Fair Cleopatra next, last of that race,
Whom Julius Caesar set in royal place;
She with her paramour, Mark Anthony,
Held for a time the Egyptian monarchy,
Till great Augustus had with him a fight 3370
At Actium, where his navy's put to flight;
He seeing his honour lost, his kingdom end,
Did by his sword his life soon after send.
His brave virago asps sets to her arms,
To take her life and quit her from all harms; 3375
For 'twas not death nor danger she did dread,
But some disgrace in triumph to be led.
Here ends at last the Grecian monarchy,
Which by the Romans had its destiny:
Thus king and kingdoms have their times and dates, 3380
Their standings, overturnings, bounds, and fates;
Now up, now down, now chief, and then brought under,
The heavens thus rule, to fill the world with wonder.
The Assyrian monarchy long time did stand,
But yet the Persian got the upper hand; 3385
The Grecian them did utterly subdue,
And millions were subjected unto few.
The Grecian longer than the Persian stood;
Then came the Roman like a raging flood,
And with the torrent of his rapid course, 3390
Their crowns, their titles, riches bears by force.

The first was likened to a head of gold,
Next arms and breast of silver to behold,
The third, belly and thighs of brass in sight,
And last was iron, which breaketh all with might;   3395
The stone out of the mountain then did rise,
And smote those feet, those legs, those arms, and thighs;
Then gold, silver, brass, iron, and all the store
Became like chaff upon the threshing floor.
The first a lion, second was a bear,   3400
The third a leopard, which four wings did rear;
The last more strong and dreadful than the rest,
Whose iron teeth devoured every beast,
And when he had no appetite to eat,
The residue he stamped under feet;   3405
Yet shall this lion, bear, this leopard, ram,
All trembling stand before the powerful Lamb.
With these three monarchies now have I done,
But how the fourth their kingdoms from them won,
And how from small beginnings it did grow,   3410
To fill the world with terror and with woe,
My tired brain leaves to some better pen;
This task befits not women like to men.
For what is past, I blush, excuse to make,
But humbly stand, some grave reproof to take;   3415
Pardon to crave for errors, is but vain,
The subject was too high, beyond my strain.
To frame apology for some offense,
Converts our boldness into impudence.
This my presumption some now to requite,   3420
Ne sutor ultra crepidam may write.

THE END OF THE GRECIAN MONARCHY

After some days of rest, my restless heart
To finish what's begun, new thoughts impart;
And maugre all resolves, my fancy wrought   3425
This fourth to th' other three, now might be brought.
Shortness of time and inability
Will force me to a confused brevity.
Yet in this chaos one shall easily spy
The vast limbs of a mighty monarchy.   3430
What e'er is found amiss take in good part,
As faults proceeding from my head, not heart.

Stout Romulus, Rome's founder and first king,
Whom vestal Rhea to the world did bring,
His father was not Mars as some devised,
But Aemulus in armour all disguised;   3440
Thus he deceived his niece, she might not know
The double injury he then did do.
Where sheperds once had cotes, and sheep their folds,
Where swains and rustic peasants kept their holds,
A city fair did Romulus erect,   3445
The mistress of the world in each respect;
His brother Remus there by him was slain,
For leaping o'er the wall with some disdain.
The stones at first was cemented with blood,
And bloody hath it proved, since first it stood.   3450
This city built and sacrifices done,
A form of government, he next begun;
A hundred senators he likewise chose,
And with the style of *Patres,* honoured those;
His city to replenish, men he wants;   3455
Great privileges then to all he grants,
That will within those strong built walls reside,
And this new gentle government abide.
Of wives there was so great a scarcity,
They to their neighbors sue for a supply;   3460
But all disdain alliance then to make,
So Romulus was forced this course to take:
Great shows he makes at tilt and tournament,
To see these sports, the Sabines all are bent.
Their daughters by the Romans then were caught;   3465

Then to recover them a field was fought,
But in the end, to final peace they come,
And Sabines as one people dwelt in Rome.
The Romans now more potent 'gin to grow,
And Fidenates they wholly overthrow. 3470
But Romulus then comes unto his end.
Some feigning to the gods he did ascend;
Others, the seven and thirtieth of his reign,
Affirm, that by the senate he was slain.

Numa Pompilius 3475

Numa Pompilius next chose they king,
Held for his piety some sacred thing;
To Janus he that famous temple built:
Kept shut in peace, set ope when blood was spilt;
Religious rites and customs instituted, 3480
And priests and *flamines* likewise he deputed,
Their augurs strange, their gestures and attire,
And vestal maids to keep the holy fire.
The nymph Aegeria this to him told,
So to delude the people he was bold; 2485
Forty-three years he ruled with general praise,
Accounted for a god in after days.

Tullius Hostilius

Tullis Hostilius was third Roman king,
Who martial discipline in use did bring; 3490
War with the ancient Albans he did wage,
This strife to end six brothers did engage.
Three called Horatii on the Romans' side,
And Curiatii three, Albans provide:
The Romans conquer, th' other yield the day, 3495
Yet in their compact after false they play.

The Romans sore incensed, their general slay,
And from old Alba fetch the wealth away;
Of Latin Kings this was long since the seat,
But now demolished, to make Rome great.   3500
Thirty-two years did Tullius reign, then die,
Left Rome in wealth and power still growing high.

Ancus Martius

Next Ancus Martius sits upon the throne,
Nephew unto Pompilius dead and gone;   3505
Rome he enlarged, new built again the wall,
Much stronger and more beautiful withal;
A stately bridge he over Tiber made,
Of boats and oars no more they need the aid.
Fair Ostia he built this town; it stood   3510
Close by the mouth of famous Tiber flood.
Twenty-four years time of his royal race,
Then unto death unwillingly gives place.

Tarquinius Priscus

Tarquin, a Greek at Corinth born and bred,   3515
Who from his country for sedition fled,
Is entertained at Rome, and in short time,
By wealth and favour doth to honour climb;
He after Martius' death the kingdom had.
A hundred senators he more did add.   3520
Wars with the Latins he again renews,
And nations twelve of Tuscany subdues.
To such rude triumphs as young Rome then had,
Some state and splendor did this Priscus add.
Thirty-eight years this stranger born did reign,   3525
And after all, by Ancus' sons was slain.

Servius Tullius

Next Servius Tullius gets into the throne,
Ascends not up by merits of his own,
But by the favour and the special grace   3530
Of Tanaquil, late queen, obtains the place.
He ranks the people into each degree,
As wealth had made them of ability;
A general muster takes, which by account,
To eighty thousand souls then did amount.   3535
Forty-four years did Servius Tullius reign,
And then by Tarquin Priscus' son was slain.

Tarquinius Superbus the last
King of the Romans

Tarquin the proud, from manners called so,   3540
Sat on the throne, when he had slain his foe.
Sextus, his son, did most unworthily
Lucretia force, mirror of chastity.
She loathed so the fact, she loathed her life,
And shed her guiltless blood with guilty knife.   3545
Her husband, sore incensed to quit this wrong,
With Junius Brutus rose, and being strong,
The Tarquins they from Rome by force expel,
In banishment perpetual to dwell;
The government they change, a new one bring,   3550
And people swear ne'er to accept of king.

An Apology

To finish what's begun, was my intent,
My thoughts and my endeavours thereto bent;
Essays I many made but still gave out,   3555

The more I mused, the more I was in doubt;
The subject large, my mind and body weak,
With many moe discouragements did speak.
All thoughts of further progress laid aside,
Though oft persuaded, I as oft denied;   3560
At length resolved, when many years had past,
To prosecute my story to the last;
And for the same, I hours not few did spend,
And weary lines (though lank) I many penned;
But 'fore I could accomplish my desire,   3565
My papers fell a prey to th' raging fire.
And thus my pains (with better things) I lost,
Which none had cause to wail, nor I to boast.
No more I'll do sith I have suffered wrack,
Although my monarchies their legs do lack;   3570
Nor matter is't this last, the world now sees,
Hath many ages been upon his knees.

A DIALOGUE BETWEEN OLD ENGLAND AND NEW; CONCERNING THEIR PRESENT TROUBLES, ANNO, 1642

New England

Alas, dear Mother, fairest queen and best,   5
With honour, wealth, and peace, happy and blest;
What ails thee hang thy head and cross thine arms?
And sit i' th' dust, to sigh these sad alarms?
What deluge of new woes thus overwhelm
The glories of thy ever famous realm?   10
What means this wailing tone, this mournful guise?
Ah, tell thy daughter, she may sympathize.

Old England

Art ignorant indeed of these my woes?
Or must my forced tongue these griefs disclose? 15
And must myself dissect my tattered state,
Which 'mazed Christendom stands wond'ring at?
And thou a child, a limb, and dost not feel
My fainting weak'ned body now to reel?
This physic purging potion I have taken   20
Will bring consumption or an ague quaking,
Unless some cordial thou fetch from high,
Which present help may ease my malady.
If I decease, doth think thou shalt survive?
Or by my wasting state dost think to thrive?   25
Then weigh our case, if't be not justly sad;
Let me lament alone, while thou art glad.

New England

And thus (alas) your state you much deplore
In general terms, but will not say wherefore.   30
What medicine shall I seek to cure this woe,
If th' wound's so dangerous I may not know.
But you perhaps, would have me guess it out:
What hath some Hengist like that Saxon stout
By fraud or force usurped thy flow'ring crown,   35
Or by tempestous wars thy fields trod down?
Or hath Canutus, that brave valiant Dane,
The regal, peaceful scepter from thee ta'en?
Or is't a Norman, whose victorious hand
With English blood bedews thy conquered land?   40
Or is't intestine wars that thus offend?
Do Maud and Stephen for the crown contend?
Do barons rise and side against their king,
And call in foreign aid to help the thing?
Must Edward be deposed? or is't the hour   45
That second Richard must be clapt in th' tower?
Or is't the fatal jar, again begun,
That from the red white pricking roses sprung?
Must Richmond's aid, the nobles now implore,
To come and break the tushes of the boar?   50
If none of these, dear mother, what's your woe?
Pray do you fear Spain's bragging Armado?
Doth your ally, fair France, conspire your wrack,
Or do the Scots play false behind your back?
Doth Holland quit you ill for all your love?   55
Whence is the storm from earth or heaven above?
Is't drought, is't famine, or is't pestilence?
Doth feel the smart, or fear the consequence?
Your humble child entreats you, show your grief,
Though arms, nor purse she hath for your relief,   60

Such is her poverty, yet shall be found
A suppliant for your help, as she is bound.

Old England

I must confess some of those sores you name,
My beauteous body at this present maim;   65
But foreign foe, nor feigned friend I fear,
For they have work enough (thou know'st) elsewhere.
Nor is it Alcie's son, nor Henry's daughter,
Whose proud contention cause this slaughter,
Nor nobles siding to make John no king,   70
French Lewis unjustly to the crown to bring;
No Edward, Richard, to lose rule and life,
Nor no Lancastrians to renew old strife;
No Duke of York, nor Earl of March to soil
Their hands in kindred's blood whom they did foil;   75
No crafty tyrant now usurps the seat,
Who nephews slew that so he might be great;
No need of Tudor roses to unite,
None knows which is the red, or which the white;
Spain's braving fleet, a second time is sunk;   80
France knows how oft my fury she hath drunk
By Edward Third and Henry Fifth of fame,
Her lilies in mine arms avouch the same.
My sister Scotland hurts me now no more
Though she hath been injurious heretofore;   85
What Holland is I am in some suspense,
But trust not much unto his excellence.
For wants, sure some I feel, but more I fear,
And for the pestilence, who knows how near;
Famine and plague, two sisters of the sword,   90
Destruction to a land doth soon afford;
They're for my punishment ordained on high,

Unless our tears prevent it speedily.
But yet I answer not what you demand,
To show the grievance of my troubled land.   95
Before I tell th' effect, I'll show the cause
Which are my sins, the breach of sacred laws.
Idolatry, supplanter of a nation,
With foolish superstitious adoration,
Are liked and countenanced by men of might,   100
The Gospel trodden down and hath no right;
Church offices were sold and bought for gain,
That Pope had hope to find Rome here again.
For oaths and blasphemies, did ever ear
From Belzebub himself such language hear?   105
What scorning of the saints of the Most High?
What injuries did daily on them lie?
What false reports, what nick-names did they take
Not for their own, but for their master's sake?
And thou, poor soul, wert jeered among the rest,   110
Thy flying for the truth was made a jest.
For Sabbath-breaking and for drunkenness,
Did ever land profaneness more express?
From crying blood yet cleansed am not I,
Martyrs and others, dying causelessly.   115
How many princely heads on blocks laid down
For nought but title to a fading crown?
'Mongst all the cruelties by great ones done
Oh, Edward's youths, and Clarence hapless son,
O Jane, why didst thou die in flow'ring prime?   120
Because of royal stem, that was thy crime.
For bribery, adultery, and lies,
Where is the nation, I can't paralyze.
With usury, extortion, and oppression,
These be the Hydras of my stout transgression.   125
These be the bitter fountains, heads, and roots,
Whence flowed the source, the springs, the boughs and fruits

Of more than thou canst hear or I relate,
That with high hand I still did perpetrate,
For these were threatened the woeful day   130
I mocked the preachers, put it far away;
The sermons yet upon record do stand
That cried destruction to my wicked land;
I then believed not, now I feel and see,
The plague of stubborn incredulity.   135
Some lost their livings, some in prison pent,
Some fined, from house and friends to exile went.
Their silent tongues to heaven did vengeance cry,
Who saw their wrongs and hath judged righteously
And will repay it sevenfold in my lap: 140
This is forerunner of my afterclap.
Nor took I warning by my neighbour's falls.
I saw sad Germany's dismantled walls,
I saw her people famished, nobles slain,
Her fruitful land, a barren heath remain.   145
I saw, unmoved, her armies foiled and fled,
Wives forced, babes tossed, her houses calcined.
I saw strong Rochelle yielded to her foe,
Thousands of starved Christians there also.
I saw poor Ireland bleeding out her last,   150
Such cruelties as all reports have past;
Mine heart obdurate stood not yet aghast.
Now sip I of that cup, and just 't may be
The bottom dregs reserved are for me.

New England   155

To all you've said, sad Mother, I assent,
Your fearful sins great cause there's to lament,
My guilty hands, in part, hold up with you,
A sharer in your punishment's my due.
But all you say amounts to this effect,   160

Not what you feel, but what you do expect,
Pray in plain terms, what is your present grief?
Then let's join heads and hearts for your relief.

Old England

Well to the matter then, there's grown of late   165
'Twixt king and peers a question of state,
Which is the chief, the law, or else the king.
One said, "It's he," the other no such thing.
'Tis said, my better part in Parliament
To ease my groaning land, showed their intent,   170
To crush the proud, and right to each man deal,
To help the Church and stay the commonweal.
So many obstacles came in their way,
As puts me to a stand what I should say;
Old customs, new prerogatives stood on,   175
Had they not held law fast, all had been gone,
Which by their prudence stood them in such stead
They took high Strafford lower by the head.
And to their Laud be't spoke, they held i'th' tower
All England's metropolitan that hour;   180
This done, an act they would have passed fain,
No prelate should his bishopric retain;
Here tugged they hard, indeed, for all men saw
This must be done by Gospel, not by law.
Next the militia they urged sore,   185
This was denied (I need not say wherefore).
The King, displeased, at York himself absents,
They humbly beg return, show their intents;
The writing, printing, posting to and fro,
Shows all was done, I'll therefore let it go.   190
But now I come to speak of my disaster,
Contention grown, 'twixt subjects and their master;
They worded it so long, they fell to blows,

That thousands lay on heaps, here bleeds my woes,
I that no wars so many years have known, 195
Am now destroyed and slaught'red by mine own;
But could the field alone this strife decide,
One battle two or three I might abide,
But these may be beginnings of more woe.
Who knows, but this may be my overthrow. 200
Oh pity me in this sad perturbation,
My plundred towns, my houses' devastation,
My weeping virgins and my young men slain;
My wealthy trading fall'n, my dearth of grain,
The seedtime's come, but ploughman hath no hope 205
Because he knows not who shall in his crop.
The poor they want their pay, their children bread,
Their woeful mothers' tears unpitied.
If any pity in thy heart remain,
Or any childlike love thou dost retain, 210
For my relief, do what there lies in thee,
And recompense that good I've done to thee.

New England

Dear Mother, cease complaints and wipe your eyes,
Shake off your dust, cheer up, and now arise; 215
You are my mother nurse, and I your flesh,
Your sunken bowels gladly would refresh;
Your griefs I pity, but soon hope to see,
Out of your troubles much good fruit to be,
To see those latter days of hoped for good, 220
Though now beclouded all with tears and blood.
After dark Popery the day did clear,
But now the sun in's brightness shall appear.
Blest be the nobles of thy noble land,
With ventured lives for truth's defence that stand. 225
Blest be thy commons, who for common good,

And thy infringed laws have boldly stood.
Blest be thy counties, who did aid thee still,
With hearts and states to testify their will.
Blest be thy preachers, who do cheer thee on,   230
O cry, "the sword of God and Gideon";
And shall I not on them wish Mero's curse,
That help thee not with prayers, arms, and purse?
And for myself let miseries abound,
If mindless of thy state I e'er be found.   235
These are the days the Church's foes to crush,
To root out Popelings head, tail, branch, and rush;
Let's bring Baal's vestments forth to make a fire,
Their miters, surplices, and all their tire,
Copes, rochets, crosiers, and such empty trash,   240
And let their names consume, but let the flash
Light Christendom, and all the world to see
We hate Rome's whore with all her trumpery.
Go on brave Essex with a loyal heart,
Not false to king, nor to the better part;   245
But those that hurt his people and his crown,
As duty binds, expell and tread them down.
And ye brave nobles chase away all fear,
And to this hopeful cause closely adhere;
O Mother, can you weep, and have such peers?   250
When they are gone, then drown yourself in tears.
If now you weep so much, that then no more
The briny ocean will o'erflow your shore.
These, these are they I trust, with Charles our King,
Out of all mists such glorious days shall bring;   255
That dazzled eyes beholding much shall wonder
At that thy settled peace, thy wealth and splendor.
Thy Church and weal established in such manner,
That all shall joy, that thou displayed'st thy banner;
And discipline erected so I trust,   260

That nursing kings shall come and lick thy dust.
Then justice shall in all thy courts take place,
Without respect of person or of case;
Then bribes shall cease, and suits shall not stick long,
Patience and purse of clients oft to wrong.   265
Then high commissions shall fall to decay,
And pursuivants and catchpoles want their pay.
So shall thy happy nation ever flourish,
When truth and righteousness they thus shall nourish,
When thus in peace, thine armies brave send out   270
To sack proud Rome and all her vassals rout;
There let thy name, thy fame, and glory shine,
As did thine ancestors' in Palestine;
And let her spoils full pay with interest be,
Of what unjustly once she polled from thee.   275
Of all the woes thou canst let her be sped,
And on her pour the vengeance threat'ned;
Bring forth the beast that ruled the world with's beck,
And tear his flesh and set your feet on's neck;
And make his filthy den so desolate,   280
To th' 'stonishment of all that knew his state.
This done, with brandished swords to Turkey go,
For then what is't but English blades dare do,
And lay her waste for so's the sacred doom,
And do to Gog as thou hast done to Rome.   285
Oh Abraham's seed, lift up your heads on high,
For sure the day of your redemption's nigh;
The scales shall fall from your long blinded eyes,
And Him you shall adore who now despise.
Then fullness of the nations in shall flow,   290
And Jew and Gentile to one worship go;
Then follows days of happiness and rest;
Whose lot doth fall to live therein is blest:
No Canaanite shall then be found i' th' land,

And holiness on horses' bells shall stand.
If this make way thereto, then sigh no more,
But if at all, thou didst not see't before;
Farewell, dear Mother, rightest cause prevail,
And in a while, you'll tell another tale.

AN ELEGY UPON THAT HONORABLE AND RENOWNED KNIGHT SIR PHILIP SIDNEY, WHO WAS UNTIMELY SLAIN AT THE SIEGE OF ZUTPHEN, ANNO 1586

5

When England did enjoy her halcyon days,
Her noble Sidney wore the crown of bays;
As well an honour to our British land,
As she that swayed the scepter with her hand;
Mars and Minerva did in one agree,   10
Of arms and arts he should a pattern be,
Calliope with Terpsichore did sing,
Of poesy, and of music, he was king;
His rhetoric struck Polymnia dead,
His eloquence made Mercury wax red: 15
His logic from Euterpe won the crown,
More worth was his than Clio could set down.
Thalia and Melpomene, say truth,
(Witness *Arcadia* penned in his youth)
Are not his tragic comedies so acted,   20
As if your ninefold wit had been compacted.
To show the world, they never saw before,
That this one volume should exhaust your store;
His wiser days condemned his witty works,
Who knows the spells that in his rhetoric lurks,   25
But some infatuate fools soon caught therein;
Fond Cupid's dame had never such a gin,
Which makes severer eyes but slight that story,
And men of morose minds envy his glory.
But he's a beetle-head that can't descry   30
A world of wealth within that rubbish lie,
And doth his name, his work, his honour wrong,

The brave refiner of our British tongue,
That sees not learning, valour and morality,
Justice, friendship, and kind hospitality,   35
Yea, and divinity within his book;
Such were prejudicate and did not look.
In all records his name I ever see
Put with an epithet of dignity,
Which shows his worth was great, his honour such,   40
The love his country ought him was as much.
Then let none disallow of these my strains
Whilst English blood yet runs within my veins.
O brave Achilles, I wish some Homer would
Engrave in marble with characters of gold   45
The valiant feats thou didst on Flanders' coast,
Which at this day fair Belgia may boast.
The more I say, the more thy worth I stain,
Thy fame and praise is far beyond my strain.
O Zutphen, Zutphen that most fatal city,   50
Made famous by thy death, much more the pity.
Ah! in his blooming prime death plucked this rose,
Ere he was ripe, his thread cut Atropos.
Thus man is born to die, and dead is he,
Brave Hector by the walls of Troy we see.   55
O who was near thee but did sore repine
He rescued not with life that life of thine.
But yet impartial Fates this boon did give,
Though Sidney died his valiant name should live;
And live it doth in spite of death, through fame,   60
Thus being overcome, he overcame.
Where is that envious tongue, but can afford
Of this our noble Scipio some good word.
Great Bartas this unto thy praise adds more,
In sad sweet verse thou didst his death deplore.   65
And Phoenix Spenser doth unto his life,
His death present in sable to his wife.

Stella the fair, whose streams from conduits fell
For the sad loss of her dear Astrophel.
Fain would I show how he fame's paths did tread,   70
But now into such lab'rinths I am lead,
With endless turns, the way I find not out,
How to persist my Muse is more in doubt;
Which makes me now with Sylvester confess,
But Sidney's Muse can sing his worthiness.   75
The Muses' aid I craved; they had no will
To give to their detractor any quill;
With high disdain, they said they gave no more,
Since Sidney had exhausted all their store.
They took from me the scribbling pen I had,   80
(I to be eased of such a task was glad)
Then to revenge this wrong, themselves engage,
And drave me from Parnassus in a rage.
Then wonder not if I no better sped,
Since I the Muses thus have injured.   85
I, pensive for my fault, sat down, and then
Errata through their leave threw me my pen;
My poem to conclude, two lines they deign,
Which writ, she bade return't to them again;
So Sidney's fame I leave to England's rolls,   90
His bones do lie interred in stately Paul's.

His Epitaph

Here lies in fame under this stone,
Philip and Alexander both in one;
Heir to the Muses, the son of Mars in truth,   95
Learning, valour, wisdom, all in virtuous youth:
His praise is much, this shall suffice my pen,
That Sidney died 'mong most renowned of men.

Among the happy wits this age hath shown,
Great, dear, sweet Bartas, thou art matchless known;
My ravished eyes and heart with faltering tongue,
In humble wise have vowed their service long,   5
But knowing th' task so great, and strength but small,
Gave o'er the work before begun withal.
My dazzled sight of late reviewed thy lines,
Where art, and more than art, in nature shines;
Reflection from their beaming altitude   10
Did thaw my frozen heart's ingratitude;
Which rays, darting upon some richer ground,
Had caused flowers and fruits soon to abound;
But barren I my daisy here do bring,
A homely flower in this my latter spring,   15
If summer or my autumn age do yield
Flowers, fruits, in garden, orchard, or in field,
They shall be consecrated in my verse,
And prostrate offered at great Bartas' herse;
My muse unto a child I may compare,   20
Who sees the riches of some famous fair,
He feeds his eyes, but understanding lacks
To comprehend the worth of all those knacks;
The glittering plate and jewels he admires,
The hats and fans, the plumes and ladies' tires,   25
And thousand times his mazed mind doth wish
Some part (at least) of that brave wealth was his,
But seeing empty wishes nought obtain,
At night turns to his mother's cot again,
And tells her tales (his full heart over-glad)   30
Of all the glorious sights his eyes have had;
But finds too soon his want of eloquence,

The silly prattler speaks no word of sense;
But seeing utterance fail his great desires,
Sits down in silence, deeply he admires.   35
Thus weak brained I, reading thy lofty style,
Thy profound learning, viewing other while,
Thy art in natural philosophy,
Thy saint-like mind in grave divinity,
Thy piercing skill in high astronomy,   40
And curious insight in anatomy,
Thy physic, music, and state policy,
Valour in war, in peace good husbandry.
Sure lib'ral nature did with art not small,
In all the arts make thee most liberal.   45
A thousand thousand times my senseless senses
Moveless stand charmed by thy sweet influences;
More senseless than the stones to Amphion's lute,
Mine eyes are sightless, and my tongue is mute,
My full astonished heart doth pant to break,   50
Through grief it wants a faculty to speak;
Volleys of praises could I echo then,
Had I an angel's voice, or Bartas' pen;
But wishes can't accomplish my desire,
Pardon if I adore, when I admire.   55
O France, thou didst in him more glory gain
Than in thy Martel, Pipin, Charlemagne,
Than in St. Louis, or thy last Henry Great,
Who tamed his foes in wars, in blood and sweat.
Thy fame is spread as far, I dare be bold,   60
In all the zones, the temp'rate, hot, and cold.
Their trophies were but heaps of wounded slain,
Thine, the quintessence of an heroic brain.
The oaken garland ought to deck their brows,
Immortal bays to thee all men allows.   65
Who in thy triumphs never won by wrongs,
Lead'st millions chained by eyes, by ears, by tongues.

Oft have I wond'red at the hand of heaven,
In giving one what would have served seven.
If e'er this golden gift was show'red on any, 70
Thy double portion would have served many.
Unto each man his riches is assigned
Of name, of state, of body and of mind;
Thou hadst thy part of all, but of the last,
O pregnant brain, O comprehension vast, 75
Thy haughty style and rapted wit sublime
All ages wond'ring at, shall never climb.
Thy sacred works are not for imitation,
But monuments to future admiration.
Thus Bartas' fame shall last while stars do stand, 80
And whilst there's air, or fire, or sea, or land.
But lest mine ignorance should do thee wrong,
To celebrate thy merits in my song,
I'll leave thy praise to those shall do thee right,
Good will, not skill, did cause me bring my mite. 85

His Epitaph

Here lies the pearl of France, Parnassus' glory;
The world rejoiced at's birth, at's death was sorry.
Art and Nature joined, by heaven's high decree,
Now showed what once they ought, humanity; 90
And Nature's law, had it been revocable,
To rescue him from death, Art had been able.
But Nature vanquished Art, so Bartas died;
But Fame outliving both, he is revived.

IN HONOUR OF THAT HIGH AND MIGHTY PRINCESS QUEEN ELIZABETH OF HAPPY MEMORY

The Proem

Although, great Queen, thou now in silence lie   5
Yet thy loud herald Fame doth to the sky
Thy wondrous worth proclaim in every clime,
And so hath vowed while there is world or time.
So great's thy glory and thine excellence,
The sound thereof rapts every human sense,   10
That men account it no impiety,
To say thou wert a fleshly deity.
Thousands bring offerings (though out of date)
Thy world of honours to accumulate;
'Mongst hundred hecatombs of roaring verse,   15
Mine bleating stands before thy royal herse.
Thou never didst nor canst thou now disdain
T' accept the tribute of a loyal brain.
Thy clemency did erst esteem as much
The acclamations of the poor as rich,   20
Which makes me deem my rudeness is no wrong,
Though I resound thy praises 'mongst the throng.

The Poem

No Phoenix pen, nor Spenser's poetry,
No Speed's nor Camden's learned history,   25
Eliza's works wars, praise, can e'er compact;
The world's the theatre where she did act.
No memories nor volumes can contain
The 'leven Olympiads of her happy reign.
Who was so good, so just, so learn'd, so wise,   30

From all the kings on earth she won the prize.
Nor say I more than duly is her due,
Millions will testify that this is true.
She hath wiped off th' aspersion of her sex,
That women wisdom lack to play the rex.   35
Spain's monarch, says not so, nor yet his host;
She taught them better manners, to their cost.
The Salic law, in force now had not been,
If France had ever hoped for such a queen.
But can you, doctors, now this point dispute,   40
She's argument enough to make you mute.
Since first the Sun did run his ne'er run race,
And earth had, once a year, a new old face,
Since time was time, and man unmanly man,
Come show me such a Phoenix if you can.   45
Was ever people better ruled than hers?
Was ever land more happy freed from stirs?
Did ever wealth in England more abound?
Her victories in foreign coasts resound;
Ships more invincible than Spain's, her foe,   50
She wracked, she sacked, she sunk his Armado;
Her stately troops advanced to Lisbon's wall,
Don Anthony in's right there to install.
She frankly helped Frank's brave distressed king;
The states united now her fame do sing.   55
She their protectrix was; they well do know
Unto our dread virago, what they owe.
Her nobles sacrificed their noble blood,
Nor men nor coin she spared to do them good.
The rude untamed Irish, she did quell,   60
Before her picture the proud Tyrone fell.
Had ever prince such counsellors as she?
Herself Minerva caused them so to be.
Such captains and such soldiers never seen,
As were the subjects of our Pallas queen.   65

Her seamen through all straits the world did round;
Terra incognita might know the sound.
Her Drake came laden home with Spanish gold;
Her Essex took Cadiz, their Herculean hold.
But time would fail me, so my tongue would too,   70
To tell of half she did, or she could do.
Semiramis to her is but obscure,
More infamy than fame she did procure.
She built her glory but on Babel's walls,
World's wonder for a while, but yet it falls.   75
Fierce Tomris (Cyrus' headsman) Scythians' queen,
Had put her harness off, had she but seen
Our Amazon in th' Camp of Tilbury,
Judging all valour and all majesty
Within that princess to have residence,   80
And prostrate yielded to her excellence.
Dido, first foundress of proud Carthage walls
(Who living consummates her funerals),
A great Eliza, but compared with ours,
How vanisheth her glory, wealth, and powers.   85
Profuse, proud Cleopatra, whose wrong name,
Instead of glory, proved her country's shame,
Of her what worth in stories to be seen,
But that she was a rich Egyptian queen.
Zenobya, potent empress of the East,   90
And of all these without compare the best,
Whom none but great Aurelius could quell;
Yet for our Queen is no fit parallel.
She was a Phoenix queen, so shall she be,
Her ashes not revived, more Phoenix she.   95
Her personal perfections, who would tell
Must dip his pen in th' Heleconian well,
Which I may not, my pride doth but aspire
To read what others write and so admire.
Now say, have women worth? or have they none?   100

Or had they some, but with our Queen is't gone?
Nay masculines, you have thus taxed us long,
But she, though dead, will vindicate our wrong.
Let such as say our sex is void of reason,
Know 'tis a slander now but once was treason. 105
But happy England which had such a queen;
Yea happy, happy, had those days still been.
But happiness lies in a higher sphere,
Then wonder not Eliza moves not here.
Full fraught with honour, riches and with days 110
She set, she set, like Titan in his rays.
No more shall rise or set so glorious sun
Until the heaven's great revolution;
If then new things their old forms shall retain,
Eliza shall rule Albion once again. 115

Her Epitaph

Here sleeps the queen, this is the royal bed
Of th' damask rose, sprung from the white and red,
Whose sweet perfume fills the all-filling air.
This rose is withered, once so lovely fair. 120
On neither tree did grow such rose before,
The greater was our gain, our loss the more.

Another

Here lies the pride of queens, pattern of kings,
So blaze it, Fame, here's feathers for thy wings. 125
Here lies the envied, yet unparalleled prince,
Whose living virtues speak (though dead long since).
If many worlds, as that fantastic framed,
In every one be her great glory famed.

DAVID'S LAMENTATION FOR
SAUL AND JONATHAN
II SAM. 1:19

Alas, slain is the head of Israel,
Illustrious Saul, whose beauty did excel;   5
Upon thy places mountainous and high,
How did the mighty fall, and falling die?
In Gath let not this thing be spoken on,
Nor published in the streets of Ascalon,
Lest daughters of the Philistines rejoice,   10
Lest the uncircumcised lift up their voice.
O Gilbo Mounts, let never pearled dew,
Nor fruitful showers your barren tops bestrew,
Nor fields of off'rings ever on you grow,
Nor any pleasant thing e'er may you show;   15
For there the mighty ones did soon decay,
The shield of Saul was vilely cast away,
There had his dignity so sore a foil,
As if his head ne'er felt the sacred oil.
Sometimes from crimson blood of ghastly slain,   20
The bow of Jonathan ne'er turned in vain:
Nor from the fat and spoils of mighty men
With bloodless sword did Saul turn back again.
Pleasant and lovely were they both in life,
And in their death was found no parting strife.   25
Swifter than swiftest eagles so were they,
Stronger than lions ramping for their prey.
O Israel's dames, o'erflow your beauteous eyes
For valiant Saul who on Mount Gilbo lies,
Who clothed you in cloth of richest dye,   30
And choice delights full of variety,
On your array put ornaments of gold,

Which made you yet more beauteous to behold.
Oh! how in battle did the mighty fall
In midst of strength not succoured at all.   35
O lovely Jonathan! How wast thou slain?
In places high, full low thou didst remain.
Distressed for thee I am, dear Jonathan,
Thy love was wonderful, surpassing man,
Exceeding all the love that's feminine,   40
So pleasant hast thou been, dear brother mine.
How are the mighty fall'n into decay?
And warlike weapons perished away?

TO THE MEMORY OF MY DEAR
AND EVER HONOURED FATHER
THOMAS DUDLEY ESQ.
WHO DECEASED, JULY 31, 1653,
AND OF HIS AGE 77   5

By duty bound and not by custom led
To celebrate the praises of the dead,
My mournful mind, sore pressed, in trembling verse
Presents my lamentations at his hearse,
Who was my father, guide, instructor too,   10
To whom I ought whatever I could do.
Nor is't relation near my hand shall tie;
For who more cause to boast his worth than I?
Who heard or saw, observed or knew him better?
Or who alive than I a greater debtor?   15
Let malice bite and envy gnaw its fill,
He was my father, and I'll praise him still.
Nor was his name or life lead so obscure
That pity might some trumpeters procure
Who after death might make him falsely seem   20
Such as in life no man could justly deem.
Well known and loved, where e'er he lived, by most
Both in his native and in foreign coast,
These to the world his merits could make known,
So needs no testimonial from his own;   25
But now or never I must pay my sum;
While others tell his worth, I'll not be dumb.
One of thy Founders, him New England know,
Who stayed thy feeble sides when thou wast low,
Who spent his state, his strength and years with care   30
That after-comers in them might have share.
True patriot of this little commonweal,

Who is't can tax thee ought, but for thy zeal?
Truth's friend thou wert, to errors still a foe,
Which caused apostates to malign so.   35
Thy love to true religion e'er shall shine;
My father's God, be God of me and mine.
Upon the earth he did not build his nest,
But as a pilgrim, what he had, possessed.
High thoughts he gave no harbour in his heart,   40
Nor honours puffed him up when he had part;
Those titles loathed, which some too much do love,
For truly his ambition lay above.
His humble mind so loved humility,
He left it to his race for legacy;   45
And oft and oft with speeches mild and wise
Gave his in charge that jewel rich to prize.
No ostentation seen in all his ways,
As in the mean ones of our foolish days,
Which all they have and more still set to view,   50
Their greatness may be judged by what they shew.
His thoughts were more sublime, his actions wise,
Such vanities he justly did despise.
Nor wonder 'twas, low things ne'er much did move
For he a mansion had, prepared above,   55
For which he sighed and prayed and longed full sore
He might be clothed upon for evermore.
Oft spake of death, and with a smiling cheer
He did exult his end was drawing near;
Now fully ripe, as shock of wheat that's grown,   60
Death as a sickle hath him timely mown,
And in celestial barn hath housed him high,
Where storms, nor show'rs, nor ought can damnify.
His generation served, his labours cease;
And to his fathers gathered is in peace.   65
Ah happy soul, 'mongst saints and angels blest,
Who after all his toil is now at rest.

His hoary head in righteousness was found;
As joy in heaven, on earth let praise resound.
Forgotten never be his memory,   70
His blessing rest on his posterity;
His pious footsteps, followed by his race,
At last will bring us to that happy place
Where we with joy each other's face shall see,
And parted more by death shall never be.   75

His Epitaph

Within this tomb a patriot lies
That was both pious, just, and wise,
To truth a shield, to right a wall,
To sectaries a whip and maul,
A magazine of history,
A prizer of good company,
In manners pleasant and severe;
The good him loved, the bad did fear,
And when his time with years was spent,
If some rejoiced, more did lament.

AN EPITAPH ON MY DEAR AND
EVER-HONOURED MOTHER
MRS. DOROTHY DUDLEY,
WHO DECEASED DECEMBER 27,
1643, AND OF HER AGE, 61   5

            Here lies,
A worthy matron of unspotted life,
A loving mother and obedient wife,
A friendly neighbor, pitiful to poor,
Whom oft she fed and clothed with her store;   10
To servants wisely awful, but yet kind,
And as they did, so they reward did find.
A true instructor of her family,
The which she ordered with dexterity.
The public meetings ever did frequent,   15
And in her closet constant hours she spent;
Religious in all her words and ways,
Preparing still for death, till end of days:
Of all her children, children lived to see,
Then dying, left a blessed memory.   20

CONTEMPLATIONS

Some time now past in the autumnal tide,
When Phoebus wanted but one hour to bed,
The trees all richly clad, yet void of pride,
Where gilded o'er by his rich golden head.   5
Their leaves and fruits seemed painted, but was true,
Of green, of red, of yellow, mixed hue;
Rapt were my senses at this delectable view.

2

I wist not what to wish, yet sure thought I,
If so much excellence abide below,   10
How excellent is He that dwells on high,
Whose power and beauty by his works we know?
Sure he is goodness, wisdom, glory, light,
That hath this under world so richly dight;
More heaven than earth was here, no winter and no night. 15

3

Then on a stately oak I cast mine eye,
Whose ruffling top the clouds seemed to aspire;
How long since thou wast in thine infancy?
Thy strength, and stature, more thy years admire,
Hath hundred winters past since thou wast born?   20
Or thousand since thou brakest thy shell of horn?
If so, all these as nought, eternity doth scorn.

4

Then higher on the glistering Sun I gazed,
Whose beams was shaded by the leavie tree;
The more I looked, the more I grew amazed,   25
And softly said, "What glory's like to thee?"
Soul of this world, this universe's eye,
No wonder some made thee a deity;
Had I not better known, alas, the same had I.

5

Thou as a bridegroom from thy chamber rushes,   30
And as a strong man, joys to run a race;
The morn doth usher thee with smiles and blushes;

The Earth reflects her glances in thy face.
Birds, insects, animals with vegative,
Thy heat from death and dullness doth revive,   35
And in the darksome womb of fruitful nature dive.

6

Thy swift annual and diurnal course,
Thy daily straight and yearly oblique path,
Thy pleasing fervor and thy scorching force,
All mortals here the feeling knowledge hath.   40
Thy presence makes it day, thy absence night,
Quaternal seasons caused by thy might:
Hail creature, full of sweetness, beauty, and delight.

7

Art thou so full of glory that no eye
Hath strength thy shining rays once to behold?   45
And is thy splendid throne erect so high,
As to approach it, can no earthly mould?
How full of glory then must thy Creator be,
Who gave this bright light luster unto thee?
Admired, adored for ever, be that Majesty.   50

8

Silent alone, where none or saw, or heard,
In pathless paths I lead my wand'ring feet,
My humble eyes to lofty skies I reared
To sing some song, my mazed Muse thought meet.
My great Creator I would magnify,   55
That nature had thus decked liberally;
But Ah, and Ah, again, my imbecility!

9

I heard the merry grasshopper then sing.
The black-clad cricket bear a second part;
They kept one tune and played on the same string,   60
Seeming to glory in their little art.
Shall creatures abject thus their voices raise
And in their kind resound their Maker's praise,
Whilst I, as mute, can warble forth no higher lays?

10

When present times look back to ages past,   65
And men in being fancy those are dead,
It makes things gone perpetually to last,
And calls back months and years that long since fled.
It makes a man more aged in conceit
Than was Methuselah, or's grandsire great,   70
While of their persons and their acts his mind doth treat.

11

Sometimes in Eden fair he seems to be,
Sees glorious Adam there made lord of all,
Fancies the apple, dangle on the tree,
That turned his sovereign to a naked thrall.   75
Who like a miscreant's driven from that place,
To get his bread with pain and sweat of face,
A penalty imposed on his backsliding race.

12

Here sits our grandame in retired place,
And in her lap her bloody Cain new-born;   80

The weeping imp oft looks her in the face,
Bewails his unknown hap and fate forlorn;
His mother sighs to think of Paradise,
And how she lost her bliss to be more wise,
Believing him that was, and is, father of lies.   85

13

Here Cain and Abel come to sacrifice,
Fruits of the earth and fatlings each do bring,
On Abel's gift the fire descends from skies,
But no such sign on false Cain's offering;
With sullen hateful looks he goes his ways,   90
Hath thousand thoughts to end his brother's days,
Upon whose blood his future good he hopes to raise.

14

There Abel keeps his sheep, no ill he thinks;
His brother comes, then acts his fratricide;
The virgin Earth of blood her first draught drinks,   95
But since that time she often hath been cloyed.
The wretch with ghastly face and dreadful mind
Thinks each he sees will serve him in his kind,
Though none on earth but kindred near then could he find.

15

Who fancies not his looks now at the bar,   100
His face like death, his heart with horror fraught,
Nor malefactor ever felt like war,
When deep despair with wish of life hath fought,
Branded with guilt and crushed with treble woes,
A vagabond to Land of Nod he goes.   105
A city builds, that walls might him secure from foes.

16

Who thinks not oft upon the father's ages,
Their long descent, how nephews' sons they saw,
The starry observations of those sages,
And how their precepts to their sons were law,   110
How Adam sighed to see his progeny,
Clothed all in his black sinful livery,
Who neither guilt nor yet the punishment could fly.

17

Our life compare we with their length of days
Who to the tenth of theirs doth now arrive?   115
And though thus short, we shorten many ways,
Living so little while we are alive;
In eating, drinking, sleeping, vain delight
So unawares comes on perpetual night,
And puts all pleasures vain unto eternal flight.   120

18

When I behold the heavens as in their prime,
And then the earth (though old) still clad in green,
The stones and trees, insensible of time,
Nor age nor wrinkle on their front are seen;
If winter come and greenness then do fade,   125
A spring returns, and they more youthful made;
But man grows old, lies down, remains where once he's laid.

19

By birth more noble than those creatures all,
Yet seems by nature and by custom cursed,
No sooner born, but grief and care makes fall   130

That state obliterate he had at first;
Nor youth, nor strength, nor wisdom spring again,
Nor habitations long their names retain,
But in oblivion to the final day remain.

20

Shall I then praise the heavens, the trees, the earth   135
Because their beauty and their strength last longer?
Shall I wish there, or never to had birth,
Because they're bigger, and their bodies stronger?
Nay, they shall darken, perish, fade and die,
And when unmade, so ever shall they lie,   140
But man was made for endless immortality.

21

Under the cooling shadow of a stately elm
Close sat I by a goodly river's side,
Where gliding streams the rocks did overwhelm,
A lonely place, with pleasures dignified.   145
I once that loved the shady woods so well,
Now thought the rivers did the trees excel,
And if the sun would ever shine, there would I dwell.

22

While on the stealing stream I fixt mine eye,
Which to the longed-for ocean held its course,   150
I marked, nor crooks, nor rubs that there did lie
Could hinder ought, but still augment its force.
"O happy flood," quoth I, "that holds thy race
Till thou arrive at thy beloved place,
Nor is it rocks or shoals that can obstruct thy pace,   155

23

Nor is't enough, that thou alone mayst slide,
But hundred brooks in thy clear waves do meet,
So hand in hand along with thee they glide
To Thetis' house, where all embrace and greet.
Thou emblem true of what I count the best,   160
O could I lead my rivulets to rest,
So may we press to that vast mansion, ever blest."

24

Ye fish, which in this liquid region 'bide,
That for each season have your habitation,
Now salt, now fresh where you think best to glide   165
To unknown coasts to give a visitation,
In lakes and ponds you leave your numerous fry;
So nature taught, and yet you know not why,
You wat'ry folk that know not your felicity.

25

Look how the wantons frisk to taste the air,   170
Then to the colder bottom straight they dive;
Eftsoon to Neptune's glassy hall repair
To see what trade they great ones there do drive,
Who forage o'er the spacious sea-green field,
And take the trembling prey before it yield,   175
Whose armour is their scales, their spreading fins
    their shield.

26

While musing thus with contemplation fed,
And thousand fancies buzzing in my brain,

The sweet-tongued Philomel perched o'er my head
And chanted forth a most melodious strain   180
Which rapt me so with wonder and delight,
I judged my hearing better than my sight,
And wished me wings with her a while to take my flight.

27

"O merry Bird," said I, "that fears no snares,
That neither toils nor hoards up in thy barn,   185
Feels no sad thoughts nor cruciating cares
To gain more good or shun what might thee harm.
Thy clothes ne'er wear, thy meat is everywhere,
Thy bed a bough, thy drink the water clear,
Reminds not what is past, nor what's to come dost fear."   190

28

"The dawning morn with songs thou dost prevent,
Sets hundred notes unto thy feathered crew,
So each one tunes his pretty instrument,
And warbling out the old, begin anew,
And thus they pass their youth in summer season,   195
Then follow thee into a better region,
Where winter's never felt by that sweet airy legion."

29

Man at the best a creature frail and vain,
In knowledge ignorant, in strength but weak,
Subject to sorrows, losses, sickness, pain,   200
Each storm his state, his mind, his body break,
From some of these he never finds cessation,
But day or night, within, without, vexation,
Troubles from foes, from friends, from dearest, near'st
    relation.

30

And yet this sinful creature, frail and vain,   205
This lump of wretchedness, of sin and sorrow,
This weatherbeaten vessel wracked with pain,
Joys not in hope of an eternal morrow;
Nor all his losses, crosses, and vexation,
In weight, in frequency and long duration   210
Can make him deeply groan for that divine translation.

31

The mariner that on smooth waves doth glide
Sings merrily and steers his bark with ease,
As if he had command of wind and tide,
And now become great master of the seas: 215
But suddenly a storm spoils all the sport,
And makes him long for a more quiet port,
Which 'gainst all adverse winds may serve for fort.

32

So he that saileth in this world of pleasure,
Feeding on sweets, that never bit of th' sour,   220
That's full of friends, of honour, and of treasure,
Fond fool, he takes this earth ev'n for heav'n's bower.
But sad affliction comes and makes him see
Here's neither honour, wealth, nor safety;
Only above is found all with security.   225

33

O Time the fatal wrack of mortal things,
That draws oblivion's curtains over kings;
Their sumptuous monuments, men know them not,

Their names without a record are forgot,
Their parts, their ports, their pomp's all laid in th' dust   230
Nor wit nor gold, nor buildings scape times rust;
But he whose name is graved in the white stone
Shall last and shine when all of these are gone.

THE FLESH AND THE SPIRIT

In secret place where once I stood
Close by the banks of Lacrim flood,
I heard two sisters reason on
Things that are past and things to come;   5
One flesh was called, who had her eye
On worldly wealth and vanity;
The other Spirit, who did rear
Her thoughts unto a higher sphere:
Sister, quoth Flesh, what liv'st thou on,   10
Nothing but meditation?
Doth contemplation feed thee so
Regardlessly to let earth go?
Can speculation satisfy
Notion without reality?   15
Dost dream of things beyond the moon,
And dost thou hope to dwell there soon?
Hast treasures there laid up in store
That all in th' world thou count'st but poor?
Art fancy sick, or turned a sot   20
To catch at shadows which are not?
Come, come, I'll show unto thy sense,
Industry hath its recompense.
What canst desire, but thou may'st see
True substance in variety?   25
Dost honour like? Acquire the same,
As some to their immortal fame,
And trophies to thy name erect
Which wearing time shall ne'er deject.
For riches doth thou long full sore?   30
Behold enough of precious store.
Earth hath more silver, pearls, and gold,

Than eyes can see or hands can hold.
Affect's thou pleasure? Take thy fill,
Earth hath enough of what you will.   35
Then let not go, what thou may'st find
For things unknown, only in mind.
Spir. Be still thou unregenerate part,
Disturb no more my settled heart,
For I have vowed (and so will do)   40
Thee as a foe still to pursue.
And combat with thee will and must,
Until I see thee laid in th' dust.
Sisters we are, yea, twins we be,
Yet deadly feud 'twixt thee and me;   45
For from one father are we not,
Thou by old Adam wast begot,
But my arise is from above,
Whence my dear Father I do love.
Thou speak'st me fair, but hat'st me sore,   50
Thy flatt'ring shows I'll trust no more.
How oft thy slave, hast thou me made,
When I believed what thou hast said,
And never had more cause of woe
Than when I did what thou bad'st do.   55
I'll stop mine ears at these thy charms,
And count them for my deadly harms.
Thy sinful pleasures I do hate,
Thy riches are to me no bait,
Thine honours do, nor will I love;   60
For my ambition lies above.
My greatest honour it shall be
When I am victor over thee,
And triumph shall with laurel head,
When thou my captive shalt be led,   65
How I do live, thou need'st not scoff,
For I have meat thou know'st not of;

The hidden manna I do eat,
The word of life it is my meat.
My thoughts do yield me more content   70
Than can thy hours in pleasure spent.
Nor are they shadows which I catch,
Nor fancies vain at which I snatch,
But reach at things that are so high,
Beyond thy dull capacity;   75
Eternal substance I do see,
With which enriched I would be.
Mine eye doth pierce the heavens and see
What is invisible to thee.
My garments are not silk nor gold,   80
Nor such like trash which earth doth hold,
But royal robes I shall have on,
More glorious than the glist'ring sun;
My crown not diamonds, pearls, and gold,
But such as angels' heads enfold.   85
The city where I hope to dwell,
There's none on earth can parallel;
The stately walls both high and strong,
Are made of precious jasper stone;
The gates of pearl, both rich and clear,   90
And angels are for porters there;
The streets thereof transparent gold,
Such as no eye did e'er behold;
A crystal river there doth run,
Which doth proceed from the Lamb's throne.   95
Of life, there are the waters sure,
Which shall remain forever pure,
Nor sun, nor moon, they have no need,
For glory doth from God proceed.
No candle there, nor yet torchlight,   100
For there shall be no darksome night.
From sickness and infirmity

For evermore they shall be free;
Nor withering age shall e'er come there,
But beauty shall be bright and clear;
This city pure is not for thee,
For things unclean there shall not be.
If I of heaven may have my fill,
Take thou the world and all that will.

105

THE VANITY OF ALL WORDLY THINGS

As he said vanity, so vain say I,
Oh! vanity, O vain all under sky;
Where is the man can say, "Lo, I have found
On brittle earth a consolation sound"?   5
What is't in honour to be set on high?
No, they like beasts and sons of men shall die,
And whilst they live, how oft doth turn their fate;
He's now a captive that was king of late.
What is't in wealth great treasures to obtain?   10
No, that's but labour, anxious care, and pain.
He heaps up riches, and he heaps up sorrow,
It's his today, but who's his heir tomorrow?
What then? Content in pleasures canst thou find?
More vain than all, that's but to grasp the wind.   15
The sensual senses for a time they please,
Meanwhile the conscience rage, who shall appease?
What is't in beauty? No that's but a snare,
They're foul enough today, that once were fair.
What is't in flow'ring youth, or manly age?   20
The first is prone to vice, the last to rage.
Where is it then, in wisdom, learning, arts?
Sure if on earth, it must be in those parts;
Yet these the wisest man of men did find
But vanity, vexation of mind.   25
And he that knows the most doth still bemoan
He knows not all that here is to be known.
What is it then? to do as stoics tell,
Nor laugh, nor weep, let things go ill or well?
Such stoics are but stocks, such teaching vain,   30
While man is man, he shall have ease or pain.
If not in honour, beauty, age, nor treasure,

Nor yet in learning, wisdom, youth, nor pleasure,
Where shall I climb, sound, seek, search, or find
That *summum bonum* which may stay my mind? 35
There is a path no vulture's eye hath seen,
Where lion fierce, nor lion's whelps have been,
Which leads unto that living crystal fount,
Who drinks thereof, the world doth nought account.
The depth and sea have said " 'tis not in me," 40
With pearl and gold it shall not valued be.
For sapphire, onyx, topaz who would change;
It's hid from eyes of men, they count it strange.
Death and destruction the fame hath heard,
But where and what it is, from heaven's declared; 45
It brings to honour which shall ne'er decay,
It stores with wealth which time can't wear away.
It yieldeth pleasures far beyond conceit,
And truly beautifies without deceit.
Nor strength, nor wisdom, nor fresh youth shall fade, 50
Nor death shall see, but are immortal made.
This pearl of price, this tree of life, this spring,
Who is possessed of shall reign a king.
Nor change of state nor cares shall ever see,
But wear his crown unto eternity. 55
This satiates the soul, this stays the mind,
And all the rest, but vanity we find.

FINIS

THE AUTHOR TO HER BOOK

Thou ill-formed offspring of my feeble brain,
Who after birth didst by my side remain,
Till snatched from thence by friends, less wise than true,
Who thee abroad, exposed to public view,   5
Made thee in rags, halting to th' press to trudge,
Where errors were not lessened (all may judge).
At thy return my blushing was not small,
My rambling brat (in print) should mother call,
I cast thee by as one unfit for light,   10
Thy visage was so irksome in my sight;
Yet being mine own, at length affection would
Thy blemishes amend, if so I could:
I washed thy face, but more defects I saw,
And rubbing off a spot still made a flaw.   15
I stretched thy joints to make thee even feet,
Yet still thou run'st more hobbling than is meet;
In better dress to trim thee was my mind,
But nought save homespun cloth i' th' house I find.
In this array 'mongst vulgars may'st thou roam.   20
In critic's hands beware thou dost not come,
And take thy way where yet thou art not known;
If for thy father asked, say thou hadst none;
And for thy mother, she alas is poor,
Which caused her thus to send thee out of door.   25

UPON A FIT OF SICKNESS,
ANNO 1632 *AETATIS SUAE,* 19

Twice ten years old not fully told
  since nature gave me breath,
My race is run, my thread is spun,
  lo, here is fatal death.
All men must die, and so must I;   5
  this cannot be revoked.
For Adam's sake this word God spake
  when he so high provoked.
Yet live I shall, this life's but small,
  in place of highest bliss,   10
Where I shall have all I can crave,
  no life is like to this.
For what's this life but care and strife
  since first we came from womb?
Our strength doth waste, our time doth haste,   15
  and then we go to th' tomb.
O bubble blast, how long can'st last?
  that always art a breaking,
No sooner blown, but dead and gone,
  ev'n as a word that's speaking.   20
O whilst I live this grace me give,
  I doing good may be,
Then death's arrest I shall count best,
  because it's Thy decree;
Bestow much cost there's nothing lost,   25
  to make salvation sure,
O great's the gain, though got with pain,
  comes by profession pure.
The race is run, the field is won,
  the victory's mine I see;   30
Forever known, thou envious foe,
  the foil belongs to thee.

UPON SOME DISTEMPER OF BODY

In anguish of my heart replete with woes,
And wasting pains, which best my body knows,
In tossing slumbers on my wakeful bed,
Bedrenched with tears that flowed from mournful head,   5
Till nature had exhausted all her store,
Then eyes lay dry, disabled to weep more;
And looking up unto his throne on high,
Who sendeth help to those in misery;
He chased away those clouds and let me see   10
My anchor cast i' th' vale with safety.
He eased my soul of woe, my flesh of pain,
And brought me to the shore from troubled main.

BEFORE THE BIRTH OF ONE
OF HER CHILDREN

All things within this fading world hath end,
Adversity doth still our joys attend;
No ties so strong, no friends so dear and sweet,   5
But with death's parting blow is sure to meet.
The sentence past is most irrevocable,
A common thing, yet oh, inevitable.
How soon, my Dear, death may my steps attend,
How soon't may be thy lot to lose thy friend,   10
We both are ignorant, yet love bids me
These farewell lines to recommend to thee,
That when that knot's untied that made us one,
I may seem thine, who in effect am none.
And if I see not half my days that's due,   15
What nature would, God grant to yours and you;
The many faults that well you know I have
Let be interred in my oblivious grave;
If any worth or virtue were in me,
Let that live freshly in thy memory   20
And when thou feel'st no grief, as I no harms,
Yet love thy dead, who long lay in thine arms.
And when thy loss shall be repaid with gains
Look to my little babes, my dear remains.
And if thou love thyself, or loved'st me,   25
These O protect from step-dame's injury.
And if chance to thine eyes shall bring this verse,
With some sad sighs honour my absent hearse;
And kiss this paper for thy love's dear sake,
Who with salt tears this last farewell did take.   30

A. B.

TO MY DEAR AND LOVING HUSBAND

If ever two were one, then surely we.
If ever man were loved by wife, then thee;
If ever wife was happy in a man,
Compare with me, ye women, if you can. 5
I prize thy love more than whole mines of gold
Or all the riches that the East doth hold.
My love is such that rivers cannot quench,
Nor ought but love from thee, give recompense.
Thy love is such I can no way repay, 10
The heavens reward thee manifold, I pray.
Then while we live, in love let's so persevere
That when we live no more, we may live ever.

A LETTER TO HER HUSBAND, ABSENT UPON PUBLIC EMPLOYMENT

My head, my heart, mine eyes, my life, nay, more,
My joy, my magazine of earthly store,
If two be one, as surely thou and I,
How stayest thou there, whilst I at Ipswich lie?
So many steps, head from the heart to sever,   5
If but a neck, soon should we be together.
I, like the Earth this season, mourn in black,
My Sun is gone so far in's zodiac,
Whom whilst I 'joyed, nor storms, nor frost I felt,
His warmth such frigid colds did cause to melt.   10
My chilled limbs now numbed lie forlorn;
Return, return, sweet Sol, from Capricorn;
In this dead time, alas, what can I more
Than view those fruits which through thy heat I bore?
Which sweet contentment yield me for a space,   15
True living pictures of their father's face.
O strange effect! now thou art southward gone,
I weary grow the tedious day so long;
But when thou northward to me shalt return,
I wish my Sun may never set, but burn   20
Within the Cancer of my glowing breast,
The welcome house of him my dearest guest.
Where ever, ever stay, and go not thence,
Till nature's sad decree shall call thee hence;
Flesh of thy flesh, bone of thy bone,   25
I here, thou there, yet both but one.

                              A. B.

ANOTHER

Phoebus make haste, the day's too long, be gone,
The silent night's the fittest time for moan;
But stay this once, unto my suit give ear,
And tell my griefs in either hemisphere.
(And if the whirling of thy wheels don't drown'd)   5
The woeful accents of my doleful sound,
If in thy swift carrier thou canst make stay,
I crave this boon, this errand by the way,
Commend me to the man more loved than life,
Show him the sorrows of his widowed wife;   10
My dumpish thoughts, my groans, my brakish tears
My sobs, my longing hopes, my doubting fears,
And if he love, how can he there abide?
My interest's more than all the world beside.
He that can tell the stars or ocean sand,   15
Or all the grass that in the meads do stand,
The leaves in th' woods, the hail, or drops of rain,
Or in a corn-field number every grain,
Or every mote that in the sunshine hops,
May count my sighs, and number all my drops.   20
Tell him the countless steps that thou dost trace,
That once a day thy spouse thou may'st embrace;
And when thou canst not treat by loving mouth,
Thy rays afar salute her from the south.
But for one month I see no day (poor soul)   25
Like those far situate under the pole,
Which day by day long wait for thy arise,
O how they joy when thou dost light the skies.
O Phoebus, hadst thou but thus long from thine
Restrained the beams of thy beloved shine,   30
At thy return, if so thou could'st or durst,

Behold a Chaos blacker than the first.
Tell him here's worse than a confused matter,
His little world's a fathom under water.
Nought but the fervor of his ardent beams   35
Hath power to dry the torrent of these streams.
Tell him I would say more, but cannot well,
Oppressed minds abruptest tales do tell.
Now post with double speed, mark what I say,
By all our loves conjure him not to stay.   40

ANOTHER

As loving hind that (hartless) wants her deer,
Scuds through the woods and fern with hark'ning ear,
Perplext, in every bush and nook doth pry,
Her dearest deer, might answer ear or eye;
So doth my anxious soul, which now doth miss   5
A dearer dear (far dearer heart) than this.
Still wait with doubts, and hopes, and failing eye,
His voice to hear or person to descry.
Or as the pensive dove doth all alone
(On withered bough) most uncouthly bemoan   10
The absence of her love and loving mate,
Whose loss hath made her so unfortunate,
Ev'n thus do I, with many a deep sad groan,
Bewail my turtle true, who now is gone,
His presence and his safe return still woos,   15
With thousand doleful sighs and mournful coos.
Or as the loving mullet, that true fish,
Her fellow lost, nor joy nor life do wish,
But launches on that shore, there for to die,
Where she her captive husband doth espy.   20
Mine being gone, I lead a joyless life,
I have a loving peer, yet seem no wife;
But worst of all, to him can't steer my course,
I here, he there, alas, both kept by force.
Return my dear, my joy, my only love,   25
Unto thy hind, thy mullet, and thy dove,
Who neither joys in pasture, house, nor streams,
The substance gone, O me, these are but dreams.
Together at one tree, oh let us browse,
And like two turtles roost within one house,   30
And like the mullets in one river glide,

Let's still remain but one, till death divide.
Thy loving love and dearest dear,
At home, abroad, and everywhere.

A. B.

TO HER FATHER WITH
SOME VERSES

Most truly honoured, and as truly dear,
If worth in me or ought I do appear,
Who can of right better demand the same
Than may your worthy self from whom it came?   5
The principal might yield a greater sum,
Yet handled ill, amounts but to this crumb;
My stock's so small I know not how to pay,
My bond remains in force unto this day;
Yet for part payment take this simple mite,   10
Where nothing's to be had, kings loose their right.
Such is my debt I may not say forgive,
But as I can, I'll pay it while I live;
Such is my bond, none can discharge but I,
Yet paying is not paid until I die.   15

A. B.

IN REFERENCE TO HER CHILDREN,
23 JUNE, 1659

I had eight birds hatched in one nest,
Four cocks there were, and hens the rest.
I nursed them up with pain and care, 5
Nor cost, nor labour did I spare,
Till at the last they felt their wing,
Mounted the trees, and learned to sing;
Chief of the brood then took his flight
To regions far and left me quite. 10
My mournful chirps I after send,
Till he return, or I do end:
Leave not thy nest, thy dam and sire,
Fly back and sing amidst this choir.
My second bird did take her flight, 15
And with her mate flew out of sight;
Southward they both their course did bend,
And seasons twain they there did spend,
Till after blown by southern gales,
They norward steered with filled sails. 20
A prettier bird was no where seen,
Along the beach among the treen.
I have a third of colour white,
On whom I placed no small delight;
Coupled with mate loving and true, 25
Hath also bid her dam adieu;
And where Aurora first appears,
She now hath perched to spend her years.
One to the academy flew
To chat among that learned crew; 30
Ambition moves still in his breast
That he might chant above the rest,

Striving for more than to do well,
That nightingales he might excel.
My fifth, whose down is yet scarce gone, 35
Is 'mongst the shrubs and bushes flown,
And as his wings increase in strength,
On higher boughs he'll perch at length.
My other three still with me nest,
Until they're grown, then as the rest, 40
Or here or there they'll take their flight,
As is ordained, so shall they light.
If birds could weep, then would my tears
Let others know what are my fears
Lest this my brood some harm should catch, 45
And be surprised for want of watch,
Whilst pecking corn and void of care,
They fall un'wares in fowler's snare,
Or whilst on trees they sit and sing,
Some untoward boy at them do fling, 50
Or whilst allured with bell and glass,
The net be spread, and caught, alas.
Or lest by lime-twigs they be foiled,
Or by some greedy hawks be spoiled.
O would my young, ye saw my breast, 55
And knew what thoughts there sadly rest,
Great was my pain when I you bred,
Great was my care when I you fed,
Long did I keep you soft and warm,
And with my wings kept off all harm, 60
My cares are more and fears than ever,
My throbs such now as 'fore were never.
Alas, my birds, you wisdom want,
Of perils you are ignorant;
Oft times in grass, on trees, in flight, 65
Sore accidents on you may light.
O to your safety have an eye,

So happy may you live and die.
Meanwhile my days in tunes I'll spend,
Till my weak lays with me shall end.   70
In shady woods I'll sit and sing,
And things that past to mind I'll bring.
Once young and pleasant, as are you,
But former toys (no joys) adieu.
My age I will not once lament,   75
But sing, my time so near is spent.
And from the top bough take my flight
Into a country beyond sight,
Where old ones instantly grow young,
And there with seraphims set song;   80
No seasons cold, nor storms they see;
But spring lasts to eternity.
When each of you shall in your nest
Among your young ones take your rest,
In chirping language, oft them tell,   85
You had a dam that loved you well,
That did what could be done for young,
And nursed you up till you were strong,
And 'fore she once would let you fly,
She showed you joy and misery;   90
Taught what was good, and what was ill,
What would save life, and what would kill.
Thus gone, amongst you I may live,
And dead, yet speak, and counsel give:
Farewell, my birds, farewell adieu,   95
I happy am, if well with you.

                              A. B.

IN MEMORY OF MY DEAR GRANDCHILD ELIZABETH BRADSTREET, WHO DECEASED AUGUST, 1665, BEING A YEAR AND HALF OLD

Farewell dear babe, my heart's too much content,
Farewell sweet babe, the pleasure of mine eye,
Farewell fair flower that for a space was lent,
Then ta'en away unto eternity.
Blest babe, why should I once bewail thy fate,   10
Or sigh thy days so soon were terminate,
Sith thou art settled in an everlasting state.

2

By nature trees do rot when they are grown,
And plums and apples thoroughly ripe do fall,
And corn and grass are in their season mown,   15
And time brings down what is both strong and tall.
But plants new set to be eradicate,
And buds new blown to have so short a date,
Is by His hand alone that guides nature and fate.

IN MEMORY OF MY DEAR
GRANDCHILD ANNE BRADSTREET
WHO DECEASED JUNE 20, 1669,
BEING THREE YEARS AND
SEVEN MONTHS OLD   5

With troubled heart and trembling hand I write,
The heavens have changed to sorrow my delight.
How oft with disappointment have I met,
When I on fading things my hopes have set.
Experience might 'fore this have made me wise,   10
To value things according to their price.
Was ever stable joy yet found below?
Or perfect bliss without mixture of woe?
I knew she was but as a withering flower,
That's here today, perhaps gone in an hour;   15
Like as a bubble, or the brittle glass,
Or like a shadow turning as it was.
More fool then I to look on that was lent
As if mine own, when thus impermanent.
Farewell dear child, thou ne'er shall come to me,   20
But yet a while, and I shall go to thee;
Mean time my throbbing heart's cheered up with this:
Thou with thy Saviour art in endless bliss.

ON MY DEAR GRANDCHILD
SIMON BRADSTREET, WHO DIED
ON 16 NOVEMBER, 1669, BEING BUT
A MONTH, AND ONE DAY OLD

No sooner came, but gone, and fall'n asleep,   5
Acquaintance short, yet parting caused us weep;
Three flowers, two scarcely blown, the last i' th' bud,
Cropt by th' Almighty's hand; yet is He good.
With dreadful awe before Him let's be mute,
Such was His will, but why, let's not dispute,   10
With humble hearts and mouths put in the dust,
Let's say He's merciful as well as just.
He will return and make up all our losses,
And smile again after our bitter crosses
Go pretty babe, go rest with sisters twain;   15
Among the blest in endless joys remain.

A. B.

TO THE MEMORY OF MY DEAR DAUGHTER-IN-LAW, MRS. MERCY BRADSTREET, WHO DECEASED SEPT. 6, 1669, IN THE 28 YEAR OF HER AGE

And live I still to see relations gone,
And yet survive to sound this wailing tone;
Ah, woe is me, to write thy funeral song,
Who might in reason yet have lived long,
I saw the branches lopped the tree now fall,   10
I stood so nigh, it crushed me down withal.
My bruised heart lies sobbing at the root,
That thou, dear son, hath lost both tree and fruit.
Thou, then on seas sailing to foreign coast,
Was ignorant what riches thou hadst lost.   15
But ah too soon those heavy tidings fly,
To strike thee with amazing misery;
Oh, how I sympathize with thy sad heart,
And in thy griefs still bear a second part;
I lost a daughter dear, but thou a wife,   20
Who loved thee more (it seemed) than her own life.
Thou being gone, she longer could not be,
Because her soul she'd sent along with thee.
One week she only passed in pain and woe,
And then her sorrows all at once did go;   25
A babe she left before she soared above,
The fifth and last pledge of her dying love,
Ere nature would, it hither did arrive,
No wonder it no longer did survive.
So with her children four, she's now at rest,   30
All freed from grief (I trust) among the blest;
She one hath left, a joy to thee and me,

The heavens vouchsafe she may so ever be.
Cheer up, dear son, thy fainting bleeding heart,
In Him alone that caused all this smart;   35
What though thy strokes full sad and grievous be,
He knows it is the best for thee and me.

A. B.

TO MY DEAR CHILDREN

This book by any yet unread,
I leave for you when I am dead,
That being gone, here you may find
What was your living mother's mind.   5
Make use of what I leave in love,
And God shall bless you from above.
A. B.

My dear children,

I, knowing by experience that the exhortations of parents take most effect when the speakers leave to speak, and those especially sink deepest which are spoke latest, and being ignorant whether on my death bed I shall have opportunity to speak to any of you, much less to all, thought it the best, whilst I was able, to compose some short matters (for what else to call them I know not) and bequeath to you, that when I am no more with you, yet I may be daily in your remembrance (although that is the least in my aim in what I now do), but that you may gain some spiritual advantage by my experience. I have not studied in this you read to show my skill, but to declare the truth, not to set forth myself, but the glory of God. If I had minded the former, it had been perhaps better pleasing to you, but seeing the last is the best, let it be best pleasing to you.

The method I will observe shall be this: I will begin with God's dealing with me from my childhood to this day.

In my young years, about 6 or 7 as I take it, I began to make conscience of my ways, and what I knew was sinful, as lying, disobedience to parents, etc., I avoided it. If at any time I was overtaken with the like evils, it was as a great trouble, and I could not be at rest 'till by prayer I had confessed it unto God. I was also troubled at the neglect of private duties though too often tardy that way. I also found much comfort in reading the Scriptures, especially those places I thought most concerned my condition, and as I grew to have more understanding, so the more solace I took in them.

In a long fit of sickness which I had on my bed I often communed with my heart and made my supplication to the most High who set me free from that affliction.

But as I grew up to be about 14 or 15, I found my heart more carnal, and sitting loose from God, vanity and the follies of youth take hold of me.

About 16, the Lord laid His hand sore upon me and smote me with the smallpox. When I was in my affliction, I besought the Lord and confessed my pride and vanity, and He was entreated of me and again restored me. But I rendered not to Him according to the benefit received.

After a short time I changed my condition and was married, and came into this country, where I found a new world and new manners, at which my heart rose. But after I was convinced it was the way of God, I submitted to it and joined to the church at Boston.

After some time I fell into a lingering sickness like a consumption together with a lameness, which correction I saw the Lord sent to humble and try me and do me good, and it was not altogether ineffectual.

It pleased God to keep me a long time without a child, which was a great grief to me and cost me many prayers and tears before I obtained one, and after him gave me many more of whom I now take the care, that as I have brought you into the world, and with great pains, weakness, cares, and fears brought you to this, I now travail in birth again of you till Christ be formed in you.

Among all my experiences of God's gracious dealings with me, I have constantly observed this, that He hath never suffered me long to sit loose from Him, but by one affliction or other hath made me look home, and search what was amiss; so usually thus it hath been with me that I have no sooner felt my heart out of order, but I have expected correction for it, which most commonly hath been upon my own person in sickness, weakness, pains, sometimes on my soul, in doubts and fears of God's displeasure and my sincerity towards Him; sometimes He hath smote a child with a sickness, sometimes chastened by losses in estate, and these times (through His great mercy) have been the times of my greatest getting and advantage; yea, I have found them the times when the Lord hath manifested the most love to me. Then have I gone to searching and have said with David, "Lord, search me and try me, see what ways of wickedness are in me, and lead me in the way everlasting," and seldom or never but I have found either some sin I lay under which God would have reformed, or some duty neglected which He would have performed, and by His help I have laid vows and bonds upon my soul to perform His righteous commands.

If at any time you are chastened of God, take it as thankfully and joyfully as in greatest mercies, for if ye be His, ye shall reap the greatest benefit by it. It hath been no small support to me in times of darkness when the Almighty hath hid His face from me that yet I have had abundance of sweetness and refreshment after affliction and more circumspection in my walking after I have been afflicted. I have been with God like an untoward child, that no longer than the rod has been on my back (or at least in sight) but I have been apt to forget Him and myself, too. Before I was afflicted, I went astray, but now I keep Thy statutes.

I have had great experience of God's hearing my prayers and returning comfortable answers to me, either in granting the thing I prayed for, or else in satisfying my mind without it, and I have been confident it hath been from Him, because I have found my heart through His goodness enlarged in thankfulness to Him.

I have often been perplexed that I have not found that constant joy in my pilgrimage and refreshing which I supposed most of the servants of God have, although He hath not left me altogether without the witness of His holy spirit, who hath oft given me His word and set to His seal that it shall be well with me. I have sometimes tasted of that hidden manna that the world knows not, and have set up my Ebenezer, and have resolved with myself that against such a promise, such tastes of sweetness, the gates of hell shall never prevail; yet have I many times sinkings and droopings, and not enjoyed that felicity that sometimes I have done. But when I have been in darkness and seen no light, yet have I desired to stay myself upon the Lord, and when I have been in sickness and pain, I have thought if the Lord would but lift up the light of His countenance upon me, although He ground me to powder, it would be but light to me; yea, oft have I thought were I in hell itself and could there find the love of God toward me, it would be a heaven. And could I have been in heaven without the love of God, it would have been a hell to me, for in truth it is the absence and presence of God that makes heaven or hell.

Many times hath Satan troubled me concerning the verity of the Scriptures, many times by atheism how I could know whether there was a God; I never saw any miracles to confirm me, and those which I read of, how did I know but they were feigned? That there is a God my reason would soon tell me by the wondrous works that I see, the vast frame of the heaven and the earth, the order of all things, night and day, summer and winter, spring and autumn, the daily providing for this great household upon the earth, the preserving and directing of all to its proper end. The consideration of these things would with amazement certainly resolve me that there is an Eternal Being. But how should I know He is such a God as I worship in Trinity, and such a Saviour as I rely upon? Though this hath thousands of times been suggested to me, yet God hath helped me over. I have argued thus with myself. That there is a God, I see. If ever this God hath revealed himself, it must be in His word, and this must be it or none. Have I not found that operation by it that no human invention can work upon the soul, hath not judgments befallen divers who have scorned and contemned it, hath it not been preserved through all ages maugre all the heathen tyrants and all of the enemies who have opposed it? Is there any story but that which shows the beginnings of times, and how the world came to be as we see? Do we not know the prophecies in it fulfilled which could not have been so long foretold by any but God Himself?

When I have got over this block, then have I another put in my way, that admit this be the true God whom we worship, and that be his word, yet why may not the Popish religion be the right? They have the same God, the same Christ, the same word. They only enterpret it one way, we another.

This hath sometimes stuck with me, and more it would, but the vain fooleries that are in their religion together with their lying miracles and cruel persecutions of the saints, which admit were they as they term them, yet not so to be dealt withal.

The consideration of these things and many the like would soon turn me to my own religion again.

But some new troubles I have had since the world has been filled with blasphemy and sectaries, and some who have been accounted sincere Christians have been carried away with them, that sometimes I have said, "Is there faith upon the earth?" and I have not known what to think; but then I have remembered the works of Christ that so it must be, and if it were possible, the very elect should be deceived. "Behold," saith our Saviour, "I have told you before." That hath stayed my heart, and I can now say, "Return, O my Soul, to thy rest, upon this rock Christ Jesus will I build my faith, and if I perish, I perish"; but I know all the Powers of Hell shall never prevail against it. I know whom I have trusted, and whom I have believed, and that He is able to keep that I have committed to His charge.

Now to the King, immortal, eternal and invisible, the only wise God, be honour, and glory for ever and ever, Amen.

This was written in much sickness and weakness, and is very weakly and imperfectly done, but if you can pick any benefit out of it, it is the mark which I aimed at.

HERE FOLLOW SEVERAL OCCASIONAL MEDITATIONS

1

By night when others soundly slept,
And had at once both ease and rest,
My waking eyes were open kept   5
And so to lie I found it best.

2

I sought Him whom my soul did love,
With tears I sought Him earnestly;
He bowed His ear down from above.
In vain I did not seek or cry.   10

3

My hungry soul He filled with good,
He in His bottle put my tears,
My smarting wounds washed in His blood,
And banished thence my doubts and fears.

4

What to my Savior shall I give,   15
Who freely hath done this for me?
I'll serve Him here whilst I shall live
And love Him to eternity.

FOR DELIVERANCE FROM A FEVER

When sorrows had begirt me round,
And pains within and out,
When in my flesh no part was found,
Then didst Thou rid me out.   5
My burning flesh in sweat did boil,
My aching head did break,
From side to side for ease I toil,
So faint I could not speak.
Beclouded was my soul with fear   10
Of Thy displeasure sore,
Nor could I read my evidence
Which oft I read before.
"Hide not Thy face from me!" I cried,
"From burnings keep my soul.   15
Thou know'st my heart, and hast me tried;
I on Thy mercies roll."
"O heal my soul," Thou know'st I said,
"Though flesh consume to nought,
What though in dust it shall be laid,   20
To glory t' shall be brought."
Thou heard'st, Thy rod Thou didst remove
And spared my body frail,
Thou show'st to me Thy tender love,
My heart no more might quail.   25
O, praises to my mighty God,
Praise to my Lord, I say,
Who hath redeemed my soul from pit,
Praises to Him for aye.

FROM ANOTHER SORE FIT

In my distress I sought the Lord
When naught on earth could comfort give,
And when my soul these things abhorred,
Then, Lord, Thou said'st unto me, "Live."   5

Thou knowest the sorrows that I felt;
My plaints and groans were heard of Thee,
And how in sweat I seemed to melt
Thou help'st and Thou regardest me.

My wasted flesh Thou didst restore,   10
My feeble loins didst gird with strength,
Yea, when I was most low and poor,
I said I shall praise Thee at length.

What shall I render to my God
For all His bounty showed to me?   15
Even for His mercies in His rod,
Where pity most of all I see.

My heart I wholly give to Thee;
O make it fruitful, faithful Lord.
My life shall dedicated be   20
To praise in thought, in deed, in word.

Thou know'st no life I did require
Longer than still Thy name to praise,
Nor ought on earth worthy desire,
In drawing out these wretched days.   25

Thy name and praise to celebrate,
O Lord, for aye is my request.
O grant I do it in this state,
And then with Thee, which is the best.

DELIVERANCE FROM A FIT OF FAINTING

Worthy art Thou, O Lord, of praise,
   But ah! It's not in me.
My sinking heart I pray Thee raise
   So shall I give it Thee.   5

My life as spider's webb's cut off,
   Thus fainting have I said,
And living man no more shall see
   But be in silence laid.

My feeble spirit Thou didst revive,   10
   My doubting Thou didst chide,
And though as dead mad'st me alive,
   I here a while might 'bide.

Why should I live but to Thy praise?
   My life is hid with Thee.   15
O Lord, no longer be my days
   Than I may fruitful be.

MEDITATIONS WHEN MY SOUL HATH BEEN REFRESHED WITH THE CONSOLATIONS WHICH THE WORLD KNOWS NOT

Lord, why should I doubt any more when Thou hast given me such assured pledges of Thy love? First, Thou art my Creator, I Thy creature, Thou my master, I Thy servant. But hence arises not my comfort, Thou art my Father, I Thy child; "Ye shall be My sons and daughters," saith the Lord Almighty. Christ is my brother, I ascend unto my Father, and your Father, unto my God and your God; but lest this should not be enough, thy maker is thy husband. Nay more, I am a member of His body, He my head. Such privileges had not the Word of Truth made them known, who or where is the man that durst in his heart have presumed to have thought it? So wonderful are these thoughts that my spirit fails in me at the consideration thereof, and I am confounded to think that God, who hath done so much for me, should have so little from me. But this is my comfort, when I come to Heaven, I shall understand perfectly what He hath done for me, and then shall I be able to praise Him as I ought. Lord, having this hope, let me purify myself as Thou art pure, and let me be no more afraid of death, but even desire to be dissolved and be with Thee, which is best of all.

July 8th., 1656

I had a sore fit of fainting, which lasted 2 or 3 days, but not in that extremity which at first it took me, and so much the sorer it was to me because my dear husband was from home (who is my chiefest comforter on earth) but my God, who never failed me, was not absent but helped me and graciously manifested His love to me, which I dare not pass by without remembrance, that it may be a support to me when I shall have occasion to read this hereafter and to others that shall read it when I shall possess that I now hope for, that so they may be encouraged to trust in Him who is the only portion of His servants.

O Lord, let me never forget Thy goodness, nor question Thy faithfulness to me, for Thou art my God, Thou hast said, and shall not I believe it?

Thou hast given me a pledge of that inheritance Thou hast promised to bestow upon me. O never let Satan prevail against me, but strengthen my faith in Thee till I shall attain the end of my hopes, even the salvation of my soul. Come, Lord Jesus, come quickly.

What God is like to Him I serve?
What Saviour like to mine?
O never let me from Thee swerve,
For truly I am Thine.

My thankful mouth shall speak Thy praise,   5
My tongue shall talk of Thee;
On high my heart O do Thou raise
For what Thou'st done for me.

Go worldlings to your vanities,
And heathen to your gods;   10
Let them help in adversities
And sanctify their rods;

My God He is not like to yours
Yourselves shall judges be;
I find His love, I know His power—   15
A succorer of me

He is not man that He should lie,
Nor son of man to unsay;
His word He plighted hath on high,
And I shall live for aye.   20

And for His sake that faithful is,
That died but now doth live,
The first and last that lives for aye,
Me lasting life shall give.

My soul, rejoice thou in thy God,
  Boast of Him all the day,
Walk in His law, and kiss His rod
  Cleave close to Him alway.

What though thy outward man decay,   5
  Thy inward shall wax strong.
Thy body vile it shall be changed,
  And glorious made erelong.

With angel's wings thy soul shall mount
  To bliss unseen by eye,   10
And drink at unexhausted fount
  Of joy unto eternity.

Thy tears shall all be dried up,
  Thy sorrows all shall fly,
Thy sins shall ne'er be summoned up   15
  Nor come in memory.

Then shall I know what Thou hast done
  For me, unworthy me,
And praise Thee shall ev'n as I ought
  For wonders that I see.   20

Base world, I trample on thy face,
  Thy glory I despise,
No gain I find in ought below,
  For God hath made me wise.

Come Jesus quickly, Blessed Lord.   25
  Thy face when shall I see?
O let me count each hour a day
  'Till I dissolved be.

August 28, 1656

After much weakness and sickness when my spirits were worn out, and many times my faith weak likewise, the Lord was pleased to uphold my drooping heart, and to manifest His love to me, and this is that which stays my soul that this condition that I am in is the best for me, for God doth not afflict willingly, nor take delight in grieving the children of men; He hath no benefit by my adversity, nor is He the better for my prosperity, but He doth it for my advantage, and that I may be a gainer by it. And if He knows that weakness and a frail body is the best to make me a vessel fit for His use why should I not bear it, not only willingly but joyfully? The Lord knows I dare not desire that health that sometimes I have had, lest my heart should be drawn from Him, and set upon the world.

Now I can wait, looking every day when my Saviour shall call for me. Lord grant that while I live I may do that service I am able in this frail body, and be in continual expectation of my change, and let me never forget Thy great love to my soul so lately expressed, when I could lie down and bequeath my soul to Thee, and death seemed no terrible thing. O let me ever see Thee that art invisible, and I shall not be unwilling to come, though by so rough a messenger.

May 11, 1657

I had a sore sickness and weakness took hold of me which hath by fits lasted all this spring till this 11, May; yet hath my God given me many a respite and some ability to perform the duties I owe to Him and the work of my family.

Many a refreshment have I found in this my weary pilgrimage, and in this Valley of Baca many pools of water. That which now I chiefly labour for is a contented thankful heart under my affliction and weakness, seeing it is the will of God it should be thus. Who am I that I should repine at His pleasure, especially seeing it is for my spiritual advantage, for I hope my soul shall flourish while my body decays, and the weakness of this outward man shall be a means to strengthen my inner man.

Yet a little while and He that shall come will come and will not tarry.

May 13, 1657

As spring the winter doth succeed
And leaves the naked trees do dress,
The earth all black is clothed in green.
At sunshine each their joy express. 5

My sun's returned with healing wings,
My soul and body doth rejoice,
My heart exults and praises sings
To Him that heard my wailing voice.

My winter's past, my storms are gone, 10
And former clouds seem now all fled,
But if they must eclipse again,
I'll run where I was succored.

I have a shelter from the storm,
A shadow from the fainting heat, 15
I have access unto His throne,
Who is a God so wondrous great.

O hath Thou made my pilgrimage
Thus pleasant, fair, and good,
Blessed me in youth and elder age, 20
My Baca made a springing flood.

O studious am what I shall do
To show my duty with delight;
All I can give is but Thine own
And at the most a simple mite. 25

Sept. 30, 1657

It pleased God to visit me with my old distemper of weakness and fainting, but not in that sore manner sometimes He hath. I desire not only willingly but thankfully to submit to Him, for I trust it is out of His abundant love to my straying soul which in prosperity is too much in love with the world. I have found by experience I can no more live without correction than without food. Lord, with Thy correction give instruction and amendment, and then Thy strokes shall be welcome. I have not been refined in the furnace of affliction as some have been, but have rather been preserved with sugar than brine, yet will He preserve me to His heavenly kingdom.

Thus, dear children, have ye seen the many sicknesses and weaknesses that I have passed through to the end that if you meet with the like you may have recourse to the same God who hath heard and delivered me, and will do the like for you if you trust in Him; and when He shall deliver you out of distress, forget not to give Him thanks, but to walk more closely with Him than before. This is the desire of your loving mother.

A. B.

UPON MY SON SAMUEL HIS GOING
FOR ENGLAND, NOV. 6, 1657

Thou mighty God of sea and land,
I here resign into Thy hand
The son of prayers, of vows, of tears,   5
The child I stayed for many years.
Thou heard'st me then and gav'st him me;
Hear me again, I give him Thee.
He's mine, but more, O Lord, Thine own,
For sure Thy grace on him is shown.   10
No friend I have like Thee to trust,
For mortal helps are brittle dust.
Preserve, O Lord, from storms and wrack,
Protect him there, and bring him back,
And if Thou shalt spare me a space   15
That I again may see his face,
Then shall I celebrate Thy praise
And bless Thee for't even all my days.
If otherwise I go to rest,
Thy will be done, for that is best.   20
Persuade my heart I shall him see
Forever happified with Thee.

May 11, 1661

It hath pleased God to give me a long time of respite for these 4 years that I have had no great fit of sickness, but this year from the middle of January till May I have been by fits very ill and weak. The first of this month I had a fever seized upon me which indeed was the longest and sorest that ever I had, lasting 4 days, and the weather being very hot made it the more tedious, but it pleased the Lord to support my heart in His goodness, and hear my prayers, and to deliver me out of adversity. But alas! I cannot render unto the Lord according to all His loving kindness, nor take the cup of salvation with thanksgiving as I ought to do. Lord, Thou that knowest all things know'st that I desire to testify my thankfulness not only in word, but in deed, that my conversation may speak that Thy vows are upon me.

My thankful heart with glorying tongue
Shall celebrate Thy name,
Who hath restored, redeemed, recured
From sickness, death, and pain.

I cried, Thou seem'st to make some stay,   5
I sought more earnestly
And in due time Thou succour'st me
And sent'st me help from high.

Lord, whilst my fleeting time shall last,
Thy goodness let me tell,   10
And new experience I have gained
My future doubts repel.

An humble, faithful life, O Lord,
Forever let me walk;

Let my obedience testify   15
My praise lies not in talk.

Accept, O Lord, my simple mite,
For more I cannot give.
What Thou bestow'st I shall restore,
For of thine alms I live.   20

FOR THE RESTORATION OF MY DEAR HUSBAND FROM A BURNING AGUE, JUNE 1, 1661

Whence fears and sorrows me beset
Then didst Thou rid me out;   5
When heart did faint and spirits quail,
Thou comforts me about.

Thou rais'st him up I feared to lose,
Regav'st me him again,
Distempers Thou didst chase away,   10
With strength didst him sustain.

My thankful heart with pen record
The goodness of thy God,
Let thy obedience testify
He taught thee by His rod.   15

And with His staff did thee support
That thou by both may'st learn,
And 'twixt the good and evil way
At last, thou might'st discern.

Praises to Him who hath not left   20
My soul as destitute,
Nor turned His ear away from me,
But granted hath my suit.

UPON MY DAUGHTER HANNAH WIGGIN HER RECOVERY FROM A DANGEROUS FEVER

Blest be Thy name who didst restore
 To health my daughter dear,   5
When death did seem ev'n to approach,
 And life was ended near.

Grant she remember what Thou'st done
 And celebrate Thy praise
And let her conversation say   10
 She loves Thee all Thy days.

ON MY SON'S RETURN OUT OF
ENGLAND, JULY 17, 1661

All praise to Him who hath now turned
My fears to joys, my sighs to song,
My tears to smiles, my sad to glad;   5
He's come for whom I waited long.

Thou didst preserve him as he went,
In raging storms didst safely keep,
Didst that ship bring to quiet port.
The other sank low in the deep.   10

From dangers great Thou didst him free
Of pirates who were near at hand,
And order'st so the adverse wind
That he before them got to land.

In country strange Thou didst provide,   15
And friends raised him in every place,
And courtesies of sundry sorts
From such as 'fore ne'er saw his face.

In sickness when he lay full sore,
His help and his physician wert.   20
When royal ones that time did die,
Thou healed'st his flesh and cheered his heart.

From trouble and encumbers Thou
Without all fraud didst set him free,
That without scandal he might come   25
To th' land of his nativity.

On eagles' wings him hither brought
Through want and dangers manifold,
And thus hath granted my request
That I Thy mercies might behold.   30

O help me pay my vows, O Lord,
That ever I may thankful be
And may put him in mind of what
Thou'st done for him, and so for me.

In both our hearts erect a frame   35
Of duty and of thankfulness,
That all Thy favours great received
Our upright walking may express.

   O Lord, grant that I may never forget Thy loving kindness
in this particular, and how graciously Thou hast answered
my desires.

UPON MY DEAR AND LOVING HUSBAND HIS GOING INTO ENGLAND JAN. 16, 1661

O thou Most High who rulest all
And hear'st the prayers of thine,   5
O hearken, Lord, unto my suit
And my petition sign.

Into Thy everlasting arms
Of mercy I commend
Thy servant, Lord. Keep and preserve   10
My husband, my dear friend.

At Thy command, O Lord, he went,
Nor nought could keep him back.
Then let Thy promise joy his heart,
O help and be not slack.   15

Uphold my heart in Thee, O God.
Thou art my strength and stay,
Thou see'st how weak and frail I am,
Hide not Thy face away.

I in obedience to Thy will   20
Thou knowest did submit.
It was my duty so to do;
O Lord, accept of it.

Unthankfulness for mercies past
Impute Thou not to me.   25
O Lord, Thou know'st my weak desire
Was to sing praise to Thee.

Lord, be Thou pilot to the ship
And send them prosperous gales.
In storms and sickness, Lord, preserve.   30
Thy goodness never fails.

Unto Thy work he hath in hand
Lord, grant Thou good success
And favour in their eyes to whom
He shall make his address.   35

Remember, Lord, Thy folk whom Thou
To wilderness hast brought;
Let not Thine own inheritance
Be sold away for nought.

But tokens of Thy favour give,   40
With joy send back my dear
That I and all Thy servants may
Rejoice with heavenly cheer.

Lord, let my eyes see once again
Him whom Thou gavest me   45
That we together may sing praise
Forever unto Thee.

And the remainder of our days
Shall consecrated be
With an engaged heart to sing   50
All praises unto Thee.

IN MY SOLITARY HOURS IN MY
DEAR HUSBAND HIS ABSENCE

O Lord, Thou hear'st my daily moan
   And see'st my dropping tears.
My troubles all are Thee before,   5
   My longings and my fears.

Thou hitherto hast been my God;
   Thy help my soul hath found.
Though loss and sickness me assailed,
   Through Thee I've kept my ground.   10

And Thy abode Thou'st made with me;
   With Thee my soul can talk;
In secret places Thee I find
   Where I do kneel or walk.

Though husband dear be from me gone,   15
   Whom I do love so well,
I have a more beloved one
   Whose comforts far excel.

O stay my heart on Thee, my God,
   Uphold my fainting soul,   20
And when I know not what to do,
   I'll on Thy mercies roll.

My weakness, Thou dost know full well
   Of body and of mind;
I in this world no comfort have,   25
   But what from Thee I find.

Though children Thou has given me,
　　And friends I have also,
Yet if I see Thee not through them,
　　They are no joy, but woe. 30

O shine upon me, blessed Lord,
　　Ev'n for my Saviour's sake;
In Thee alone is more than all,
　　And there content I'll take.

O hear me, Lord, in this request 35
　　As Thou before hast done,
Bring back my husband, I beseech,
　　As Thou didst once my son.

So shall I celebrate Thy praise
　　Ev'n while my days shall last 40
And talk to my beloved one
　　Of all Thy goodness past.

So both of us Thy kindness, Lord,
　　With praises shall recount
And serve Thee better than before 45
　　Whose blessings thus surmount.

But give me, Lord, a better heart,
　　Then better shall I be,
To pay the vows which I do owe
　　Forever unto Thee. 50

Unless Thou help, what can I do
　　But still my frailty show?
If Thou assist me, Lord, I shall
　　Return Thee what I owe.

IN THANKFUL ACKNOWLEDGMENT
FOR THE LETTERS I RECEIVED
FROM MY HUSBAND OUT OF
ENGLAND

O Thou that hear'st the prayers of Thine   5
And 'mongst them hast regarded mine,
Hast heard my cries and seen my tears,
Has known my doubts and all my fears,
Thou hast relieved my fainting heart
Nor paid me after my desert;   10
Thou hast to shore him safely brought
For whom I Thee so oft besought.
Thou wast the pilot to the ship,
And raised him up when he was sick,
And hope Thou'st given of good success   15
In this his business and address,
And that Thou wilt return him back
Whose presence I so much do lack.
For all these mercies I Thee praise
And so desire ev'n all my days.   20

IN THANKFUL REMEMBRANCE
FOR MY DEAR HUSBAND'S SAFE
ARRIVAL. SEPT. 3, 1662

What shall I render to Thy name
    Or how Thy praises speak? 5
My thanks how shall I testify?
    O Lord, Thou know'st I'm weak.

I owe so much, so little can
    Return unto Thy name,
Confusion seizes on my soul, 10
    And I am filled with shame.

O Thou that hearest prayers, Lord,
    To Thee shall come all flesh,
Thou hast me heard and answered,
    My plaints have had access. 15

What did I ask for but Thou gav'st?
    What could I more desire?
But thankfulness even all my days
    I humbly this require.

Thy mercies, Lord, have been so great 20
    In number numberless,
Impossible for to recount
    Or any way express.

O help Thy saints that sought Thy face
    T' return unto Thee praise 25
And walk before Thee as they ought,
    In strict and upright ways.

FOR MY DEAR SON SIMON
BRADSTREET

Parents perpetuate their lives in their posterity and their manners; in their imitation children do naturally rather follow the failings than the virtues of their predecessors, but I am persuaded better things of you. You once desired me to leave something for you in writing that you might look upon, when you should see me no more; I could think of nothing more fit for you nor of more ease to myself than these short meditations following. Such as they are, I bequeath to you; small legacies are accepted by true friends, much more by dutiful children. I have avoided encroaching upon others' conceptions because I would leave you nothing but mine own, though in value they fall short of all in this kind; yet I presume they will be better prized by you for the author's sake. The Lord bless you with grace here and crown you with glory hereafter, that I may meet you with rejoicing at that great day of appearing, which is the continual prayer of

your affectionate mother,

A. B.

March 20, 1664

MEDITATIONS DIVINE
AND MORAL

I

There is no object that we see, no action that we do, no good that we enjoy, no evil that we feel or fear, but we may make some spiritual advantage of all; and he that makes such improvement is wise as well as pious.

2

Many can speak well, but few can do well. We are better scholars in the theory than the practic part, but he is a true Christian that is a proficient in both.

3

Youth is the time of getting, middle age of improving and old age of spending; a negligent youth is usually attended by an ignorant middle age, and both by an empty old age. He that hath nothing to feed on but vanity and lies must needs lie down in the bed of sorrow.

4

A ship that bears much sail and little or no ballast is easily overset, and that man whose head hath great abilities and his heart little or no grace is in danger of foundering.

5

It is reported of the peacock that, priding himself in his gay feathers, he ruffles them up, but spying his black feet, he soon lets fall his plumes; so he that glories in his gifts and adornings should look upon his corruptions, and that will damp his high thoughts.

6

The finest bread hath the least bran, the purest honey the least wax, and the sincerest Christian the least self-love.

7

The hireling that labours all the day comforts himself that when night comes he shall both take his rest and receive his reward; the painful Christian that hath wrought hard in God's vineyard and hath born the heat and drought of the day, when he perceives his sun apace to decline and the shadows of his evening to be stretched out, lifts up his head with joy, knowing his refreshing is at hand.

8

Downy beds make drowsy persons, but hard lodging keeps the eyes open; a prosperous state makes a secure Christian, but adversity makes him consider.

9

Sweet words are like honey: a little may refresh, but too much gluts the stomach.

10

Diverse children have their different natures: some are like flesh which nothing but salt will keep from putrefaction, some again like tender fruits that are best preserved with sugar. Those parents are wise that can fit their nurture according to their nature.

11

That town which thousands of enemies without hath not been able to take hath been delivered up by one traitor within, and that man which all the temptations of Satan without could not hurt hath been foiled by one lust within.

12

Authority without wisdom is like a heavy axe without an edge: fitter to bruise than polish.

13

The reason why Christians are so loath to exchange this world for a better is because they have more sense than faith: they see what they enjoy; they do but hope for that which is to come.

14

If we had no winter, the spring would not be so pleasant; if we did not sometimes taste of adversity, prosperity would not be so welcome.

15

A low man can go upright under that door where a taller is glad to stoop; so a man of weak faith and mean abilities may undergo a cross more patiently than he that excels him both in gifts and graces.

16

That house which is not often swept makes the cleanly inhabitant soon loath it, and that heart which is not continually purifying itself is no fit temple for the spirit of God to dwell in.

17

Few men are so humble as not to be proud of their abilities, and nothing will abase them more than this: what hast thou, but what thou hast received? Come, give an account of thy stewardship.

18

He that will undertake to climb up a steep mountain with a great burden on his back will find it a wearisome if not an impossible task; so he that thinks to mount to heaven clogged with the cares and riches of this life, 'tis no wonder if he faint by the way.

19

Corn, till it have past through the mill and been ground to powder, is not fit for bread. God so deals with his servants: he grinds them with grief and pain till they turn to dust, and then are they fit manchet for his mansion.

20

God hath suitable comforts and supports for His children according to their several conditions. If He will make His face to shine upon them, He then makes them lie down in green pastures and leads them besides the still waters. If they stick in deep mire and clay, and all His waves and billows go over their heads, He then leads them to the rock which is higher than they.

21

He that walks among briars and thorns will be very careful where he sets his foot, and he that passes through the wilderness of this world had need ponder all his steps.

22

Want of prudence as well as piety hath brought men into great inconveniences, but he that is well stored with both seldom is so ensnared.

23

The skillful fisher hath his several baits for several fish, but there is a hook under all; Satan, that great Angler, hath his sundry baits for sundry tempers of men, which they all catch greedily at, but few perceives the hook till it be too late.

24

There is no new thing under the sun: there is nothing that can be said or done, but either that or something like it hath been both done and said before.

25

An aching head requires a soft pillow, and a drooping heart a strong support.

26

A sore finger may disquiet the whole body, but an ulcer within destroys it; so an enemy without may disturb a commonwealth, but dissentions within overthrow it.

27

It is a pleasant thing to behold the light, but sore eyes are not able to look upon it; the pure in heart shall see God, but the defiled in conscience shall rather choose to be buried under rocks and mountains than to behold the presence of the Lamb.

28

Wisdom with an inheritance is good, but wisdom without an inheritance is better than an inheritance without wisdom.

29

Lightning doth usually precede thunder, and storms rain, and strokes do not often fall till after threatening.

30

Yellow leaves argue want of sap and gray hairs want of moisture; so dry and sapless performances are symptoms of little spiritual vigor.

31

Iron, till it be thoroughly heat, is uncapable to be wrought; so God sees good to cast some men into the furnace of affliction and then beats them on His anvil into what frame he pleases.

32

Ambitious men are like hops that never rest climbing so long
as they have anything to stay upon, but take away their props,
and they are of all the most dejected.

33

Much labour wearies the body, and many thoughts oppress
the mind; man aims at profit by the one and content in the
other, but often misses of both and finds nothing but vanity
and vexation of spirit.

34

Dim eyes are the concomitants of old age, and shortsighted-
ness in those that are eyes of a republic fortells a declining
state.

35

We read in Scriptures of three sorts of arrows: the arrow of
an enemy, the arrow of pestilence, and the arrow of a slander-
ous tongue. The two first kill the body, the last the good
name; the two former leave a man when he is once dead, but
the last mangles him in his grave.

36

Sore labourers have hard hands and old sinners have brawny
consciences.

37

Wickedness comes to its height by degrees. He that dares say
of a less sin "Is it not a little one?" will ere long say of a
greater, "Tush, God regards it not."

38

Some children are hardly weaned; although the teat be rubbed with wormwood or mustard, they will either wipe it off, or else suck down sweet and bitter together. So is it with some Christians: let God embitter all the sweets of this life, that so they might feed upon more substantial food, yet they are so childishly sottish that they are still hugging and sucking these empty breasts that God is forced to hedge up their way with thorns or lay affliction on their loins that so they might shake hands with the world, before it bid them farewell.

39

A prudent mother will not cloth her little child with a long and cumbersome garment; she easily forsees what events it is like to produce, at the best, but falls and bruises or perhaps somewhat worse. Much more will the allwise God proportion His dispensations according to the stature and strength of the person He bestows them on. Large endowments of honour, wealth, or a healthful body would quite overthrow some weak Christian; therefore God cuts their garments short to keep them in such a trim that they might run the ways of His commandment.

40

The spring is a lively emblem of the resurrection: after a long winter we see the leafless trees and dry stocks (at the approach of the sun) to resume their former vigor and beauty in a more ample manner than what they lost in the autumn; so shall it be at that great day after a long vacation, when the Sun of righteousness shall appear; those dry bones shall arise in far more glory than that which they lost at their creation, and in this transcends the spring that their leaf shall never fail nor their sap decline.

41

A wise father will not lay a burden on a child of seven years old which he knows is enough for one of twice his strength; much less will our heavenly Father (who knows our mold) lay such afflictions upon his weak children as would crush them to the dust, but according to the strength he will proportion the load. As God hath His little children, so He hath His strong men, such as are come to a full stature in Christ, and many times He imposes weighty burdens on their shoulders, and yet they go upright under them, but it matters not whether the load be more or less if God afford His help.

42

"I have seen an end of all perfection," said the royal prophet, but he never said, "I have seen an end of all sinning." What he did say may be easily said by many, but what he did not say cannot truly be uttered by any.

43

Fire hath its force abated by water, not by wind, and anger must be allayed by cold words and not by blustering threats.

44

A sharp appetite and a thorough concoction is a sign of a healthful body; so a quick reception and a deliberate cogitation argues a sound mind.

45

We often see stones hang with drops not from any innate moisture, but from a thick air about them; so may we sometime see marble-hearted sinners seem full of contrition, but it is not from any dew of grace within but from some black clouds that impends them, which produces these sweating effects.

46

The words of the wise, saith Solomon, are as nails and as goads, both used for contrary ends; the one holds fast, the other puts forward. Such should be the precepts of the wise masters of assemblies to their hearers, not only to bid them hold fast the form of sound doctrine, but also so to run that they might obtain.

47

A shadow in the parching sun and a shelter in a blustering storm are of all seasons the most welcome; so a faithful friend in time of adversity is of all other most comfortable.

48

There is nothing admits of more admiration than God's various dispensation of His gifts among the sons of men, betwixt whom He hath put so vast a disproportion that they scarcely seem made of the same lump or sprung out of the loins of one Adam, some set in the highest dignity that mortality is capable of, and some again so base that they are viler than the earth, some so wise and learned that they seem like angels among men, and some again so ignorant and sottish that they are more like beasts than men, some pious saints, some incarnate devils, some exceeding beautiful, and some extremely deformed, some so strong and healthful that their bones are full of marrow and their breasts of milk, and some again so weak and feeble that while they live they are accounted among the dead; and no other reason can be given of all this but so it pleased Him whose will is the perfect rule of righteousness.

49

The treasures of this world may well be compared to husks, for they have no kernal in them, and they that feed upon them may soon stuff their throats, but cannot fill their bellies. They may be choked by them, but cannot be satisfied with them.

50

Sometimes the sun is only shadowed by a cloud that we cannot see his luster although we may walk by his light, but when he is set, we are in darkness till he arise again. So God doth sometime veil His face but for a moment that we cannot behold the light of His countenance as at some other time, yet He affords so much light as may direct our way, that we may go forwards to the city of habitation, but when He seems to set and be quite gone out of sight, then must we needs walk in darkness and see no light; yet then must we trust in the Lord and stay upon our God, and when the morning (which is the appointed time) is come, the Sun of righteousness will arise with healing in His wings.

51

The eyes and the ears are the inlets or doors of the soul, through which innumerable objects enter; yet is not that spacious room filled, neither doth it ever say it is enough, but like the daughters of the horseleach, cries, "Give, give"; and which is most strange, the more it receives, the more empty it finds itself and sees an impossibility ever to be filled but by Him in whom all fullness dwells.

52

Had not the wisest of men taught us this lesson that all is vanity and vexation of spirit, yet our own experience would soon have spelled it out, for what do we obtain of all these things, but it is with labour and vexation? When we enjoy them it is vanity and vexation, and if we loose them, then they are less than vanity and more than vexation, so that we have good cause often to repeat that sentence: vanity of vanities, vanity of vanities, all is vanity.

53

He that is to sail into a far country, although the ship, cabin, and provision be all convenient and comfortable for him, yet he hath no desire to make that his place of residence, but longs to put in at that port where his business lies. A Christian is sailing through this world unto his heavenly country, and here he hath many conveniences and comforts, but he must beware of desiring to make this the place of his abode, lest he meet with such tossings that may cause him to long for shore before he sees land. We must, therefore, be here as strangers and pilgrims, that we may plainly declare that we seek a city above and wait all the days of our appointed time till our change shall come.

54

He that never felt what it was to be sick or wounded doth not much care for the company of the physician or surgeon, but if he perceive a malady that threatens him with death, he will gladly entertain him whom he slighted before; so he that never felt the sickness of sin, nor the wounds of a guilty conscience cares not how far he keeps from him that hath skill to cure it, but when he finds his diseases to disrest him, and

that he must needs perish if he have no remedy, will unfeign-
edly bid him welcome that brings a plaster for his sore or a
cordial for his fainting.

55

We read of ten lepers that were cleansed but of one that re-
turned thanks; we are more ready to receive mercies than we
are to acknowledge them. Men can use great importunity
when they are in distresses and show great ingratitude after
their successes, but he that ordereth his conversation aright
will glorify him that heard him in the day of his trouble.

56

The remembrance of former deliverances is a great support in
present distresses. "He that delivered me," saith David, "from
the paw of the lion and the paw of the bear will deliver me
from this uncircumcised Philistine," and "He that hath de-
livered me," saith Paul, "will deliver me." God is the same
yesterday, today, and forever; we are the same that stand in
need of Him, today as well as yesterday, and so shall forever.

57

Great receipts call for great returns; the more that any man
is intrusted withal, the larger his accounts stands upon God's
score. It therefore behoves every man so to improve his talents
that when his great Master shall call him to reckoning, He
may receive His own with advantage.

58

Sin and shame ever go together. He that would be freed from
the last must be sure to shun the company of the first.

59

God doth many times both reward and punish for one and the same action, as we see in Jehu; he is rewarded with a kingdom to the fourth generation for taking vengeance on the house of Ahab; and "Yet a little while," saith God, "and I will avenge the blood of Jezreel upon the house of Jehu." He was rewarded for the matter, and yet punished for the manner, which should warn him that doth any special service for God to fix his eye on the command and not on his own ends, lest he meet with Jehu's reward, which will end in punishment.

60

He that would be content with a mean condition must not cast his eye upon one that is in a far better estate than himself, but let him look upon him that is lower than he is, and if he see, that such a one bears poverty comfortably, it will help to quiet him, but if that will not do, let him look on his own unworthiness and that will make him say with Jacob: I am less than the least of Thy mercies.

61

Corn is produced with much labour (as the husbandman well knows), and some land asks much more pains than some other doth to be brought into tilth; yet all must be ploughed and harrowed. Some children (like sour land) are of so tough and morose a disposition that the plough of correction must make long furrows on their back and the harrow of discipline go often over them before they be fit soil to sow the seed of morality much less of grace in them. But when by prudent nurture they are brought into a fit capacity, let the seed of good instruction and exhortation be sown in the spring of their youth, and a plentiful crop may be expected in the harvest of their years.

62

As a man is called the little world, so his heart may be called the little commonwealth; his more fixed and resolved thoughts are like to inhabitants, his slight and flitting thoughts are like passengers that travel to and fro continually; here is also the great court of justice erected, which is alway kept by conscience, who is both accuser, excuser, witness, and judge, whom no bribes can pervert nor flattery cause to favour, but as he finds the evidence, so he absolves or condemns; yea, so absolute is this court of judicature that there is no appeal from it, no not to the court of heaven itself, for if our conscience condemn us, He also who is greater than our conscience will do it much more, but he that would have boldness to go to the throne of grace to be accepted there must be sure to carry a certificate from the court of conscience that he stands right there.

63

He that would keep a pure heart and lead a blameless life must set himself alway in the awful presence of God. The consideration of His all-seeing eye will be a bridle to restrain from evil and spur to quicken on to good duties. We certainly dream of some remoteness betwixt God and us, or else we should not so often fail in our whole course of life as we do, but he that with David sets the Lord alway in his sight will not sin against Him.

64

We see in orchards some trees so fruitful that the weight of their burden is the breaking of their limbs, some again are but meanly loaden, and some have nothing to show but leaves only, and some among them are dry stock; so is it in the church, which is God's orchard; there are some eminent

Christians that are so frequent in good duties that many times, the weight thereof impairs both their bodies and estates, and there are some (and they sincere ones, too) who have not attained to that fruitfulness, although they aim at perfection, and again there are others that have nothing to commend them but only a gay profession, and these are but leavie Christians which are in as much danger of being cut down as the dry stock, for both cumber the ground.

65

We see in the firmament there is but one sun among a multitude of stars and those stars also to differ much one from the other in regard of bigness and brightness, yet all receive their light from that one sun; so is it in the church both militant and triumphant: there is but one Christ, who is the sun of righteousness, in the midst of an unnumerable company of saints and angels; those saints have their degrees, even in this life: some are stars of the first magnitude, and some of a less degree, and others (and they indeed the most in number) but small and obscure, yet all receive their luster (be it more or less) from that glorious sun that enlightens all in all, and if some of them shine so bright while they move on earth, how transcendently splendid shall they be when they are fixt in their heavenly spheres!

66

Men that have walked very extravagantly and at last bethink themselves of turning to God, the first thing which they eye is how to reform their ways rather than to beg forgiveness for their sins. Nature looks more at a compensation than at a pardon, but he that will not come for mercy without money and without price, but bring his filthy rags to barter for it, shall meet with miserable disappointment, going away empty bearing the reproach of his pride and folly.

67

All the works and doings of God are wonderful, but none more awful than His great work of election and reprobation; when we consider how many good parents have had bad children, and again how many bad parents have had pious children, it should make us adore the sovereignty of God, who will not be tied to time nor place, nor yet to persons, but takes and chooses, when and where and whom He pleases; it should also teach the children of godly parents to walk with fear and trembling, lest they through unbelief fall short of a promise; it may also be a support to such as have or had wicked parents, that if they abide not in unbelief, God is able to gaff them in. The upshot of all should make us with the apostle to admire the justice and mercy of God and say how unsearchable are His ways and His footsteps past finding out.

68

The gifts that God bestows on the sons of men are not only abused but most commonly employed for a clean contrary end than that which they were given for, as health, wealth, and honour, which might be so many steps to draw men to God in consideration of His bounty towards them, but have driven them the further from Him that they are ready to say: we are lords, we will come no more at Thee. If outward blessings be not as wings to help us mount upwards, they will certainly prove clogs and weights that will pull us lower downward.

69

All the comforts of this life may be compared to the gourd of Jonah, that notwithstanding we take great delight for a season in them and find their shadow very comfortable, yet there is some worm or other, of discontent, of fear, or grief that lies at the root, which in great part withers the pleasure which else we should take in them, and well it is that we perceive a decay in their greenness, for were earthly comforts permanent, who would look for heavenly?

70

All men are truly said to be tenants at will, and it may as truly be said that all have a lease of their lives, some longer, some shorter, as it pleases our great Landlord to let. All have their bounds set, over which they cannot pass, and till the expiration of that time, no dangers, no sickness, no pains, nor troubles shall put a period to our days. The certainty that that time will come, together with the uncertainty, how, where, and when, should make us so to number our days as to apply our hearts to wisdom, that when we are put out of these houses of clay we may be sure of an everlasting habitation that fades not away.

71

All weak and diseased bodies have hourly mementos of their mortality, but the soundest of men, have likewise their nightly monitor by the emblem of death, which is their sleep (for so is death often called), and not only their death, but their grave is lively represented before their eyes by beholding their bed, the morning may mind them of the resurrection, and the sun approaching of the appearing of the Sun of righteousness, at whose coming they shall all rise out of their beds, the long night shall fly away, and the day of eternity shall never end. Seeing these things must be, what manner of persons ought we to be, in all good conversation?

72

As the brands of a fire, if once severed, will of themselves go out although you use no other means to extinguish them, so distance of place together with length of time (if there be no intercourse) will cool the affections of intimate friends, though there should be no displeasance between them.

73

A good name is as a precious ointment, and it is a great favour to have a good repute among good men; yet it is not that which commends us to God, for by His balance we must be weighed, and by His judgment we must be tried, and as He passes the sentence, so shall we stand.

74

Well doth the apostle call riches "deceitful" riches, and they may truly be compared to deceitful friends who speak fair and promise much but perform nothing, and so leave those in the lurch that most relied on them; so is it with the wealth, honours, and pleasures of this world which miserably delude men and make them put great confidence in them, but when death threatens and distress lays hold upon them, they prove like the reeds of Egypt that pierce instead of supporting, like empty wells in the time of drought that those that go to find water in them return with their empty pitchers ashamed.

75

It is admirable to consider the power of faith, by which all things are (almost) possible to be done; it can remove mountains (if need were); it hath stayed the course of the sun, raised the dead, cast out devils, reversed the order of nature, quenched the violence of the fire, made the water become firm footing for Peter to walk on; nay, more than all these, it hath overcome the omnipotent Himself, as when Moses intercedes for the people, God saith to him, "Let me alone, that I may destroy them," as if Moses had been able by the hand of

faith to hold the everlasting arms of the mighty God of Jacob.
Yea Jacob himself when he wrestled with God face to face in
Penuel, "Let me go," saith that Angel. "I will not let thee go,"
replies Jacob, "till thou bless me." Faith is not only thus
potent but it is so necessary that without faith there is no
salvation; therefore with all our seekings and gettings, let
us above all seek to obtain this pearl of price.

76

Some Christians do by their lusts and corruptions as the
Israelites did by the Canaanites, not destroy them but put
them under tribute, for that they could do (as they thought)
with less hazard and more profit; but what was the issue,
they became a snare unto them, pricks in their eyes and thorns
in their sides, and at last overcame them and kept them under
slavery; so it is most certain that those that are disobedient
to the command of God and endeavour not to the utmost to
drive out all their accursed inmates but make a league with
them, they shall at last fall into perpetual bondage under
them unless the great deliverer Christ Jesus come to their
rescue.

77

God hath by his providence so ordered that no one country
hath all commodities within itself, but what it wants another
shall supply that so there may be a mutual commerce through
the world. As it is with countries so it is with men; there was
never yet any one man that had all excellences, let his parts
natural and acquired, spiritual and moral, be never so large,
yet he stands in need of something which another man hath
(perhaps meaner than himself) which shows us perfection is
not below, as also that God will have us beholden one to
another.

HERE FOLLOWS SOME VERSES UPON THE BURNING OF OUR HOUSE JULY 10TH, 1666. COPIED OUT OF A LOOSE PAPER

In silent night when rest I took   5
For sorrow near I did not look
I wakened was with thund'ring noise
And piteous shrieks of dreadful voice.
That fearful sound of "Fire!" and "Fire!"
Let no man know is my desire.   10
I, starting up, the light did spy,
And to my God my heart did cry
To strengthen me in my distress
And not to leave me succorless.
Then, coming out, beheld a space   15
The flame consume my dwelling place.
And when I could no longer look,
I blest His name that gave and took,
That laid my goods now in the dust.
Yea, so it was, and so 'twas just.   20
It was His own, it was not mine,
Far be it that I should repine;
He might of all justly bereft
But yet sufficient for us left.
When by the ruins oft I past   25
My sorrowing eyes aside did cast,
And here and there the places spy
Where oft I sat and long did lie:
Here stood that trunk, and there that chest,
There lay that store I counted best.   30
My pleasant things in ashes lie,
And them behold no more shall I.

Under thy roof no guest shall sit,
Nor at thy table eat a bit.
No pleasant tale shall e'er be told,   35
Nor things recounted done of old.
No candle e'er shall shine in thee,
Nor bridegroom's voice e'er heard shall be.
In silence ever shall thou lie,
Adieu, Adieu, all's vanity.   40
Then straight I 'gin my heart to chide,
And did thy wealth on earth abide?
Didst fix thy hope on mold'ring dust?
The arm of flesh didst make thy trust?
Raise up thy thoughts above the sky   45
That dunghill mists away may fly.
Thou hast an house on high erect,
Framed by that mighty Architect,
With glory richly furnished,
Stands permanent though this be fled.   50
It's purchased and paid for too
By Him who hath enough to do.
A price so vast as is unknown
Yet by His gift is made thine own;
There's wealth enough, I need no more,   55
Farewell, my pelf, farewell my store.
The world no longer let me love,
My hope and treasure lies above.

A. B.

AS WEARY PILGRIM

As weary pilgrim, now at rest,
  Hugs with delight his silent nest,
His wasted limbs now lie full soft
  That mirey steps have trodden oft,
Blesses himself to think upon   5
  His dangers past, and travails done.
The burning sun no more shall heat,
  Nor stormy rains on him shall beat.
The briars and thorns no more shall scratch,
  Nor hungry wolves at him shall catch.   10
He erring paths no more shall tread,
  Nor wild fruits eat instead of bread.
For waters cold he doth not long
  For thirst no more shall parch his tongue.
No rugged stones his feet shall gall,   15
  Nor stumps nor rocks cause him to fall.
All cares and fears he bids farewell
  And means in safety now to dwell.
A pilgrim I, on earth perplexed
  With sins, with cares and sorrows vext,   20
By age and pains brought to decay,
  And my clay house mold'ring away.
Oh, how I long to be at rest
  And soar on high among the blest.
This body shall in silence sleep,   25
  Mine eyes no more shall ever weep,
No fainting fits shall me assail,
  Nor grinding pains my body frail,
With cares and fears ne'er cumb'red be
  Nor losses know, nor sorrows see.   30

What though my flesh shall there consume,
   It is the bed Christ did perfume,
And when a few years shall be gone,
   This mortal shall be clothed upon.
A corrupt carcass down it lays,   35
   A glorious body it shall rise.
In weakness and dishonour sown,
   In power 'tis raised by Christ alone.
Then soul and body shall unite
   And of their Maker have the sight.   40
Such lasting joys shall there behold
   As ear ne'er heard nor tongue e'er told.
Lord make me ready for that day,
   Then come, dear Bridegroom, come away.

Aug. 31, 1669.   45